# CHILDREN FRAMING CHILDHOODS

## Working-Class Kids' Visions of Care

### Wendy Luttrell

First published in Great Britain in 2020 by

Policy Press
University of Bristol
1-9 Old Park Hill
Bristol
BS2 8BB
UK
t: +44 (0)117 954 5940
pp-info@bristol.ac.uk
www.policypress.co.uk

North America office:
Policy Press
c/o The University of Chicago Press
1427 East 60th Street
Chicago, IL 60637, USA
t: +1 773 702 7700
f: +1 773-702-9756
sales@press.uchicago.edu
www.press.uchicago.edu

British Library Cataloguing in Publication Data
A catalogue record for this book is available from the British Library

Library of Congress Cataloging-in-Publication Data
A catalog record for this book has been requested

ISBN 978-1-4473-5330-0 paperback
ISBN 978-1-4473-5285-3 hardcover
ISBN 978-1-4473-5333-1 ePub
ISBN 978-1-4473-5332-4 ePdf

Cover design by Andrew Corbett
Front cover image: photo taken by Kendra, age 17, © Wendy Luttrell
Printed and bound in Great Britain by CMP, Poole
Policy Press uses environmentally responsible print partners

This book is dedicated to my grandkids, Cobi and Nova. They bring me unfettered joy with their hilarious expressions and acute perceptiveness of the world around them. Theirs will be a world beyond our imagination; I trust they will take hold of it with the care and dignity shown by the kids in this book.

# Contents

# Notes on digital and visual elements

This book comes with an website (childrenframingchildhoods.com) that collects together photographs taken by the kids who participated in the research project upon which this book is based. The website includes the photographs printed in each chapter, a selection of photographs of the kids' homeplaces and special objects as discussed in Chapter 2, and an example of one individual child's photographs spanning across time. I encourage people to view the galleries on the website before they read the book, to let their eyes be drawn to what grabs their attention and to ask themselves why this might be. My hope is that people will immerse themselves in the images and then come back to the text to gain a deeper understanding of the social contexts and conditions within which these photographs were created, as well as an appreciation for the layered meanings and intentions that the kids shared with me and with each other about their pictures. This movement between image and text invites readers/viewers to reflect on their ways of seeing while considering the interpretations I offer.

The website also houses five videos that I created in collaboration with others. As the project developed, I began to think about how I could use visual and creative means to express some of my ideas about the research. I came to realize the power and possibilities of multimodal inquiry and representation, a process that I have called "collaborative seeing." These videos intentionally blur the borders between research and art, analysis and evocation, looking and feeling, ethics and aesthetics, seeing and knowing. Each video or "digital interlude" is placed in relationship to a thematically related chapter, but each of them can also be viewed apart and out of sequence from those chapters. Throughout the text I have indicated where watching a digital interlude might enhance readers' engagement with the sights, sounds, feel, and aliveness of the people, places, and ideas that are presented. People who wish to see an overview of the research project, its stance toward knowledge creation, data collection, analysis, and forms of representation, should start with Digital Interlude #5. Those who wish to arrive with me at the school site where the project began in 2003 should start with Digital Interlude #1.

The process of making these interludes is described in the Postlude, not as a guide or recipe for others to follow, but as an invitation to release creative experimentation, guided by ethical imperatives.

I am grateful to the kids for allowing me copyright ownership of their images so that they can be widely viewed. The photographs and videos on the website are protected under a Creative Commons license that allows for free access and distribution as long as people abide by the conditions specified. These include the following: the work must be given attribution, the work must be used for noncommercial purposes, and no derivatives (for example, re-mixing and re-purposing) of the work can be made.

# List of figures and tables

## Figures

*Chapter 6*

*Postlude*

## Tables

*Appendix*

# Acknowledgments

Writing acknowledgments is a practice of gratitude. Aside from expressing my appreciation for the people who made this book possible, I want to signal an obvious but not always recognized fact: a book is always part of something much larger than its author.

The glue that binds the pages of this book is thick: it consists of more people than I can list here. Some of these people have been cited for their intellectual contributions and others for their direct participation in the project. Their names appear in the chapters, endnotes, and reference list.

Above all, I am indebted to the young people who entrusted me with their words, images, and ideas. I can only hope my gratitude, sense of awe, and joy from working with them comes across in this book.

There are two people I wish were alive to see this book come to fruition. The day I returned the copy-edited pages to the Press, I received news that my mentor, colleague, friend, and chosen kin to my family, Naomi Quinn, had died. I was heartbroken, and am still reckoning with her loss. Naomi had confidence in me as a thinker and writer long before I did. She nourished my intellectual "light" and actively refused the academic borders and hierarchies that can be soul-crushing. A tough but tender critic, Naomi was more than generous with her time, talents, and advice. I admired her more than I think she knew.

Elliot Mishler is the second person who nourished this work. He welcomed me into the monthly Narrative Working Group meetings held in his Cambridge, MA home. People gathered to share their works-in-progress and be inspired by the way Elliot gently joined us in our thinking. He had an extraordinary listening ear—for words, stories, silences and sighs—and he taught us all by example how to operate as an interpretive community. After I presented one night, Elliot encouraged me to focus on individual case studies, for which I am forever grateful. Like Naomi, Elliot's commitment to social justice was woven into his everyday life, scholarship, and career. They set the standard for what I aspire to offer others.

This book would not have seen the light of day were it not for Cathy Reissman and Marjorie DeVault, members of my writing group. They have stood alongside me with encouragement, critical commentary, care, and concern from the beginning of this project in 2003. Each of them brought to it her distinctive set of insights as sociologists, feminists, editors (of endless drafts), and confidants; I consider them silent partners in a joint venture. I believe my desire to make them proud and to honor their amazing investment in this work kept me moving forward at a time when I would otherwise have given up. I am beyond thankful.

Cathy introduced me to an editor, Jennifer McFadden, as the book was beginning to cohere. Jennifer was the quintessential cheerleader, or, better yet, the doula who guided my breathing, thoughts, words, and organization in pushing this book out. Aside from her editorial skills, Jennifer brought to the book a perspective deeply informed by discourse analysis. I am indebted to the interest she took in the worlds and words of the kids, as well as mine.

Susie Nielsen gave me the courage to move from a researcher's stance into the realm of artistic practice. Susie is an accomplished visual artist and I am drawn to her work, as well as her way of working. She uses oil, acrylic, screen-printing and enamel to create layers. To describe a series of her work entitled *Unmeasured*, she wrote that she is "always trying to remove meaning and create a new opportunity to understand something in a different way ... Process drives my work. I am building up and then removing. Scraping away specifics, hoping to leave an ambiguous moment—hinting." Collaborating with Susie, first on an exhibition of the kids' photographs and then on Digital Interlude #4, taught me so much about another form of layering: the power of ambiguity, and reciprocal vision.

Beyond all measure is the contribution of Victoria Restler. Our mentoring relationship brought the kind of mutual growth that one hopes for but rarely experiences. The way Victoria joins together her artistic, scholarly, political and humanist "eye" is, simply put, brilliant. Victoria was part of the Collaborative Seeing Studio (https://collaborativeseeingstudio.commons.gc.cuny.edu) and a member of the research team for the second phase of work on the book. Victoria also read and generously commented on every chapter, even as she was researching and writing and I was commenting on her dissertation. There are places in this book where our thoughts and words intermingle; I have tried to make sure proper attribution has been made. She also viewed and gave invaluable feedback on all but one of the digital interludes and introduced me to artists who stretched my imagination (including Ukeles and Gomez, whose work appears in this book). It is hard to do justice to her all-encompassing role in this project.

With Emily Clark, I have enjoyed and benefited by another kind of mentoring relationship, one that is still ongoing. Her willingness to venture into collaborative video editing grew into a full-blown artist residency at my home in Wellfleet, MA. Emily is a creative and playful problem-solver, whether the problem involves photography, video, sound production, or finding the right window shades to block unwanted shadows. I can't wait to read and view her dissertation!

I was fortunate to have research assistants at two institutions—the Harvard Graduate School of Education and the Urban Education PhD program at the Graduate Center of the City University of New York. I am especially grateful to Julie Broussard, Carla Shalaby, Sherry Deckman, Milagros Seraus-Roache, Demet Arpacik, and Karen Zaino for their hard work. Each, in her own way, went above and beyond the call of duty.

Members of the Collaborative Seeing Studio sustained and inspired me—David Chapin, Emily Clark, Ivana Espinet, Gene Fellner, Claire Fontaine, Asilia Franklin-Phipps, Helen Kwah, Scott Lizama, Victoria Restler, Rondi Silva, and Tran Templeton.

I am thankful to a wide circle of friends and colleagues who read pieces of the manuscript and/or viewed the videos, including the late Jean Anyon, Susan Bell, Dympna Devine, Lisa Dodson, Michelle Fine, Idé O'Carroll, Annie Rogers, and John and Rosemary Wilson.

I owe Isobel Bainton, Commissioning Editor at Policy Press, a special acknowledgment for seeing the potential in this project and supporting my unconventional vision and requests for the book. Sarah Bird graciously took over when Isobel went on maternity leave and buoyed my confidence as I struggled to finally let the book go. Thanks to Sarah for that last important nudge. Working with Vaarunika Dharmapala, Production Editor, has been a true pleasure. Vaarunika really "gets" the book and the ties between its visual aesthetics and its message. Her simultaneous wide-angle lens and attention to detail is a rare combination. Thanks to Jessica Miles, Digital Marketing Manager, for her work on the accompanying website, and to Shannon Kneis, Assistant Editor, for threading the needle that stitches things together. As is obvious, it takes a village to produce a book and I am grateful to everyone's unseen labor at the Press.

I want to thank the following funders: the American Council of Learned Societies (ACLS) for a fellowship to complete the book; the PSC–CUNY (Professional Staff Congress–City University of New York) Research Awards that supported the second phase of the research and its digital elements; and the William F. Milton Fund Award, Harvard University, for supporting part of the first phase of research.

To my three children, Mikaela, Liam and Emma, each of you, in your way, is a source of light in my life that is hard to put into words. I have marveled at your unique forms of resilience and persistence, how hard you each work to make a better world in unsettling times. I thank you for your presence and patience. The lessons I have learned from loving each of you make me stronger, wiser, and open-hearted.

Finally, to my husband, Robert Shreefter, you are my enduring not-so-silent partner in love and life. Our bond is the strong and lasting glue that allows me to persist, repair, revise, and renew, as I believe is also the case for you. Thank you for your support for and recognition of my work (and the time it takes). Your artistic interventions are found throughout the book, including the suggestion to use a computer curser icon to highlight the digital interludes in the text, which Vaarunika and I both agreed was the perfect solution. Your talents are unparalleled— as a printer-maker, bookmaker, literacy and arts educator, curator, published poet, and lively, humorous "schmoozer," whose genuine interest in people's life stories, not to mention your memory for what you have been told, dazzles my mind. I simply can't imagine my life or this book without you.

# Prelude

## Worcester, Massachusetts
## Fall, 2003

As the front doors of Park Central School swing shut behind me, I check my bag—the camera I brought with me is heavy against my hip. Traffic through Worcester was bad this morning, and my watch says I'm five minutes late. I am nervous, excited, impatient. As I wait for Dr. Galinsky, the principal of PCS, I take in the scene of this K–6 school—its bright but battered hallways, the shuffling and murmuring of kids[1] and teachers settling down to their morning routines, the familiar smells of paper, floor polish, wet shoes.

I am here at Dr. Galinsky's generous invitation. I am part of an interdisciplinary team of faculty at the Harvard Graduate School of Education, and we are designing a new core course for graduate students called *Thinking Like an Educator*. The initiative is based in a belief that "perspectives embodied by particular actors, disciplinary traditions, and levels of analysis contribute to a deep and actionable understanding of complex educational realities" (Boix Mansilla, 2004). I want to be sure that children count among the important actors whose perspectives are considered, and it's that concern that brings me to PCS on this crisp fall day: to understand how kids frame their childhoods. How do they see their school, but also how they see their homes, their identities, their priorities. I mean these questions literally: How do things look from where children stand? What is most important to them? What can educators learn if we take their perspectives into account?

Dr. Galinsky—or "Dr. G.", as her students call her—shares my interest in these questions, and she likes my idea of giving kids cameras to record, represent, and reflect on their everyday lives. Our hope is that their photos will serve as a window onto the school culture, and at the same time allow me and my colleagues to ask other, more complex questions: How do the children express and establish their identities? What role, if any, do gender, race, immigrant status, and relative economic advantage play in the children's representations? What can we learn from young people's depictions of everyday life at home and in school? We both agree that there is tremendous value in

1

listening to kids' voices as a way to help educators improve teaching and learning. Dr. G. is eager for her school staff to see what the children decide to photograph and what the pictures might reveal about their lives beyond classroom walls. I plan to use the children's photographs and recorded interviews about their images as materials that will engage graduate students and teachers-in-training in assessing their own ways of seeing, and perhaps questioning their own assumptions about children growing up in working-class and immigrant communities of color.[2]

Standing in the hall at PCS, taking in the sights and sounds of this colorful, lively space, I feel the pleasant combination of eagerness and apprehension that I associate with beginning a journey—a sense of not knowing exactly what lies ahead but of being impatient to begin. I have no way of knowing how profoundly the kids I'm about to meet will come to affect me, or that they will occupy my thinking, writing, and learning for the next 15 years. I imagine that their images will lead me into their classrooms and into their homes, but I haven't considered that they will also take me into their dreams, memories, hopes, and fears. I have no idea of the magnitude of their insights, or the ways that they will transform my views of care and social justice. My perspective at the moment is a narrow one, defined by the moment in which I find myself, by the ideas about identity, development, and education I've brought with me, and by the boundaries of this hallway in this particular Massachusetts town.

From my research on the community, I understand that Park Central School is a microcosm of Worcester, the second largest city in New England. Worcester has a long history as a "working-class" town, home to immigrant families of diverse ethnic and linguistic backgrounds. Its laboring class dramatically diversified from 1880 to 1920, and since 1990 has been undergoing a second wave of immigration and expansion. Dr. G. has identified the racial, ethnic, and linguistic diversity of the student population as a point of pride and challenge for herself and her staff. She is concerned about meeting new requirements imposed by 2001's No Child Left Behind (NCLB) legislation, fearing that the standards might be beyond the reach of many of her students—a third of whom speak languages other than English at home. Alongside an influx of immigrant families, there is a high turnover rate in the student population from year to year as families move around the city in search of work and affordable housing. Ninety-two percent of her students are eligible for free and reduced school lunch, which in colloquial terms means her school serves "low-income" or "working-poor" families. According to PCS descriptors, 37 percent of its students are white, 10 percent Black, 18 percent Asian, and 35 percent Hispanic. Dr. G.

wants all students to feel "at home" in the school, and she is searching for ways to better include parents in the school culture. As I study the hallway and peer into the open doors of nearby classrooms, I see signs of "hominess"—colorful posters hanging on the walls, carpets on the floor, special items arranged on windowsills, picture frames displayed on a teacher's desk that is barely within my view.

Suddenly the office door opens, and Dr. Galinski greets me with a handshake and a smile. Behind her, a boy and a girl stand watching me with bright eyes. "Welcome to Park Central School," Dr. G. says. "I want to introduce Kendra and Alanzo, two of our fifth-graders who will be participating in your project. I've asked them to give you a tour of the school—I think they'll be excellent guides." The kids' faces break into warm grins as they shake my hand, too, and they eagerly lead me forward down the hall.

## Digital Interlude #1: Dwelling in School

childrenframingchildhoods.com/digital-interludes/dwelling-in-school

Ten-year-old Kendra is slight, but she stands tall in her floor-length black skirt and fitted red blouse, its too-long sleeves flaring at the bottom to hide her hands. Her hair is pulled back into neat plaits. Bangs frame her face, and large gold hoop earrings glint against her mahogany cheeks. Kendra has a low, soft, almost hushed voice; I have to strain to hear her. She tells me that PCS is the third elementary school she has attended since kindergarten: "So far it is my favorite." She grins, as if anticipating there will be more. Next to her stands Alanzo, also age ten, solidly built, with thick, pitch-black hair and a full, round face. His firm handshake and strong voice convey an easygoing confidence. He informs me that he has known no other school; in fact his older brothers and cousins have had some of the same teachers he has. He is wearing a red, hooded sweatshirt and bright white sneakers. Is it an accident that both are wearing red today, I wonder? They take note of my camera and assure me that I can use it whenever I want. "We already brought our permission slips," Kendra says proudly.

Kendra and Alanzo are both kids of color. In the categories used by the school, Kendra is Black, and Alanzo is Hispanic. Like many of the kids at PCS, they both live in the public housing development that stands adjacent to the school. They turn out to be first-rate guides and lively interlocutors, just as Dr. G. predicted—they are stirring

3

advocates for their school, even as they are astute witnesses to its under-resourced realities.

"We used to have lots more library books before it was flooded last year," Kendra says as they walk me quickly past the library with its lingering musty smell. As we pass by the lower grades' classrooms, I am surprised by my guides' detailed knowledge about which classes share space with other grades because of overcrowding: "Mrs. C. teaches third grade and she shares with Mrs. M.'s second-grade class for the morning and then they go to Mrs. T.'s, the other second-grade teacher, for the afternoon." They show me their fifth-grade classrooms and tell me we will have to wait to enter, or else we'll "disturb" others—but they want me to see their desks later and make me promise I won't forget. Then they usher me into the gym (which also serves as the auditorium), and Alanzo points to a red tricycle used by the pre-kindergarten kids—"I rode this bike all the time during free time when I was little," he says. I am struck by the wistful, nostalgic tone in his voice. He suggests I take a picture, as if to memorialize a time past, so I oblige. As we go down the stairs to the basement floor, I am warned that it might be "pretty dark" and "spooky," because the lighting is so low, but it would be alright. They want me to see the cafeteria and are excited that it is "pizza Friday," their favorite meal of the week.

They make a point to show me the "little kids' room" and how it is positioned next to the cafeteria—"so they don't have to walk too far." Kendra then takes me to a colorfully painted mural of animals that she calls her "favorite place," and Alanzo steers me into a broom closet he remembers once walking into thinking it was the bathroom. He laughs about how scared he had been. Passing the bathroom, we stop at a yellow laminated poster on the hallway wall: "The 5 Bs—Be Here; Be Ready; Be Safe; Be Respectful; Be Responsible." "Those are the school rules, you can take a picture of it," directs Alanzo, in an adult-like voice, and once again I take his advice. Kendra shows me the principal's office, explaining that "Dr. G. cares for" the school. "I admire her, she is nice. She takes her time and is kind to kids with problems. And she gets special things for the school"—things like the new computer lab, which is our next stop on the tour. Aside from the computers and the "big screen," Kendra and Alanzo declare excitedly, "kids like the chairs" as they plop into the cushioned chairs and swivel around in them to demonstrate. The playground outside is our last stop, and as if anticipating a question they thought I might ask, they tell me that it doesn't matter to either of them that there is no play equipment. What matters is that you can cut through the parking lot and walk to the apartment complex where they live. "Terrace Gardens," they proudly announce, pointing past the open chain-link fence. "It only takes us three minutes to get to school—you can see it from here."

Years later, as I reflect back on that first day at PCS, I can see how prescient that observation was: "you can see it from here." In fact the whole tour was a representation in miniature of what the children's images and accounts would come to show over the following years. Though their assignment that day had been to show me around the school, my wise guides did not simply walk me through the building describing where they spent a few hours each day as students. Rather, they directed my attention to the constraints and possibilities of a place they inhabited as kids, and they showed me their ways—and their teachers' and principal's ways—of making this place their own. They were attending to the elements of their schooling that would have remained invisible to me, and they were rendering them visible and affording them value.

This unspoken subtext foreshadows a key discovery of my research—the centrality and saliency of how care matters in childhood, in development, and in schooling from kids' own perspectives. I heard the elements of care expressed in Kendra's and Alanzo's protectiveness and concern about safety for the "little kids" and the importance of being close to the lunchroom, as well as their appreciation for being close to home. I heard it in their "admiration" for Dr. G. who *cares*; and in their awareness that care takes time (a resource that is increasingly diminishing in the world of school and in everyday living). I heard the links between care and "special" resources (like the new computer lab), signals to them that their lives and learning are worth investing in. It was notable to me that Kendra and Alanzo did not take such resources for granted.

Through their gestures and voices, I sensed that regardless of their school's conditions, Kendra and Alanzo were asserting their sense of belonging and standing as elders in the school world, expressing a strong affinity as full members of the school community. This was a stark contrast to the predominant "adultist" and neoliberal way of seeing and valuing schools through test scores, performance measures, or rankings—a view that reduces students and teachers to data points in a much larger scheme of standardization and accountability culture (Restler, 2017; Vinson & Ross, 2003; Taubman, 2009). Rather, Kendra and Alanzo were drawing my attention to what makes a school—books, desks, decorated walls, light (or lack thereof), play equipment (or lack thereof), food, favorite places, proximity to home, rules and relationships, a principal who is "kind" and aware of the importance of resources that make kids feel cared for. They were offering a different vision of school as a metaphorical home where feelings of belonging, security, care, and nostalgic yearning are produced. Connections of caring and care work, forged through investments of time and labor and cultivated through relationship and home-making, are critical links between home and school, child and family, individual and community. As the kids would show me time and again with their photographs and their stories, these are the things that "you can see from here"—if, that is, you know how to look.

Decades of research has established that social inequalities, especially related to class, race, and gender, shape how people learn what they feel entitled to, constrained by, and how they envision their future possibilities. For most of my life, I have been trying to untangle the connections between these forms of social inequality and people's subjective experience of their value and worth, especially in regard to education. I grew up straddling the class divide, navigating the tensions between my mother's comfortable white, Protestant, middle-class background and sensibilities and my father's white, working-class heritage, which he wore like a badge of honor covering a sense of his own limitations.

Those frictions made me a keen observer of the material and emotional nuances of class distinctions within the white communities and schools I grew up in. They also marked my childhood insecurities and affinities in ways that I didn't begin to understand until I had the privilege to attend college and searched for my own sense of belonging and identity in an elite setting I was never comfortable in. My childhood was marked by multiple moves in and around Chicago, Texas, New Jersey, Kansas, back to Chicago—a migration that left scars of disruption, loss, and longing that I learned to cover over, to make "lemonade out of lemons" in my mother's words. There was something about how Kendra and Alanzo wanted me to see their school and their place in it that compelled and resonated with me. By enlisting the PCS children as my guides and privileging their perspectives, I hoped to better understand the social dynamics and personal experiences of inclusion, exclusion, worth, and value that schooling engenders.

It is late January, 2004. Mrs. Collins, the PCS instructional technology teacher, introduces me to the first of three groups of 12 children I will work with. It is a racially and ethnically diverse selection of 10- and 11-year-olds in the fifth grade. The children all speak English fluently, with the exception of a child from Iran who is learning English during her first year in the school.

We are gathered around a table in the technology instruction room across from the new computer lab. Even before I have learned the names of each child, Jeffrey surprises me by nominating himself as my assistant. He quickly takes it upon himself to hand out the disposable, analogue cameras (now already an ancient technology), directing the kids not to open them yet. It is clear he is a leader; his classmates follow his request and seem at ease with his authority. I am immediately drawn to Jeffrey's easygoing, no-nonsense approach and am happy he took charge. Jeffrey has endearing chubby, brown-skinned cheeks, short, cropped, dark hair, and an infectious smile. He is wearing a white and green NFL football jersey that tugs at his body. In the complex racial landscape of the school I am not sure of his racial identification, but I will learn that he describes himself as "half Puerto Rican, half Black and half white" (he is Hispanic according to school categories). He gingerly handles the disposable camera and announces excitedly, "This is my first camera." Then, in a serious voice, he says to his classmates: "A camera is a big responsibility."

The palpable excitement in the room is muted by Jeffrey's earnest assessment. He points out that a camera will require special care so as not to "break it" or "lose it." Several kids ask what will happen if they do. "Not to worry," I reply, "you will be given another"—a comment that draws some surprised looks.

As the children unwrap and explore their disposable cameras, I explain that they will have their four days, from Thursday to Monday, to photograph their school, families, and communities. Jeffrey is the first to ask: "How do we know what kind of pictures to take?" A chorus of questions follows. I ask the children to imagine that they have a cousin who is moving to Worcester and coming to their school. "Take pictures of your home, school, and community that will help your cousin know what to expect." Jeffrey announces, "I have cousins in Puerto Rico." Others quickly follow his lead—having cousins in the Dominican Republic, Haiti, Colombia, New York City, Boston, Vietnam, Kenya. "We are cousins," says Danny, pointing to Tina, who looks irritated. Jeffrey is also the first to brainstorm ideas for what to photograph—"What do you do after school and on the weekends? What do you like most? Where do you feel comfortable? Who do you admire?" Later, Jeffrey adds, "What concerns you?" He speaks with quiet authority.

This conversation seemed ordinary at the time, but in retrospect, like the school tour, it foreshadowed the contours of care that would emerge from the kids' perspectives, and their feelings about the forms of care they encountered. More than a tool for documenting their lives or self-expression, the kids treated the cameras as a valued possession and personal belonging. Being attuned to the multiple ways that the kids would use their cameras would prove to be invaluable to my understanding of their meaning making.

There are many things to say about why as a sociologist I turned to using photography. Photographs are part of how we read our social worlds, construct ourselves in relation to others, and express matters of the heart.[3] Photographs communicate what may be seeable, but not easily sayable about our social worlds and the fashioning of identities. Photography is a technology that has shaped constructions of family (Hirsch, 1997; Sontag, 1977), childhood (Higonnet, 1998), and identity (Tinkler, 2008). Today, photography is a ubiquitous means of everyday communication. While this wasn't the case for the children at the beginning of the project in 2003, by the time it ended in 2013, photography had become part of the young people's social media and everyday practice.

This book is based on an extensive archive of photographs and audio-visual materials. It consists of 2,036 photographs, and 65 hours of video- and audio-taped individual and small group interviews with the kids at ages ten, 12, 16, and 18. In them, the kids discussed their photos, why they took them, and which images they wished to share with their peers and teachers. The archive also includes VoiceThreads[4] of photographs and video diaries produced by a subset of 18 participants at ages 16, 17 and 18. At each stage, the young people curated their images for a public exhibition in different settings—their school, the Worcester City Hall, Harvard Graduate School of Education, Lesley University, and the Graduate Center at City University of New York. The archive exists on a password-protected website that I have used with different groups of viewers, starting with the kids themselves as they looked back on and reflected on their childhood photographs. I have drawn from the archive to conduct teacher professional development workshops and to teach graduate students about how to conduct visual research. My goal in using the archive is to invite viewer reflexivity— prompting people to notice their identifications with and projections onto the children's images and to consider what lenses they are using to "read" and "appreciate" the images. At a time when distorted and increasingly fractious visions of "marginalized" communities proliferate, it feels all the more urgent that as educators and researchers we take the time to consider and critique what shapes our ways of seeing.

The project didn't begin as a longitudinal study; it unfolded over time as my relationship with the kids developed and I became more immersed in and compelled by their images. Behind the young people's photographs and videos are stories about and insights into historical and social contexts, as well as the creators and the subjects of the images. These stories and insights come from my dialogues with the young people over time and are integral to how I see and interpret the images. To me, the photographs and videos visualize a set of relationships and sentiments, and in this book I try to address these in all their complexity: expressions of love, pride, unity, harmony, and ease, as well as pain, discomfort, reticence, and tension. I have been equally compelled by others' reactions to these images and the stories and assumptions that lie behind an array of responses, including assumptions about deficits rather than strengths, and constraints rather than possibilities.

I have come to call my approach a practice of "collaborative seeing." The practice cannot be condensed into a single recipe or tool kit; rather it is a stance toward knowing, rooted in a "need to know more" perspective. It follows from visual theorist John Berger's claim that "the relationship between what we see and what we know is never settled" (1991: 7). My practice of collaborative seeing is fueled by the questions: Whose way of seeing is this? In what context? With what degree of authority, power, and control? Toward what purpose? With what consequences?

My interpretation of the archival materials combines different types of visual analysis, including content and narrative analysis. It is grounded in a sustained, "attentive looking, not staring" at images, as sociologist Howard Becker would put it; and in a careful "listening to" images, being attuned to the frequencies of "affect and impact" the images hold, to paraphrase historian Tina Campt. As she puts it, "listening to" photographs goes beyond visual scrutiny: "It is an ensemble of seeing, feeling, being affected, contacted, and moved beyond the distance of sight and observer" (2017: 42). Collaborative seeing also requires a regard for children's agency and self-fashioning, all the while knowing that image-making (in photography and in video) is bound by its limits and possibilities. I designed the project with this regard in mind, inviting the children to speak about their images in different settings and with different audiences. This feature of the project allowed the kids to expand, clarify, reverse and sometimes repair (any) problems they perceived in their self-representations and others' reactions to them.

Collaborative seeing is in dialogue with and puts a new spin on "giving kids cameras" research and "photovoice" methods which have burgeoned in the last 20 years by seeking to de-center adult authority, attempting to move kids' insights from the margin to the center. My hope is to offer a line of analysis that advances the theory, practice, and reflexive promise afforded by "giving kids cameras" research across the disciplines, but especially at the intersection of sociology, urban education, and critical childhood studies.

What do I mean by critical childhood studies? I will explain more in Chapter 1, but at its core, the scholarship of critical childhood studies illuminates the social and institutional forces that constrain children's freedom and imagination and devalues their intentions, agency, and subjectivity. Research in critical childhood studies aims to privilege and amplify kids' own perspectives and experiences, treating them as competent social actors in their own right (Thorne, 1993). Critical childhood research relies on innovative methods and practices that aim to minimize adults "voicing over" children's experiences and perspectives so that kids can be heard in new ways. In this book, I argue that the young people—as children and as teenagers—used their cameras to compose their identities, frame and display their valuing practices, and act on behalf of their families, friends, and communities.

Jeffrey is the first child I interview. He is holding his packet of 27 photographs as if it were a gift he is about to open. We sit together in

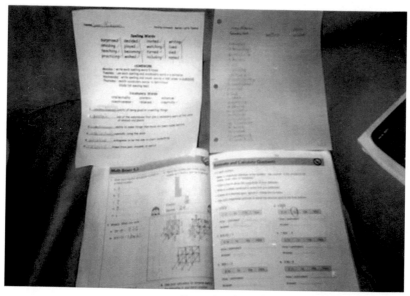

Figure A: What I do after school *Jeffrey, age 10*

the school's new computer lab, a video camera poised to record our conversation. Jeffrey adjusts his back, sits up straight at the table, and immediately takes charge. He sorts slowly and carefully through his packet of pictures, skipping over some with a laugh, while studying others as if searching for clues. He seems satisfied with his photographs, with the exception of two "mistakes," and places them in a neat stack.

We begin our dialogue, pivoting around three basic questions: "What is happening in this photograph?", "Why did you take it?", and "What is important to you about the picture?" Jeffrey's explanations follow the prompts almost verbatim.

"I took this picture [Figure A] because of what do I do after school—I do my homework. Because if you didn't have homework, you basically wouldn't learn anything." He turns from speaking to me to speaking directly to the video camera and holds up the picture for his imagined audience to view. I hear him establishing himself as a "good" student who does his homework. I am intrigued by the display of the pages and ask, "Did you put these on a couch?" He sits up straighter and grins, pleased by my question. "Yes." "Is this where you do your homework?" I ask. At this, he seems to avoid my gaze, and answers a bit sheepishly, with a little chuckle—"yes,"—as if he suspects this might not be the best answer. A photograph of the book *The Littles* is next (Figure B),

Figure B: I like to read books
*Jeffrey, age 10*

Figure C: Me helping other kids to do their work *Jeffrey, age 10*

representing what he does on the weekends. "I like to read books. That is what I mostly do on the weekend. Because every kid should like to read at their house if they are bored and have no TV." Jeffrey smiles. I ask, "Do you have a television?" "Yes, I am an only child. I'm lucky, I'm spoiled," Jeffrey replies without a hint of boastfulness.

Jeffrey is presenting himself as a "good" student who does his homework and reads on the weekends, not just because he *has* to, but because he *likes* to. And he has advice for others, especially if they are not as fortunate as he is: "Because every kid should like to read at their house if they are bored and have no TV." I hear the outlines of larger stories and debates about the relationship between media, consumption, and care, and how children should use their time. I wonder whose perspective Jeffrey is taking here. In a society where consumption expresses care and belonging for children and parents, and where social inequality can make care and belonging feel either scarce or plentiful (as sociologist Allison Pugh would put it), I sense Jeffrey's relief and gratitude for being well taken care of, that is, "lucky" and "spoiled."

As our conversation continues, Jeffrey also establishes himself as a "helper" by way of a photograph of himself recycling. "I could tell that paper doesn't belong there so I helped pick it up for the people so they won't have to come outside." There are numerous photographs of him "helping" and caring for other kids, including one of his learning-group members who he helps with his multiplication tables (Figure C).

We linger on the next photograph (Figure D), which he says is his favorite. "One thing that is important to me is firemen because if they

Figure D: What is important to me *Jeffrey, age 10*

weren't here there would be a lot of fires getting out and the firemen from far away would have to hurry up and rush by the time they get there, the fire would have burned the house." He is especially animated while describing this possibility, and he says he is proud of the fire station and admires the men who work there. He is glad the fire station is next to his grandmother's apartment, his after-school destination until his mother returns from her job as a nurse's aide.

Jeffrey's photographs do and do not speak for themselves. I read his photographs as an enactment of his multiple identities and values. His images and what he has to say about them—his visual narratives— enable us to become more attuned to what Jeffrey cares about, takes pride in, desires, wonders and worries about. I am looking and listening for what he places value upon and what gives him satisfaction ("helping"), and I pay special attention to his way of reading signs of care at home (he is "spoiled") and in his community (he is protected by the firemen). He describes some of his worries and concerns, including his concern about fighting and staying out of trouble, which I will discuss in more depth in Chapter 4. Across these two themes: being a helper and staying out of trouble I hear the outlines of larger stories against which he is making identity claims—stories about brown- and black-skinned boys who are more likely cast as "trouble" than as "helpers" or "carers" (Dumas & Nelson, 2016; Ferguson, 2000; Noguera, 2008; Luttrell, 2012; Way, 2011).

Rita Charon offers an interesting metaphor for re-thinking how we listen to children within the context of unequal power relations in an approach she calls "stereophonic listening" (2006: 97). The unequal power relation she focuses on is between medical professionals and patients as they speak about their illnesses. A stereophonic listener seeks to "hear the body and the person who inhabits it." Charon suggests that there has been "an odd diminishment of the status of storytelling in medicine ever since we decided we knew enough about the body by virtue of reducing it to its parts that we did not need to hear out its inhabitant." (2006: 261). I want to extend this same kind of listening to the unequal power relation between children and adults in research and education. Ever since adults decided we knew enough about children to be experts—a knowledge based on reducing them to discernable parts and standardizing their learning and growth—we have undermined our ability to hear out children's own perspectives:

> The classification, enumeration and collection of data concerning children are activities by no means without

13

consequences. On the contrary, classification directly affects the children being classified: this is regulation. And vice versa: this is resistance. "In medicine, the authorities who know, the doctors, tend to dominate the known about, the patients. The known about come to behave in the ways that the knower expect them to. But not always. Sometimes the known take matters into their own hands." (Hacking, 1995: 38 in Turmel, 2008: 116)

André Turmel is writing about the social technologies (recording methods, graphs, charts, tables, and so on) that focus attention on children in specific ways, as if these ways were the only way to know, understand, or value a child. The everyday activities of classification, measurement and "standardization" have come to constitute the water in which children swim in school. But it could be otherwise if, as adults, we could find better ways to nourish children's own knowing, being, and becoming. This project explores that possibility.

This is not a book *about* the kids in the traditional sense: it is not about tracing their life trajectories, categorizing or comparing them, or using their visual and verbal data to answer pre-conceived research questions. Such a book would no doubt have been interesting, but it would have depended on a very different orientation to data and to the children themselves. Indeed, in many ways this is not the book I imagined writing when I initiated this project, which I discuss more in the Postlude. The kids took me on an unexpected journey into their powerful ways of seeing at different points in their lives and from different vantage points. The perspective they offered was at once much wider and much more sharply focused than I expected, and the kids' ways of seeing care transformed and broadened my own analytic vision. This book aims to widen the scope of inquiry for others, opening imaginative spaces in which we can not only see the kids' ways of picturing care in their lives, begin to understand why it matters, but also feel compelled to respond.

Different people can and will ask different questions of the same data, especially when that data is visual (photographs, drawings, collages, videos). This comes with the territory of everyday life and is no less so in research or in art. And our eyesight is always partial, influenced by how we have been trained to see. As the art critic Herbert Read put it:

We see what we learn to see, and vision becomes a habit, a convention, a partial selection of all there is to see, and a distorted summary of the rest. We see what we want to see, and what we want to see is determined by, not the inevitable law of optics or even (as may be the case in wild animals) by an instinct for survival, but by the desire to discover or construct a credible world. (Read, 1991: 12 in Grimshaw, 2001: 8)

One regrettable, dominant habitual vision that this book engages and refuses is deficit and damage-based seeing—a way of seeing that ignores the resources of poor and working-class kids of color, their families, and communities, blames them for the state of their schools, and often results in excessive attempts to control and punish students (García & Guerra, 2004; Valencia, 2010; Weiner, 2003; Tuck, 2009). I believe this limited way of seeing happens, in large part, because the educational system has failed, since its founding, to engage Black and Brown children in helping re-train our lenses (which have all too often been white, Anglo, middle class, monolingual, color-blind, or color-evasive). Visual research has the promise, the possibility to interrupt or upend our lenses—but it does not do so automatically, necessarily, or by default. Its transformative potential is limited by its practitioners' willingness to look critically and, I argue, to see differently.

Each chapter in this book stages an encounter with different ways of seeing and angles of vision that the kids in this project offered and that I lift up for careful consideration. Throughout the text, I have also included five digital video interludes, whose sounds and images invite viewers to experience the "aliveness" of the families, school, and communities that the young people represented. Chapter 1 introduces readers to Worcester, MA, to Park Central School, and to the project through the lens of a critical childhood studies perspective, and it draws on an intersectional feminist analysis to introduce the concepts of children's agency and invisible work. Chapter 2 considers *belongings* as markers of *belonging*. In that chapter, I offer a way of seeing the children's photographs of prized possessions as a means to position themselves as the objects of others' care and as agile navigators of social and cultural differences.

Chapters 3 and 4 feature the people, rhythms, and routines—what I call "choreographies of care"—that the children made visible in their photographs and accounts about their homes and school. These two chapters draw our eyes to what care looks like, who does it, when, where, how, why it is important, the complex feelings it engenders, its rewards, costs and contradictions, and last but not least, how it is laced with power dynamics. These two chapters counteract a distorted vision and understanding of the care work that is performed by women, as working-poor mothers and as public school teachers in working-class, under-resourced schools. Additionally, these two chapters feature the care work performed by the children themselves, as boys and girls growing up in poor and working-class families and as students in under-resourced schools. This is a topic we know very little about from the perspective of young people themselves, yet it is a topic that the children made central.

Chapter 5 follows the kids into teenage-hood, inviting them to look back on their photographs from childhood and to reflect on how their lives have changed. I was surprised by the force of the young people's feelings; first, about seeing me again ("I can't believe you found me!"), and second, about seeing themselves and their family and school worlds again with new eyes. My intention was to explore the affective dimensions of childhood and schooling—those visceral feelings of lived experiences that can remain alive in memories and bodies. I came to understand these individual and collective feelings in dialogue with the young people's efforts to (re)fashion their identities and to bring their personal and social value into view. As in previous chapters, the young people's self-representations serve as insights into development—not in individual terms related to stages of maturity/independence/self-realization, but rather in terms of their collective valuing practices. This chapter also takes up the theme of temporality, especially the kids' feelings and conflicts about time as part of the process of "growing up." I argue that the young people's subjective experience of time is far more complicated than is depicted by adult concerns and anxieties about teenagers' use of time, whether it is screen and online time, or time to just "hang out."

Chapter 6 is a meditation on distorted visions of education, care, and freedom. Care in education is most often noted for its absence rather than its presence—we are accustomed to hearing various problems attributed to "students who don't care," "teachers who don't care," and/or "parents who don't care." Rarely is the state's disinvestment in care or its failure to honor its own part in the provision of care through social and workplace policies the focal point of attention (Feeley, 2014). Moreover, current neoliberal social policies and politics of school reform are training us not to see care or care work, through performance measures, data production, "teacher-proofing" (that is, de-skilling) of instruction, surveillance, zero tolerance disciplinary practices, and, as I write, alarming calls to arm teachers with guns as a means to "protect" students. Chapter 6 outlines the dangers posed by neoliberal capitalism's treatment of the activities of care as individual commodities rather than collective goods.[5]

After years of looking at and listening to the young people's images, I see the regard they have for care work and its meanings, most importantly, the freedom to care as a radical possibility within education and society. Educator and activist scholar Carla Shalaby contends, "we train youth in the image of capitalism instead of a vision of freedom—for lives as individual workers rather than solidary human beings" (2017: xvii). My hope is that Chapter 6 also broadens the conversation about home and school relationships as more than a means to promote school success, but as a means to elevate the work of care and the time it takes to nourish a democratic society so that we might construct a more credible world for the next generation.

The Postlude is a reflection on my research process over time. I account for the choices I've made, offering a portrayal of reflexivity in action. As my relationships with the young people stretched out in time, and the world around us changed (including new technologies), I found that my older ways of doing visual analysis were no longer sufficient for the task. I reflect on crossing into new theoretical, methodological, and ethical territory, stepping outside my comfort zone as a researcher, and highlight the value of creative collaboration that resulted in the digital interludes that accompany this book. These videos intentionally blur borders between research and art; analysis and evocation; looking and feeling; seeing and knowing. Characterizing my style of research in terms of what has become known as slow sociology (Garey et al, 2014), I stress the value of time and being open to life's disruptions that require care and repair as well as the joys of connectedness as "what matters most" in life and intellectual labor.

# 1

# Ways of seeing diverse working-class children and childhoods

## Introduction

When labor historian Roy Rosenzweig (1983) set out to write about the "American working-class experience" at the turn of the 20th century, he chose Worcester, Massachusetts as his focal point. He recognized the limitations of using a single community study to make claims about other urban, industrializing communities, and he knew that there could be no single story of "the American working class." His aim was not to generalize, but rather to understand social processes—class conflict, immigration, cultural change, and the shared contours of immigrant working-class culture—seen through the lens of a particular community. In this book I aim to do something similar. By situating my study in a single elementary school in Worcester, I intend to highlight social processes and patterns that shape the contours of working-class childhoods. I say childhoods because here, too, there can be no single story. In considering how the Park Central School (PCS) kids used their cameras to frame their childhoods, to represent their lives and learning as children and as teenagers, we are challenged to consider how race, ethnicity, gender, and immigrant status shape the experience of working-class childhoods. Their visions of self, family, school, and community illustrate the shared contours of seeing and valuing care in a society that is increasingly unequal.

Certain key features of Worcester's history as an industrial city and its waves of immigration provide important contexts for my project. At the turn of the 20th century, the city saw a rapid shift in the laboring class, with immigrants making up more than 70 percent of the low-wage jobs. Irish, French Canadians, and then Swedes dominated the skilled trades, and "new immigrants" from southern and eastern Europe—a religiously, ethnically, and linguistically diverse group—were forced to take unskilled positions. Members of Worcester's divided and constantly changing working class were said by Rosenzweig to be more oriented toward building solidarity within their diverse ethnic cultural worlds than within trade unions or political parties. Rosenzweig makes the point that the traditional indicators of working-class consciousness such as active trade unions and labor strikes were less prevalent in Worcester than in other industrial cities. Indeed, the prominent labor organizer Emma Goldman left Worcester and moved to Lowell as a better site for political organizing (Behrman, 1954, 1982). But what flourished in Worcester were "public modes of mutuality, conviviality, and collectivity"—what Rosenzweig calls "refuges and resources" (Rosenzweig, 1983: 223)—that were at odds with middle-class norms and elite interests. An infrastructure of churches, clubs, saloons, cafes, and charitable organizations offered alternative values and traditions, most importantly a rejection of "acquisitive individualism."[1] Rosenzweig's account emphasizes the crucial solidary character of Worcester's diverse working-class communities. Despite the ethnic enclaves and divisions between them, which employers capitalized on to pit different ethnic workers against each other, members of its working class shared the same rhythms of everyday life: "low pay, long hours, and unsafe work" (1983: 30) from which people sought respite through sociality to counteract the harshness of industrializing workplaces.

The importance of a life beyond laboring was alluded to in "Eight Hours," one of the most popular American labor songs of the late 19th and early 20th centuries. Its words reverberated throughout the streets of Worcester in 1889 when the city's trade unionists marched, and then again in 1915 when the city's machinists made their labor demands.

> We mean to make things over;
> We're tired of toil for naught;
> We may have enough to live on,
> But never an hour for thought.
>
> We want to feel the sunshine,
> We want to smell the flowers
> We are sure that God has willed it,
> And we mean to have eight hours.

The song rejects the notion of hard and endless work at the expense of the dignity of life (thinking, feeling, smelling the flowers). Like its sister labor song and slogan, "Bread and Roses," it highlights the fact that working-class struggles and demands have historically been appeals to valuing people (including children) as having more than economic worth. The appeal for time and for dignity—to be seen as a person with value beyond the marketplace—is a theme that will be highlighted by the kids in this book.

Among many illustrations of the ways that working-class demands extended beyond economic concerns, Rosenzweig describes a history of social activism related to children's quality of life in early 20th-century Worcester. Unlike other industrializing cities at the time, demands for children's play spaces in Worcester came from its working-class constituents and not from progressive social reformers. As early as 1880, Irish workers petitioned the city for play areas. Numerous working-class neighborhoods joined the cause, including Jewish residents of an East Side tenement who went on rent strike, complaining, among other things, of a lack of play space for children (1983: 144).

But if the impetus came from within the city's working-class communities, the proposal was soon co-opted by other interests with different ideas about how these public spaces should be designed and organized, including an effort to supervise play as a means to control, "Americanize," and, some would say, protect immigrant children. Middle-class reformers began promoting playgrounds as a tool for socializing working-class children into their proper roles as workers and citizens.[2] As the editor of the *Worcester Gazette*, George Booth wrote, playgrounds "bring pure gold out of the melting pot" (1983: 148).

Even as working-class demands for public play spaces were being hijacked by political interests, working-class children maintained their own perspective on the matter, as a 1912 *Worcester Telegram* article reported. According to one 11-year-old, "I can't go to the playgrounds now. They get on me nerves with so many men and women around telling you what to do." (1983: 151). Numerous children interviewed by the paper expressed a critical awareness that their own behavior and means of play were being scrutinized, judged, and regulated. It is my interest in expressions of working-class children's agency and subjectivity—their desire to conduct their lives on their own terms—that grounds my study. Paying attention to kids' efforts to exercise their agency within white, middle-class, adult-controlled institutions and conventions is what propels my questions and analysis throughout this research.

When my study began in 2003, at the turn of the 21st century, the post-industrial, working-class city of Worcester had a different racial, ethnic, linguistic, religious, and occupational landscape. Diverse immigrant communities of color had come to characterize the city. A wave of "new immigrants"—from Latin and South America and from the Asian countries of Vietnam, China, and Laos—had settled in neighborhoods and housing that were once predominantly white. A fifth of the city's residents were "foreign born," and a third spoke a language other than English at home (Worcester QuickFacts, US Census Bureau, 2003). Over the course of the decade during which I conducted my research (2003–13), the Black population of Worcester increased from 6.9 percent to 11.6 percent. The majority, non-Hispanic white population that as late as the 1970s constituted 96.8 percent of the population had dropped to 59.6 percent as of 2013.

Today, Worcester is writing a new chapter in its story of immigrant, working-class culture, struggles, refuges, and resources. Black, Asian and Hispanic-owned businesses mark the city landscape at rates almost double those of Massachusetts generally. Worcester's historic pattern of businesses serving as resources and refuges for diverse racial and ethnic communities seems to have continued into the 21st century, and a few of the participating children in this study have parents who run and work in such businesses. Overall, members of Worcester's diversified working-class population are tied to the rhythms of long hours, inflexible schedules, low pay, and limited mobility as they labor in retail, service, and "care-work" industries. These are jobs whose demands frequently render their occupants "invisible" in the neoliberal marketplace. They are also the jobs held by the parents of the kids participating in this project.

In this book I suggest that young people use their cameras to combat invisibility. In their photographs and discussions, I locate powerful appeals for dignity—for themselves, their families, their schools, and their communities. Aware that their own and their family's activities and values might be suspect, the young people seemed compelled to show their recognition of mutual care in their lives and learning, and they wished their acts of care-conscious seeing (and of rendering visible) to be witnessed and understood. I also argue that their visual narratives (photographs and videos) offer an alternative to dominant versions of individualism—in this case, the competitive, performative individualism expected and rewarded in modern American schooling. Instead, they place a high value on sociality, mutuality, reciprocity, and collectivity, expressed and documented through pictures and accounts of the care that sustains working-class families, schools, and communities. From some vantage points, this care is invisible and unacknowledged, sometimes even by those who do it (DeVault, 1991). But it depends upon who is looking and who is attaching value to that work of care. I will refer to choreographies of care made visible by the kids as a means to shine a light on the inter-related and coordinated elements—people, time, feelings, intimacies, values, and dynamics of power—that the young people invoke to frame their childhoods, learning, and growth.

In this chapter, I introduce the many threads of theoretical and contextual background that support the arguments presented in this book. These threads are tightly interwoven, and I do not attempt to neatly segment the many themes here; instead, they surface in this chapter and throughout the book in twined and iterative patterns. Here, I describe the theoretical, methodological, and political perspectives in which the work is grounded, which encompasses critical childhood studies and intersectional feminist concerns about the race-, gender-, and class-based workings of care. I present the particular school in which the study took place, and relate its demographic and infrastructural characteristics to larger trends and patterns in American education. I introduce some of the participants, including the school's principal and some of the students, and offer an early glimpse into their visions of care, schooling, childhood, and selfhood. I describe the study's adaptation of "giving kids cameras" research and address some of the advantages, challenges, and complex ethical issues that arise from visual methods. Finally, I offer a brief discussion of visuality as a tool of power and control, and I introduce the notion of "countervisuality" as an alternative way of seeing (and being seen) that "speaks back," challenging dominant viewpoints of deficits, stigma, and invisibility, and asserting value and dignity in their place.

## Taking a critical childhood perspective

The basic premise of what has been called the "new" sociology of childhood is to recognize that children are active interpreters and inventors of culture and not simply recipients of adult socialization. William Corsaro (1997), one of the founders of this school of thought, argued that children contribute to both social stability and social change through three forms of collective activity: (1) Children creatively appropriate information and language from the adult world; (2) they produce and participate in their own (peer) culture; and (3) children help facilitate the reproduction of adult culture. Each of these forms of collective activity will be evident as the kids in this study instruct us through their images and accounts. Taking a critical childhood perspective also means challenging traditional understandings of socialization and child development—that is, rather than characterizing children as "incomplete" en route to becoming adults, children are viewed for who they are in the moment, in their own terms (Adler & Adler, 1986; Ambert, 1986; Waksler, 1986; Alanen, 1988; Thorne,

1987, 2007; James & Prout, 1990; Jenks, 1992; Qvortrup et al, 1994). More traditional studies of childhood ignored the significant effects of adults always speaking for children, the ease of which "effectively silenced" children (Matthews, 2007). Child–adult relationships are understood to exist within unequal power relations born of interdependency, relationality, and oppression rather than deficiency.[3] A key tenet of critical childhood studies is to take children seriously as witnesses to their experiences, no matter where they "fit" into child development discourses.

A critical childhood perspective interrogates the changing meanings of childhood, including who counts as a child, when this status begins and ends, and recognizes that these meanings are contingent on historical, economic, cultural, and institutional contexts (Aries, 1962; Stephens, 1995). As white, Western, bourgeois society evolved, children became differentiated from adults, and this allowed for new identities to come into existence as well as new practices for governing society and individual people's lives. Children's new identities as "learners" were intertwined with schooling practices developed to manage, control, and orient them to fitting into society (Baker, 1998; Bloch et al, 2004). Much has been written about how contemporary neoliberal influences in education have recalculated children's identities and value in terms of their performance and productivity, measured by "scores" and shrinking the contours of learning into "skills" and dispositions (Devine & Luttrell, 2013; Devine, 2013; Sonu & Benson, 2016). That children's value is assigned conditionally (not inherently) based on their ability to measure up in school, is a discourse that this book aims to trouble.

Equally important is finding ways around adult-centered ways of seeing children. In 1987, sociologist Barrie Thorne published an article, "Re-Visioning Women and Social Change: Where Are the Children?" in which she observed that children's "full lives, experiences and agency have been obscured by adult standpoints" (1987: 86). She critiqued feminist and traditional forms of knowledge as "adultist" in their assumptions, including the idea that because adults have all been children, we already "know" the experiences of childhood. She also argued that research must move beyond three typical views of children as "threats to adult society; victims of adults; and learners of adult culture" (1987: 89). Despite decades of new research, these constructions of children remain dominant today.

Thorne suggested two strategies for rethinking children and childhoods. One is to examine the parallels between women's and children's situations, and the second is to clarify the ideological and actual connections between them. One important connection between women and children that this study exposes has to do with their interdependence regarding schooling. Schools are institutional, contested sites of struggle where proper or "good" childhood is co-constructed with "good" motherhood. In schools, mothers and children are judged in relationship to each other according to how they measure up (or not) to school standards and demands. And whereas many scholars (myself included) have documented mothers' experiences and perspectives on this phenomenon (David, 1993; Luttrell, 1997; Reay, 1998; Griffith & Smith, 2005; O'Brien, 2007; Dodson & Luttrell, 2011), this study features children's own viewpoints. This is a main theme in Chapter 3, where I consider how the kids picture their mothers and share their feelings and perspectives on their mothers' roles in their lives.

Another point of connection between women and children includes the extent of state as well as domestic violence against women and against children, violence that can make their survival mutually reliant. As I learned, this simple and notable fact even shaped who could participate in this project. For instance, several children whose mothers had restraining orders on former spouses or boyfriends were unable to secure parental consent, because their mothers were concerned that identifying information might expose their households to risk. Those children who could participate lived in families that were relatively stable and in homes that were safe.

Finally, a critical childhood perspective must take account of how the legacy of slavery, institutional racism, and colorism shape who is afforded the protected status of "child" to begin with. Black boys and girls have historically been granted limited consideration within the broader conception of childhood innocence—a pattern that continues today (Dumas & Nelson, 2016; Corsaro, 2015; Kehily, 2009; Majors, 2001; Morris, 2016). Robin Bernstein (2011) offers a convincing account of this racialization in her book *Racial Innocence: Performing American Childhood from Slavery to Civil Rights*. Like most scholars who reflect upon changing constructions of childhood, Bernstein identifies the shift from children being viewed as miniature adults (attributed to the work of historian Phillip Aries), to being seen as naturally sinful during the Colonial era, to being associated with a 19th-century notion of innocence, which was considered the single most important quality distinguishing children from adults. Bernstein illustrates how racial domination and de-humanization were woven into American popular culture—for example, "innocent" white children were used in advertisements to sell purity and tenderness, while Black children were portrayed as impish and invulnerable to hard work. Over time and in many different forms (for example, in books, like Harriet Beecher Stowe's *Uncle Tom's Cabin*; in theater, in film, and so on), Black children were repeatedly portrayed in ways that systematically excluded them from the domain of "childhood."

Christina Sharpe situates the roots of this exclusion in the economic system of slavery. Captured Africans—whether men, women or children—were not treated as human beings, but as "cargo" on slave ships, exposed to unspeakable violence, including being thrown overboard, murdered as part of a de-humanizing calculus to "save the rest of the cargo" (2016: 35).[4] Combing through slave trade and insurance records, including those from a ship called the *Zong* that became the subject of a complicated legal case where the ship's owner sued the insurance underwriters for "loss of property" when more than 130 Africans were thrown overboard and killed, Christina Sharpe found a disturbing detail in how records were kept:

> Purchasers are identified while Africans are reduced to the stark description of "negroe man" [*sic*] "negroe woman," or more frequently "ditto man," "ditto woman." There is one gloss to this description: "Negro girl (meager)." There are many "meagre girls," no "meagre boys." (2016: 142)

This small detail speaks volumes about the enduring societal failure to see Black boys as children, and the deadly consequences of this distorted vision. As Dumas and Nelson have put it, "Black boyhood is unimagined and unimaginable," and to assert this is to "lament that we have created a world in which Black boys cannot *be*" (2016: 28).

Indeed, research shows that people of all races see Black children as "aged" or viewed as older than they are and less innocent, more adultlike and more responsible for their actions than their white peers (Goff et al, 2014). Routine childhood behavior, like defiance, rule-breaking, limit-testing, and backtalk is seen as a criminal threat when Black kids, and especially Black boys, do it. According to a 2015 report by Kimberlé W. Crenshaw et al, this misperception causes Black children to be "pushed out, overpoliced and underprotected."[5] Even at young ages, as Ann Ferguson documents in *Bad Boys: Public Schools and the Making of Black Masculinity*, Black boys in elementary school are seen as threatening, and are over-disciplined and criminalized in what has been called the school-to-prison pipeline.[6] And as Miriam Tager (2017) illustrates, even in Pre-K settings, Black boys are viewed as less "ready" for schooling than any other group. This is not to say that other poor children and children of color, including children forcibly seized from parents at the border, are not also viewed as less "child"-like, less deserving of care, protection, and freedom to play and discover. Rather, my point is to draw attention to the enduring racialized ways of seeing and differentiating Black children that denies their access to "childhood."[7]

In adopting a critical childhood perspective, then, this study aims to address multiple challenges—avoiding "adultist" and neoliberal viewpoints and placing young people's agency, voices, and images at its center; rethinking how children's value and worth is assigned, especially in schooling; maintaining a focus on parallels and intersections between women's and children's experiences of structural oppression; and accounting for how the legacy of slavery, structural racism, and anti-Blackness inform views of childhood, gender, discipline/punishment, and learning. These lenses shape my way of seeing, listening to, and analyzing how the kids in this study speak about themselves, each other, their pictures, and their efforts to answer back to how they imagine they might be seen and unseen.

## The school

PCS might be aptly described as an ordinary[8] urban public elementary (K-6) school—that is, its gender and race/ethnicity contours parallel the profiles of public education teachers, children, and parents across the country (Figures 1.1–1.4).

Its teaching staff consisted predominantly of white, middle-class women serving native-born and immigrant children of racially, ethnically, and linguistically diverse poor and working-class families. As I mentioned in the Prelude, the 2003 demographic profile reported by the school indicated that the student population was 35 percent "Hispanic," 18 percent "Asian," 10 percent "Black," and 37 percent white.[9] If PCS displays an unusual characteristic as an urban school, it is its under-representation of Black children and its over-representation of Asian American children, an artifact of Worcester's population distribution by race and ethnicity.

The 1920s red brick building that housed PCS was iconic in its appearance. The wood and linoleum floors were clean; hallways were quiet; classrooms were bustling; the school staff was friendly; and the movement of children within and around the space was orderly. This was not a school in disarray, in crumbling physical condition, or hopelessly under-resourced, as is often the case for urban schools serving poor and working-class students.[10] But evidence of the

Children Framing Childhoods

Figure 1.1: Students and teachers in urban public schools by gender, 2003–04

## Students by gender 2003–04

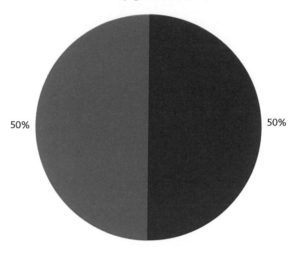

50%                    50%

## Teachers by gender 2003–04

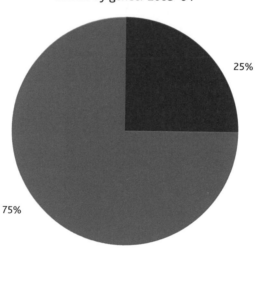

25%

75%

■ Male

■ Female

Source: NCES.ed.gov/pubs2006

Figure 1.2: Students in urban public schools by race/ethnicity, 2003–04

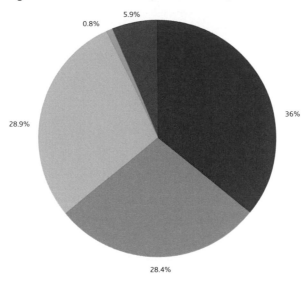

Figure 1.3: Teachers in urban public schools by race/ethnicity, 2003–04

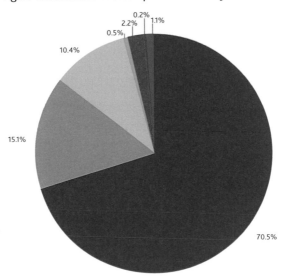

White, non-Hispanic    Black, non-Hispanic

Hispanic    American Indian/Alaska Native

Asian/Pacific Islander    Native Hawaiian/Pacific Islander

Multiple races, non-Hispanic

Source: NCES.ed.gov/pubs2006

Figure 1.4: Park Central School by race/ethnicity, 2003–04

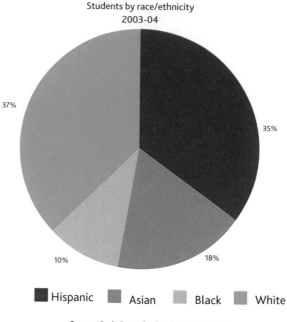

Source: Park Central School website, 2003

slow-drip effects of disinvestment could be seen in the absence of playground equipment, and there was anxious concern on the part of the principal and her staff about meeting the Adequate Yearly Progress (AYP) performance benchmarks newly required by the passage of NCLB legislation.

While NCLB sought to ensure a quality education for all students through such practices, it also established a process by which schools could be identified and labeled as "failing," creating a justification for turning schools over to the market (Lipman, 2011; Fabricant & Fine, 2012). Many schools failing to meet accountability standards—especially those in low-income communities—have been shut down, taken over by charter organizations, and/or "reconstituted" with entirely new faculty and staff (Baltodano, 2012; Rice & Croninger, 2005). In fact, Baltodano (2012) referred to NCLB as "one of the most important achievements of neoliberalism" (p. 495). When neoliberalism is applied to schools, education becomes a commodity, receptive to market forces. Within this framework, students are reconstructed as consumers—in this case, consumers of education. This framework moves conceptions of education closer to capitalistic concepts of choice and competition, and away from democratic ideals aimed at enabling students to become participatory citizens of a healthy democracy (Westbrook, 2010). These forces of neoliberalism provide a context and a particular approach to learning that will be discussed in more depth in Chapter 6.

In entering the building I sensed this was a school where adults were concerned about establishing a safe and welcoming learning environment based on mutual regard and respect. I got this feeling from the school's ambiance, its 5 Bs posters ("Be Here; Be Ready; Be Safe; Be Respectful; Be Responsible"); its nods to multiculturalism and globalization made most prominent by the "making a world of difference" bulletin board display in the main hallway; and by the bilingual Spanish-English signage on the library and bathroom doors.

## *Digital Interlude #1: Dwelling in School*

childrenframingchildhoods.com/digital-interludes/dwelling-in-school

These types of displays send powerful messages to students about the ways they do (or do not) belong in school.[11] There was also a home-like feel in the building—curtains, wallpaper borders, lamps, rugs—mitigating the institutional glare of fluorescent lights and exposed plumbing pipes. But the strongest signal of mutual regard was that Dr. G., the principal, had asked children to serve as my guides to the school, a confirmation of their potential as leaders as well as learners.

All of these features made me think that education philosopher Nel Noddings (1984) would call this a school centered on caring. Throughout my early conversations with Dr. G. I could hear references to two forms of caring that Noddings describes in her writings: aesthetic caring, on the one hand—the attention to aspects of teaching that are perceived as objective, such as "instructional goals"—and authentic caring, on the other. Authentic caring is rooted in relationships that attend to an individual child's unique needs, interests, and agency; and it was this aspect of caring that Dr. G. recognized in the project I proposed to her. What she found most appealing was the opportunity for teachers to learn from the children's photographs—their unique interests, family histories, cultural traditions, and values. When explaining the photography project to the School Board, Dr. G. emphasized its benefits to teachers:

"As educators, we must take the time to listen and to learn from our students. This project reminded our staff, once again, about the importance of learning about the lives, cultures, traditions and worldviews of our students and how these factors influence the teaching and learning process. As they do every day, our students helped us to learn.... [the project] was a powerful reminder that our vision can be cloudy or even blinded by our worldview and it is important to take the time to listen and learn through the eyes and words of others."

In Dr. G.'s description I hear an emphasis on authentic care, an insistence on taking the time (a precious commodity in the over-scheduled daily routines of school) to listen and learn, and a recognition that cross-class and cross-cultural "worldviews" require teacher reflection and revision. And as Dr. G. implies, challenging one's own worldviews doesn't occur by happenstance.[12]

As we will see in Chapter 4, Dr. G. set the tone for the school as a place for caring about caring and its multiple dimensions. Within the complex racial and ethnic landscape of the school, I was curious to learn, from the children's perspective, what their principal's emphasis on care meant to them. I was aware of Angela Valenzuela's (1999) pivotal text *Subtractive Schooling* that expanded educational theories of care by focusing on the experiences of Mexican and Mexican American high school students. Her study illustrated that white teachers and Latinx students held different orientations toward care to make sense of one another's behaviors and actions. Too often, teachers perceived students in deficit terms, as lacking care. But from the students' perspectives, caring was rooted in the concept of educación, which Valenzuela defined as "the family's role of inculcating in children a sense of moral, social, and personal responsibility [which] serves as the foundation for all other learning" (p. 23). For all immigrant and children of immigrants to be fully seen in school, Valenzuela advocated repositioning students' repertoires of knowledge, what Moll et al (1992) called "funds of knowledge" to the center of teaching and learning. Over the course our work together, I learned that the kids' perspectives were rooted in educación, but also in the multiple ways in which care linked them to others: to their teachers, school staff, classmates, family members, friends, and wider circles of community. But when I began this project, in the fall of 2003, my focus was a smaller one—I was interested in how the children saw their school and their places in it. I wanted to understand what they perceived the ethos of PCS to be. I wanted to hear about what was important to them, in their own words. In the debates about the many challenges facing American schools, I wanted to find ways to bring young people's perspectives into focus and their voices into dialogue.

In all, 36 young people lent their voices, thoughts, and images to this project. Throughout the book, I refer to them by pseudonyms, and I share some details of their backgrounds, offering their self-descriptions and my observations that I hope will help the reader to more vividly picture them and their families. (A complete list of all the participants can be found in the Appendix at the end of this book.)

## Finding a place: negotiating identities and ethics at school

I am sitting in the teacher resource room at PCS. It is April, 2003. The sunlight reflects off the sheer curtains that hang over a double window, illuminating a wooden shelf full of new literacy guidebooks. I have placed 35 of the children's photographs on a banquet-size table. Seven ten-year-old children—three girls and four boys—have each selected five photographs to share with their peers. They enter the room, bringing a palpable energy with them. Sebastian is laughing at Danny's wisecracks about his cousin, Tina, who trails behind them. Kendra and Nia get to the table first and excitedly point to each other's photographs. Isaiah joins the table last and asks Jack which photographs are his. I invite the children to walk around the table, tell each other what they notice, and ask any questions they might have of the photographer. My plan is to listen, not direct the conversation. "Try not to talk over each other so that everybody can hear," I suggest, pointing to the tape recorder. I am impressed by how much they adhere to this request—perhaps they want to ensure that their voices are captured on the tape recorder. They seem genuinely curious about who took which pictures, and they are quick to ask and answer questions about the contents of the photographs and to comment—"Where is this?" "I have that video game!" "Is that your mom?"

One particular exchange catches my ears. Jack, who is white, says, "I notice a lot of Chinese people." Danny and Tina, both the children of Vietnamese immigrants, have taken many family photographs (as well as photographs of photographs). I wait, curious to see whether they will correct Jack's ethnic assignment. They do not. But when Jack asks Nia who the three "Spanish kids" are in her photograph, she responds, "Oh, those are my sisters, but we don't speak Spanish." Then, pointing to an adult in the photograph, Nia says, "That's my uncle, he's Dominican. We are Dominican." Again I am quiet, wondering about their different ways of seeing and naming race/ethnicity but not wanting to interrupt the flow of conversation. Finally, my curiosity about how the children move in and out of using racial/ethnic markers prompts me to comment clumsily, "I see you are noticing different races and cultures of people in these photographs. What names would you give these different groups of people?" Nia responds, "There is a school rule that you can't call someone Black." "Why is that?" I ask. After some silence Kendra (who readers will remember is African American) says, "Because it isn't respecting." Jack follows: "Well, you could get into trouble."

So much is wrapped up in this exchange, including my own curiosity and uncertainty about what the children are collectively understanding and individually expressing about markers of race, ethnicity, language, and identity. I wonder about the parameters of the "school rule" and how are they making sense of it. That such a guideline exists—whether in fact or in effect—suggests attention to, if not apprehensions about, racial categories and codings. The children's discussion invokes the "color line" that W. E. B. Du Bois called the "problem of the twentieth century"[13]—and shows that it remains alive, too, as the problem of the 21st. How the children navigate its continuing challenges to the dignity afforded young people on the basis of skin color will become evident in different ways throughout my research. In this moment, I hear some children go silent (Danny and Tina) and others speaking back, not just to an individual speaker, in this case Jack, but to a larger discourse about the complicated links between language and identity (Nia and her sisters can speak English and still identify as Dominican). I will learn that these conversations about language are wrapped up with "racio-linguistic ideologies" that position some speakers as more legitimate than others.[14]

I also hear a "pedagogic voice" (Arnot & Reay, 2007) embedded in the children's perception of school rules about speaking about racial/ ethnic/linguistic differences. In the context of the school's focus on care, I hear two moral "voices" on the school rule, roughly echoing what feminist psychologist Carol Gilligan identified as an "ethic of care" and an "ethic of justice." Both guide people's thinking, feelings, and actions about social as well as personal problems, but within patriarchal society, an ethic of care has been associated with femininity and an ethic of justice with masculinity (1982). In this case, the unspoken social problem is the color line. Kendra articulates the school rule through a voice of care, focusing on the importance of preserving "respecting" relationships between people. Jack expresses the school rule through a voice of justice, speaking about what happens if one does not follow through on one's duties to be respectful. Paradoxically, in light of their association of the school rule with showing respect, something else is concealed. An underlying message of the rule is that Blackness is problematic, tainted in some way, not to be named or uttered. Whiteness, on the other hand, is unmarked and normalized. I can't help but wonder how Kendra (and Isaiah) understand their Blackness in this context and what Nia, whose photographed family members range from light brown to dark-skinned, is thinking and feeling.

Figure 1.5: My family *Tina, age 10*

In May 2003, this same group gathers to select photographs for a public exhibition. Each child has contributed a few photographs for consideration and the group is deliberating. One of Tina's photographs becomes a focal point of interest (Figure 1.5).

Pointing her finger outside the circle of her three brothers, Tina remarks, "I was here. I was going to take it just up to there. I couldn't take a picture of me." "Why?" asks the interviewer. "'Cause I didn't like myself. I look ugly." Tina shifts in her seat and looks directly at the video camera for the first time, as if addressing an "inspecting gaze" of negative judgment.[15]

It is a photograph of a family portrait. In her interview, Tina had explained that she had taken the picture so she could show her whole family because her parents' work schedule precluded the possibility of actually photographing them together. Tina instructed the interviewer to look to the left side of the picture where a child is slightly visible.

In the group conversation, Tina's photograph elicited a range of discourses and conventions through which the children's vision was being shaped.

"It looks old-fashioned," Isaiah remarked.

"It's to keep memories alive," added Nia.

Kendra asked, "Why is no one smiling?" Then after a moment of reflection she added, "Maybe they are sad about leaving their country."

Jack's reading of the photograph moved the conversation beyond the photograph in question. "I see different cultures, no offense. There are Chinese, or is it Japanese? Spanish, white, Black. I don't mean to be mean or rude or anything." "What do you mean?" I ask.

There was a moment of silence, broken by some laughter that felt like the kids might be closing ranks around Jack and against my adult intrusion. The conversation moved on, and I can only speculate about the meaning of their avoidance, especially as it pertained to the school rule.

As a white boy seeing race and ethnicity, who does Jack think he might offend? Indeed, the "offense" of seeing and speaking about race is complex, context-bound, and contingent upon the speaker and audience (which includes my whiteness and perhaps helps to explain the "closing of ranks" in this situation). Claiming to *not* see race, otherwise called colorblindness (Bonilla-Silva, 2003), is an element of white privilege that not only denies racial inequality but also negates the value of Blackness. At the same time, seeing race but neglecting to consider the effects of systemic racism—sometimes called color-muteness (Pollock, 2005) or race-avoidance (Frankenberg, 1993)—can serve to keep institutionalized racism and white supremacy intact.

Seeing and speaking, or not, about race/ethnicity and the feelings and orientations this mobilizes—respect, offense, silence, fear—are all part of how children navigate the available streams of adult racial discourse that are complex and context-bound, shifting in time and place.[16] By listening for the multiple meanings and emotions that circulated in the kids' discussion, we can hear their references to the conventions of photography, including specific affective norms such as smiling for a family portrait, as well as broader notions of history and memory. We can also hear articulated the loss and sadness associated with immigration and the morality and politics of seeing race/ethnicity.

Ultimately, the decision about whether to exhibit Tina's family portrait rested on Tina's assertion of control over "truth" and self-representation. Whereas the group voted in favor of publicly displaying the family portrait photograph, Tina refused, saying it wasn't a "real" photograph of her family: both she and her newborn brother were missing. This argument about the evidentiary value of the photograph held sway over her peers.

These exchanges, as well as others that will follow, remind us why schools are such unique sites of struggles over identity and agency—a topic that has been at the center of my research career and that I have explored from different angles (Luttrell, 1997, 2003). As sociologist of education Paul Willis writes there is no other site where:

> people of the same age are forced into a common arena, that compels individuals and groups to find a place and identity within a single complex matrix. No matter how heterogeneous their backgrounds or how differently their cultural destinies would have been played out without the unnatural social atmosphere of the school, it is within the constraints of this institution that young people negotiate their identities. (2005: 473)

Moreover, despite the fact that school experiences are to varying degrees segregated by age, race, ethnicity, gender, and social class, for many children and young people, schools remain the primary arena for directly engaging with an array of social and cultural differences (Abu El-Haj, 2006, 2015; McDermott et al, 2006).

Children's ongoing struggle to find their place in school is anxiety-ridden. Their negotiations occur not only on social terms (race, gender, class, sexuality, immigration status, language, and identity) and school terms (for example, through rules, expectations, constructions of who is "good/bad," "fast/slow," "smart/dumb," "able/disabled," "at-risk/a threat") but also on their *own* terms, as human beings with particular histories, values, traditions, and moral perspectives. Children's negotiations in school are complex and fraught engagements with larger social discourses that often operate below conscious awareness as kids wrestle with the swirls and tugs of others' (for example, parents', teachers', friends') conversations and interactions, ideas, and intentions in an effort to make their own meaning. Russian literary critic Mikhail Bakhtin (1981) calls this social process ventriloquation, an ongoing cultural and ideological process that we all pursue, "an intense struggle within us for hegemony of various available and ideological points of view, approaches, directions and values" (1981: 346).[17]

These negotiations with larger social discourses and creative appropriations of adult language were especially evident when I asked the children to provide me with self-descriptions. For example, a boy named Junior described himself as "Haitian; Haiti is my country, I talk Creole, that is my culture. I am a good kid, I pay attention more than my brother. I can speak Creole but most people can't in America. All these things that I know about Haiti makes me creative." Following this, as was my practice, I asked him to fill in the blank: Junior is _____. He offered, "friendly, short, pretty smart, fast runner, strong, likes to listen to people when people are talking. I am not disrespectful, I like that." His response, like many others', was both simple and profound in articulating not only his perceived strengths, skills, and values, but also his role in his community.

His classmate Allison struggled a bit to position herself, using the racial and linguistic landscape of the school and who "hangs out with" whom:

> "I mean, like, mostly, I'm not trying to be racist or anything, but mostly the Spanish people, they like to hang out with each other. But they sometimes will like to hang out with us. It's just, we all like to hang around with each other but then sometimes we just want to hang around with ... who we're, who we're like."

When Allison was asked whom she likes to hang around with, she identified her friends in the following way:

> "Emily is from Massachusetts and I don't know what she is. But I know what Gina is. She's Italian. She is American. And I am Italian, American, um, Irish. I am all of that. Gina

is really Italian, she knows how to speak it and she went there and everything."

Asked to fill in the blank, Allison claimed she was "a really funny person":

> "'Cause I'm really funny. I tell a lot of jokes. I'm really kind and generous to people and with my things. And I like to help. With, um, schoolwork, with people that don't get somethin'. I like to help. I make friends with the good people and the not, well, *I'm friends with everybody*, [emphasis hers] but, I don't, I don't want to be friends with the people who, like, go down to the office all the time. But I'll be nice to them if they wanna talk to me, but I don't wanna be attached to them 'cause, then, I might, they might blame it on me and then I'll have to go to the office. And that's mostly it."

We can hear Allison carefully positioning herself with other white girls, but she is sensitive to not appearing "racist" and moves from "them" and "us" to "we" to explain the dynamics of group affiliations. Meanwhile, Allison's humor, kindness, and generosity were often on display during the times I was observing. In her cohort, she was the most frequent subject of others' photographs as a "good friend," and this held across boys and girls as well as racial/ethnic lines, including the "Spanish" kids. Like Junior, Allison is attuned to her role in her community.

One aim of this book is to lift up the skillful agility of the children to make their own meanings of their surroundings, to navigate their place, belonging, and dignity in school, and to mark the invisible work they do to establish themselves as valued and respected members of their school and peer culture.

## Giving kids cameras

"Giving kids cameras" research has burgeoned in the last 25 years (Clark, 1999; Orellana, 1999; Clark–Ibanez, 2004; Cook & Hess, 2007; Prosser & Burke, 2008; Thomson, 2008; Tinkler, 2008; Luttrell & Chalfen, 2010; Yates, 2010; Mitchell, 2011; Kaplan, 2013).[18] According to Sharples et al (2003), many of these projects treat young people as "apprentice" photographers, adopting an adultist view of children as simply immature learners of adult culture or adult ways of seeing.[19]

This project was not focused on providing technical instruction or aesthetic directives; rather, the emphasis was on exploring the kids' uses of the camera and to consider what could be learned from their choices. In a school setting, especially in an era of standardization and highly scripted curricula, allowing children this kind of freedom of self-expression set the project apart from "business as usual."

I adapted some basic principles of Photovoice to guide the project (Wang & Burris, 1997; Wang, 1999; Strack et al, 2004). Photovoice is a visual methodology designed to encourage bottom-up policy and practice reforms in diverse contexts such as public health, education, housing, and neighborhood planning, among others. Photovoice puts cameras in the hands of people who don't usually have a voice in policy making, including children and young people, and enables them to record and reflect on concerns as well as strengths in domains of everyday life. My research team and I explained to the children that this was an opportunity for them to represent their point of view to adults who are in charge of making decisions and teaching children like themselves. But an important discovery of this research is how much the children took charge in shifting the audience for their images from school adults to family members and friends.

One of the aims of my project was to advance Photovoice and "giving kids cameras" research—a practice that, with some exceptions, remains under-theorized. I offer this study as an example of how to preserve multiple, sometimes competing meanings that are too often neglected, opening new methodological and analytical possibilities – an approach I came to call "collaborative seeing."

## Digital Interlude #5: Collaborative Seeing

childrenframingchildhoods.com/digital-interludes/collaborative-seeing

I encouraged, recorded, and analyzed numerous dialogues about the children's pictures and picture-taking: individual interviews in which the children would instruct us (adult researchers, teachers, and other viewers) about their choices and their images' meanings; informal conversations among the children about each other's images, intentions, and goals; more discussions among the children as they prepared to exhibit their photographs; and finally, years later, retrospective reflections during which the young people had an opportunity to revisit their childhood images and consider how they represented and transformed themselves over time. This last piece of the process highlights my embrace of a broader definition of "development," which I elaborate upon throughout the book as the young people's ongoing efforts and commitments to creating and sustaining social bonds that establish their value within otherwise hostile systems of value (including school that values competitive individualism over an ethic of collective effort).

It was clear from the start that the children associated the research team (and me in particular)[20] with adult authority and dominant educational values. While I introduced the research as a "Photovoice" project, the students called it the "Harvard Project" (and then later the "CUNY Project").[21] They spoke about completing their "assignment" of taking photographs. In their interviews, some children identified times they hadn't "stayed on task" by taking this or that photograph. Insofar as I wanted to learn how the children would take up, bend, or reject dominant school discourses that focused on performance and achievement culture, these regulatory references were telling. Most important, I wanted to open a space for conversations that do not typically take place in school settings, especially in an increasingly competitive environment driven by high-stakes testing. As participants in the project, the children were implicitly asked to engage and reflect upon their ways of seeing their surroundings, on (and in) their own terms.

Readers will remember Jeffrey's earnest assessment when the cameras were distributed that "having a camera is a big responsibility" and would require special care. I learned quickly that the children shared an orientation to the camera as more than a tool for documenting their lives; perhaps more importantly, it was also a valued possession that they used in distinctive ways. Drawing upon sociologist Allison Pugh's research on childhood consumer culture (2009), I came to understand the appeal of the camera as a token of value in what Pugh calls "economies of dignity," where children "collect or confer dignity among themselves, according to their (shifting) consensus about what sort of objects or experiences are supposed to count for it" (2009: 7).[22] Pugh makes two key claims that were borne out over the course of this project. First, children shape their own economies of dignity despite the imposition of childhood consumer culture. The value of certain goods and experiences (video games, birthday parties, clothing items) are not given, but actively negotiated between children, especially in settings where they must cross class, race, and cultural divides, as in many schools. Second, there are multiple economies of dignity depending on the context—at home, at school, in after-school programs, in the neighborhood, at church—where different signs/symbols of value are used to ensure social belonging. As I listened to these negotiations over the course of this project, I could detect the children's curiosities about—and, at times, challenges to—social divisions.

As I explained in the Prelude, the children brought numerous lenses to the prompt for picturing-taking: "Imagine you have a cousin moving to Worcester. Take pictures of your home, school, and community that will help your cousin know what to expect." In the brainstorming session on possible things to photograph, they brought up the topics of (dis)comfort, admiration, respect, and worries ("what concerns you"), and these topics set the stage for their explorations of the politics of belonging and dignity.

Aside from the prompts, we did not encourage the children to produce any particular kind of image, believing that there is merit in preserving and understanding whatever meanings children might give to their images if they are listened to carefully and systematically. Nor did I assume that there would be an authentic, single, or "neutral" voice inside a child that could somehow be elicited through an image.[23] Rather, I sought to understand which voices children would exercise when speaking about their photographs in specific contexts and in relation to specific audiences.

There are nagging and hard-to-answer questions when adult researchers give kids cameras—what ideas of childhood, self, school, and society are being brought into focus, from whose perspective, and with what purpose in mind? There is a sociological legacy for using photography in this way. W. E. Du Bois' pioneering attempt to re-create a theory of African American childhood through photography stands out in this regard. In 1923, Du Bois called for submissions of photographs "of interesting children, not necessarily pretty and dressed-up, but human and real" (Du Bois 1923, cited in Phillips, 2013: 597). Michelle Phillips (2013) writes that Du Bois' effort was to build not only a "more democratic imagery but a more democratic imaginary" of African American childhood and personhood (2013: 597). In contrast to the "many and singularly different ideas" of childhood at the time, from the child as "bond slave," "automaton," "Item of Expense," and parental "personal adornment," Du Bois sought to offer what "few people think of": "the child as Itself—as an Individual with the right and ability to feel, think and act; a being thirsty to know, curious to investigate, eager to experiment" (Du Bois 1923, cited in Phillips, 2013: 599).

In light of this history, it is curious that so few "giving kids cameras" studies consider the codes, conventions, and theories that guide children's photography, or comment on the constructions of childhood that young people in these studies are reflecting, rejecting, or inventing. Similarly, it is often hard to distinguish between children's own intentions or "readings" of their photographs and those of the adult researchers who seek to represent them (Piper & Frankham, 2007). In both cases, a form of "adultism" (albeit sometimes unwittingly) underlies the practice. While I do not claim to fully answer this question in my project, I offer some strategies that allow for a fuller appreciation of what the children in this project were doing with their cameras.

When given cameras at ages ten and 12, the children produced more family photographs than images of school or community life. In one sense, it could be argued that the children embraced the prescription that "cameras go with family life," reflecting what is said to be the earliest use of photography—the establishment of the "family album" (Sontag, 1977: 8). But, as Laura Wexler has argued, the history of the family album has always been politically (and racially) fraught:

> A century and a half into the abundant store of photographic images of American domestic life, it is well to remember that the American family album was severely out of balance from the start. The paired questions of who takes the pictures and who is in the pictures are not the only issue. The evidence from slavery suggests that the formal principles of family photography can only evolve in relation to the political principles that govern the recognition of families in the first place. Who would gain control of the domestic signifier through photography has been an issue ever since the medium was invented in 1839. (2000: 3)

In Chapters 2 and 3, which examine the children's photos of family and home, I illustrate how the young people took control of domestic signifiers to represent their families with pride and dignity—a key feature of the children's use of their cameras. Their pictures and explanations communicate their place in communal webs and choreographies of care, revealing aspects of the organization of family life that might otherwise have remained buried—including, for example, the value the children placed on their mothers' roles in "feeding the family" (DeVault, 1991). In another sense, their photographs can be read as evidence of familial ideology—presentations of harmony, togetherness, unity, and happiness (Chalfen, 1987) that reflect not only children's representational desires and choices, but also their sense of what viewers expect. Given a "flow of family life" that might not match up with projected expectations, for instance, photos could be used to create an impression of family coherence (Hirsh, 1997: 7). Indeed, the most common reason the children gave for taking a picture of a family photograph (as Tina did) was to "show my whole family" when parents (most often fathers) or other extended family members were unavailable to be photographed for numerous reasons, ranging from the demands of shift work to migration, incarceration, divorce, and death.

## The complex life of pictures and voices

In its broadest sense, this project aimed to engage young people as individuals with abilities and desires to feel, think, and act; or, put slightly differently, it engaged them as free people with free minds. Two elements of the project design stand out in this regard. First is that the children's assent was not taken for granted, but was instead established in an ongoing process. As an institution, school is a context of forced compliance, and to mitigate against this imperative, the children were encouraged to exercise their rights, both the right to "opt in" to the project as well as to "opt out" (Alderson, 1995; Valentine, 1999) at any time.[24] The children were also in charge of which photographs they would discuss with an interviewer, which photographs they would share with teachers and peers, and finally, which images they wanted to be part of a public exhibition of their work. They were also invited to edit a video clip of themselves speaking about their five favorite photographs with an interviewer.[25] I was surprised that not many children exercised this freedom, even as many children (mostly girls) covered their eyes, laughed with delight and/or embarrassment about how they looked or sounded. There were two exceptions. As Tina watched her video, she kept covering her mouth and shaking her head. At the end, she said she thought she sounded "stupid" when speaking English and asked to be re-recorded speaking Vietnamese, her mother tongue. This request surprised her fifth-grade teacher, who was unaware of her fluency in Vietnamese and was perplexed by Tina's negative feelings about speaking English, which, by all measures, was "perfect." The other exception was Angeline, the daughter of immigrants from Kenya, who asked that her video be edited. In place of her stated aspiration to become a fashion designer, Angeline wanted the video revised to express a different occupational choice—that of becoming a doctor. I have pondered over the significance of these video edits, wondering what they might reveal about how children make sense of their institutional positioning, where the primary emphasis is on educational success. I take note of the fact that Tina requests to speak in her first language because she hears herself as "stupid" in English. How has she learned to hear and assess herself in these deficit terms? Paradoxically, her desire to speak in Vietnamese is couched in school terms—to sound and be judged as "smart" and not as an exercise of cultural identity, free expression, or a free mind. Similarly, I suspect that Angeline's request is tied to a sense that her aspirations are seen and judged through societal and school lenses that value medicine over fashion.[26] Or perhaps she is simply exercising her "freedom" to change her mind.

There was an explicit discussion of the ethics of the photography "assignment" not only in the picture-taking, but also the picture-sharing. Through role-playing activities, the children practiced the ethics of picture-taking, focusing on issues of intrusion, embarrassment, and consent (Gross et al, 1988). They were encouraged to try different approaches to asking people for permission to be photographed, to explore why a person might want to say no, and to consider how this also related to their own participation in the project. We also discussed what, if any, photographs they might decide not to share with an interviewer, peer group, teacher, or in the public exhibition and why that might be. There were a few photographs the children debated. One particular conversation stood out for its complex connection between childhood innocence and children's rights. Pictures of babies and toddlers were a common subject—babies displayed propped up with pillows, wearing sunglasses, or dressed up in comical outfits; toddlers pushing toys, dancing, and making funny faces—these iconic snapshots of babyhood and its pleasures drew immediate and routinely patterned responses of glee and tender commentary about the cuteness, sweetness, and playfulness of babyhood.

It would seem that the young people in this project took up an early convention of photographic subject matter: children. Anne Higonnet writes in *Pictures of Innocence: The History and Crisis of Ideal Childhood* (1988) that the introduction of photography consolidated the ideal of childhood innocence as completely natural. She refers to this innocence as part of "Romantic childhood," an Enlightenment ideal of the child's body as innocent of adult sexuality and the child's mind as blank, which found visual expression in the 18th-century elite British portraiture of painters like Sir Joshua Reynold, Thomas Gainsborough, and Sir Henry Raeburn. Higonnet claims that this new vision of childhood began to permeate popular consciousness, helped along by new image technologies, artists, and audiences. Eventually, with "cheap, easy camera equipment and film processing, pictures of children were at almost everyone's disposal, both to look at and to make. The more people saw or made photographs of children, the more axiomatic the image of childhood innocence became" (1998: 9). And as I mentioned earlier, these proliferating images were racially tainted, featuring the innocence of white children.

But the children read more than innocence into their pictures of babies. Alanzo shared just such an axiomatic photograph of his two-year-old sister asleep, sucking her thumb. His voice grew soft and gentle as he caressed the edges of the photograph and told me in the interview that he had taken it because he loved her. Then he laughed and said that the only time she wasn't "bugging" him was when she was asleep. During the group discussion, his classmates cooed at the "cute," "adorable," "sweet" child. Then Crystal asked, "Do you think your sister might be mad you took this picture of her sucking her thumb?" This question generated a controversy. There were those who thought Alanzo shouldn't have taken the photograph without his sister's consent. "But do babies count?" others asked. Some said that all Alanzo had to do was get her permission to use it—"she can talk," and he should have the "right to show her." One child suggested that Alanzo should decide because his sister was too little to make such a decision. Still another child, anticipating the future, remarked, "when she gets older she might not like seeing herself sucking her thumb."

This exchange is laced with layers of meaning about the power and control of images. I hear the children wrestling with an emphasis on the "right to look" and the "right to be seen" and the complexities of who gets to make these decisions, in what contexts, and with what consequences. Knowing that we take and use photographs as identity statements, as a means to discover who we are or who we have been, the children seem concerned about protecting Alanzo's sister from a potential later self-discovery (as if thumb-sucking might be held against her). And indeed, the search to make sense of themselves in light of the past through photography animated the young people's conversations years later, as teenagers revisiting their own childhood images. As 17-year-old Nalanie remarked:

> "It's funny looking at these old photos. I mean, who you are is made up of your past. But there are things I don't recognize about how I look. It's really funny seeing me on the outside 'cause all I know is me on the inside. And so much has changed."[27]

Indeed, self-definitions can be contradicted, reinforced, or even created by the existence of a photograph.

It was also common for the children to hand their cameras over to a family member, friend, or teacher to establish an identity as "doing something good," as one child put it (for example, reading, recycling, completing homework, doing chores, and helping others). There was an interesting pattern that echoed one found by Richard Chalfen in his youth film project in Philadelphia during the 1970s (Chalfen, 1981). In brief, he found that working-class youth were most interested in appearing on camera and less concerned about who took the images, whereas middle-class youth were more concerned about being in control of the camera and of editing as a means to express a point or tell something about life. In a similar vein, the most advantaged children who participated in this project (in terms of parental occupation, education, and economic resources) were least likely to hand their cameras over (or to report having a family member take over the camera).

Most important, the children had their own purposes and audiences in mind for taking certain pictures. For example, during his interview, Gabriel turned away from the interviewer and spoke directly to the video camera while holding his photograph up for view: "Mommy, I took this picture for you, I'm sorry it is blurry." Whereas Gabriel addressed his mother as the primary audience for his picture of the church, in conversation with his peers he declared that he took the picture because this is where he goes to "hang with the teenagers" who invite him to join their activities even though he is "only in fifth grade." Gabriel's different identity claims were in dialogue with different audiences, and I argue that these differences must be preserved as a means to appreciate his self-definition—his attachment to his mother; his negotiation of status with his peers; and his shift in the video-taped interview away from the interviewer/educator gaze in order to claim the assignment for his own purposes.

The children's interactions with the adult interviewers—predominantly white, female graduate students in their twenties and early thirties, and me, a white middle-aged professor—provided rich insight into their identity work, including how they took charge of the interview (or not), set the pace, asserted their expertise, resisted some questions, played with power, cued into authority and status, shifted topics (for example, "I'm not ready to talk about that") or found their own purpose for the assignment, as Gabriel did.

It would not do justice to the children's agency or investment in their images to collapse the meanings of their photographs into any single theoretical framework. Nor would it do justice to the children's engagement with the "complex life"[28] of their own and each other's images. As I watched individual children carefully scrutinize an image, skip over others, and sometimes become immediately affected by an image they declared to be their "favorite" (their own or another's), I was struck by how hard it was to put what I was witnessing into words. I was reminded of the unintended details and mysteries that photographs hold for some viewers, according to Roland Barthes's classic work, *Camera Lucida* (1981)—and I wondered whether this was what I might be observing. Barthes writes about the "punctum" that "pricks" the viewer and makes her/him reach for words to say what can't easily be expressed. Barthes also uses the metaphor of a photograph serving as an "umbilical cord" of light that joins viewer and viewed into relation (1981: 81). This metaphor was useful, especially in thinking about the relationship between child photographer and his/her subject matter—a topic I address in Chapter 3.

There is an unsettled relationship between what we see, how an image makes us feel, and what we can formulate into words, and this is why I have advocated taking a "need-to-know-more stance" in this study, and in visual research more broadly. My goal is to invite reflexivity—prompting viewers/readers to notice their own identifications with, projections onto, and feelings evoked by the young people's images. For no matter who we are, our eyesight and understanding is partial.

It is, of course, well established that photography is a technology with tremendous power in directing the gaze. But photography can also redirect, contest, and unlock the gaze, and I share with many other scholars an aim to utilize visual methods to promote social awareness and justice. I am interested in how the kids' photographs offer what visual theorist Mirzoeff (2011) calls "countervisuality." He defines visuality as "the means by which authority is sutured to power." If visuality is the "way that authority envisions itself, gains and maintains power, constructs and legitimates its own worldview as natural," then "countervisuality is a kind of rebuff, a rejection—a refusal to accept visuality's claims to truth, neutrality, and authority" (Restler & Luttrell, 2018: 467).

A good example of visuality in the context of contemporary schooling can be seen in the presentation of "authoritative" information about students, teachers, learning, and teaching through the display of quantitative assessments in charts, tables, graphs, and statistics. These may be important "data points." But these images, born of neoliberal reforms and emphasis on accountability culture reduce the complex realities and humanity of learning and teaching (Restler, 2017; Vinson & Ross, 2003). I believe the young people's images and accounts offer a radically different vision of themselves in which they are not data points, not statistics or scores, but rather creative agents making powerful claims about the value of care, belonging, dignity, and an ethos of collectivity.

# 2

# The everyday politics of belonging/s

Ten-year-old Kendra, who served as my guide on my first visit to PCS, arrives to her interview wearing a crisp, white cotton top embroidered with violet flowers; this is underneath a pastel blue corduroy jumper. Her plaited hair is pulled back from her slender face; gold post earrings emphasize her delicate features. She smiles broadly when I reach to shake her hand and welcome her to the interview. She sits shyly composed, without making eye contact with the video camera. She looks intently at her set of photographs and then at me. "I am ready," she announces. Kendra is indeed ready: she has precise answers for why she took each photograph, illustrating her thorough knowledge of the "assignment"—to introduce an imaginary cousin to Worcester through photographs depicting her family, school, and community.

She gestures first to two images of the entrance to her apartment building, part of the Terrace Gardens public housing project. "This is where I am comfortable [pointing to Figure 2.1], and this is where I feel respect" [pointing to a similar photograph but without her friends, not shown here]. But when she views the next photograph [Figure 2.2], she corrects herself and starts over: "this is where I *belong* [Figure 2.1]; this is where I feel *respect* [pointing to the photograph of her

Figure 2.1: Where I belong *Kendra, age 10*

Figure 2.2: Where I feel comfortable *Kendra, age 10*

apartment without her friends, not shown here]; and this is where I feel *comfortable* [Figure 2.2]." Then she names each stuffed animal and doll lined across her bed, explaining that "Tigger," the bright yellow striped tiger, is most recent—a Christmas gift from her mother. Kendra has displayed these items to show her imaginary cousin, "but they aren't usually lined up like that."

I am struck by the constellation of feelings Kendra has linked to her home—comfort, belonging, and respect. The way Kendra uses her camera and narrates the meaning of her images establishes a way of seeing her surroundings that is similar to the tour she provided me of her school. I hear Kendra's pride in her home, as well as her awareness that others might judge it differently. The simple fact that two thirds of Kendra's pictures are taken of her home and family makes a powerful statement about what she chooses to be identified with and what she wishes to commemorate. Her photographs help to convey her values and sense of self, perhaps even more effectively than her words do. Indeed, Kendra was not alone in taking more photographs at home than in school or in the wider community, as the following graph of all student photo settings indicates (see Figure 2.3).

The children's images make clear that they used their cameras to honor their "homeplaces", a term coined by bell hooks to acknowledge home not as "property, but as places where truly all that matter[s] in life [takes] place—the warmth and comfort of shelter; the feeding of our bodies; the nourishing of our souls" (1990: 383). Written decades

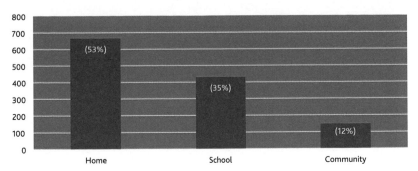

Figure 2.3: Fifth-graders' photographs by setting

ago to acknowledge Black women's care work and domesticity as a site for subversion and resistance, the elements of homeplaces that hooks outlined echo throughout the young people's accounts. The photographs of their homes and the spaces within them do not show mere rooms of buildings but "dwellings"—places within the current of life activities where worlds are made, whether in imagination or "on the ground" (Ingold, 2000: 154 in McFarlane, 2011: 660). In this chapter, I invite viewers to consider how the children are actively making their family worlds of belonging, engaging researchers and one another to show that they are cherished, protected, and cared for. At the same time, I show how easy it is to mis-read these displays.

Kendra's way of showing and speaking about her home dwelling is exemplary for the way it establishes her story of belonging. In Figure 2.1 she emphasizes her passage from home to school and back, an everyday activity that she undertakes with her best friend and a neighbor. After school, the three children do their homework together at Kendra's kitchen table. The journey from home to school and its significance as a collective endeavor among family and friends was a common theme in the children's images, and this will be discussed more in Chapter 3. The point here is that Kendra's story of belonging has a landscape and is grounded in her traveling from one place to another in the company of friends.

Figure 2.2 identifies another facet of Kendra's sense of belonging at Terrace Gardens through her careful display of prized possessions that she wants her imagined "cousin" to see. "My cousin would want to see the things that are special to me." I hear Kendra welcoming her cousin into her material world, aware of and attuned to her cousin's possible interest in (or need for) belongings/objects. At the same time, Kendra lets me know that her stuffed animals have been gifts—an indication that she is cared for, that she is special in others' eyes. Kendra also confesses that the stuffed animals are "not always lined up like that," making clear that there is hidden "labor and consciousness that bring objects to life," as historian Gaston Bachelard has argued (1957: 74). Just as "the housewife awakens the sleeping furniture" to create a home through her domestic labor and care (quoted in Auslander, 2005: 1021), Kendra has made her bed and "lined up" the stuffed animals. Her story of her dwelling and her belongings rests on invisible care work—both her own labor and that of those who care for her—and as we will see, this theme recurs throughout the children's accounts of their cherished objects.[1]

Finally, Kendra connects her sense of belonging at Terrace Gardens to "respect." She intentionally took another photograph of her building at the center of the frame and pointed to her bedroom window. Her explicit association between her home, her bedroom window, and her feelings of "respect" prompts me to think more deeply about who and what might have the power to shape the dynamic process of belonging. There is a difference, after all, between belonging and the politics of belonging (Yuval-Davis, 2011). Belonging is about an emotional (or even ontological) attachment, about feeling "at home" in a "safe" space (Ignatieff, 2001)—comfortable, rooted, among friends.[2] Belonging doesn't have to be confined to a domestic space or limited to a physical geography, especially in the age of the internet and the global migration of people.[3] The politics of belonging, on the other hand, have to do with judging or policing who belongs through the construction of boundaries and groupings of people, whether according to origin, "race," place of birth, language, culture, religion, or shared value systems, to name a few. To understand Kendra's links between her *homeplace* and her story of belonging, we must also attend to larger social forces and divisions that shape how she is making sense of her world.

Terrace Gardens, where Kendra lives, is one of three public housing projects in Worcester, designed after World War II to house returning veterans. In 2003, Terrace Gardens was in need of rehabilitation and had been targeted for capital improvements for several years, but tight state budgets had deferred repairs. The housing is referred to as the "super blocks" because there are few streets that enter each development, and each block is more densely populated than those in neighboring communities. This design "inadvertently isolated low-income families," according to a 2001 Worcester housing report,[4] reducing cohesion with surrounding neighborhoods. In recent years, housing specialists have noted the detrimental effects of this kind of public housing design because it cuts off residents from the larger community. While not made explicit in the report, the design could also be said to contribute to racial segregation: the vast majority of residents are African American or Latinx. The report mentions that "although it is sometimes believed that the super blocks have the highest crime in the city, that is not the case" (n.p.). But the high school dropout rate for those living in the super blocks is double the rate of the city at large, and only 39 percent of adult residents in the super blocks have a high school diploma or GED (n.p.).

A concentration of wage-poor families of color, an educational opportunity gap, deteriorating facilities, and city-wide perceptions of the super blocks as crime-ridden present a potent portrayal of life in Terrace Gardens. The spatial isolation and racial residential segregation create an axis of social difference that must be navigated by the children living there, and by children in similar settings all across the country.

An exchange between Kendra and a classmate about the following photograph (Figure 2.4) brings these navigations into stark relief.

During a recorded peer discussion, six children are looking through each other's photographs, describing to one another what they "notice." Allison picks up Kendra's photograph of her board games (Figure 2.4), which she has displayed in a similar fashion as her stuffed animals in Figure 2.2. Allison excitedly exclaims that she, too, has Candy Land and Monopoly but not Mancala, and that she also has Tigger. Kendra responds quickly with a smile and says Allison is welcome to come play it at her house after school and bring Tigger. Allison, who is white and lives in a multi-dwelling "three decker" near the school, says, "But my mother won't let me go to Terrace Gardens. She says it isn't safe."

Figure 2.4: My games *Kendra, age 10*

Allison's mother's view, delivered in her daughter's voice, is a commonly held local perspective. Kendra responds swiftly and matter-of-factly: "That's not true, it is the safest place that I have lived." (Recall that Kendra has already moved three times during her elementary school career). Allison embraces this response just as quickly, saying, "Good, then I will tell my mom that I can come to your house."

Both girls' conversational agility in transcending the negative perception of Terrace Gardens is noteworthy. It draws attention to the politics of belonging and the role that commodified goods—such as games and toys—play as a means for children to both uphold and reject social differences between themselves and their peers (Pugh, 2009). Kendra refutes the construction of her home as unsafe, and Allison prepares to challenge and adjust the boundaries of "safety." They also both avoid the sting and scorn of difference, with Tigger and Mancala serving as shared tokens of value that fix the social glue of belonging.

This is not the only time or way that the children navigate social differences as they examine each other's photographs. Huan lingers over Manny's photograph of his living room in Terrace Gardens. "My parents say Terrace Gardens is dangerous so I can't go there, but it looks nice." Perhaps working to avoid the social stigma of the housing project, Manny shifts the conversation: "We have the biggest apartment, and my mom's boyfriend just got us two big-screen TVs." Manny's form of establishing his worthiness differs from Kendra's, but in each case, a shared token of value and prized possession is key to challenging the boundaries of belonging.

Meanwhile, Crystal, who also resides in Terrace Gardens, expresses an alternative yearning as she examines an array of photographs. Picking up a photograph of Vivian's white-painted three-decker home (Figure 2.5), she says, "I wish I lived here—whose house is this? Who lives here?"

Vivian, the youngest of five children, and the first to be born in the United States since her parents migrated from China, answers, "I do." "Do you have your own bedroom?" Crystal inquires. Vivian shakes her head no; "my whole family [including grandparents, an aunt and uncle, and their two children] live in our apartment. But I have my own bed. See, here is my bed." "So do I," Crystal replies as they exchange photographs. Again, both girls skillfully patch over a conversational hitch that could have elicited uncomfortable feelings—but instead of exploring or exploiting their differences, each preserves her own standing through mutual agreement about the value of having one's own bed, if not bedroom. For to have a bed of one's

Figure 2.5: My apartment *Vivian, age 10*

own is to demonstrably possess a degree of privacy and autonomy (Csikszentmihalyi & Rochberg-Halton, 1981).

Drawing on the insights of sociologist Allison Pugh and her research on childhood consumer culture (2009), I understand the children's conversations as efforts to belong in their social worlds, establish a sense of worthiness, and achieve dignity in the eyes of their peers. Pugh's extensive ethnographic research followed children growing up in both affluent and low-income families in Oakland, California. She spent time in schools, in homes, after school, at birthday parties, on shopping trips, and so on, immersing herself in the everyday lives of children as well as their parents. As an urban center that is even more unequal than most American cities, Oakland has its own distinct landscape of difference, with geographically delineated class- and race-based communities. Affluent whites, Asian Americans, and some African Americans live in the hills, separated from poor African Americans, Latinx, and some Asian Americans living in the flats. Because of the close proximity of these two socioeconomic groups, Pugh's research was able to cross great divides in household resources to illustrate both the differences and similarities in how children and parents make meaning of the same consumer desires and commodities, including popular movies, toys, clothes, play equipment, and educational opportunities, to name a few. Pugh's research features the dance of both sets of players in the story of childhood consumer culture and belonging: children, who engage consumer goods and experiences as the "fabric of belonging" *vis-à-vis* their peers; and adults, who use these same goods and experiences to symbolize their care and standing as "good" parents (2009: 80–1).[5]

Pugh found that both low-income and affluent children relate to coveted belongings as a means to establish their worthiness and visibility within their social worlds and peer culture. "The deep appeal of possessions—in which the child used particular objects or events to represent good qualities about themselves—was in their ability to symbolize the children's membership in a larger community of care" (2009: 223). Pugh argues that children engaged in these symbolic efforts not simply to make themselves appear better than others, but to overcome or assuage worries about what they actually lacked—whether wealth or "the claim to someone's loving attention." She makes it clear that such efforts were not limited to low-income children. Both groups of children worked to "[portray] themselves as somebody's focal point …The difference was that affluent children used a wider variety of tactics to do so" (2009: 223).

Pugh coins the phrase "economics of dignity" to describe how children bargain over what sort of objects or experiences count as valuable and worthy (2009: 6–7). This focus on the negotiation of value is an important point of departure from earlier arguments about consumer culture. The dominant assumption has been that people buy things in order to seek status—that is, to make themselves appear better than, or at least keep up with, others. But Pugh found that children were more concerned about belonging and "joining the circle" than about being the best or having the most. We can hear this bargaining between Crystal and Vivian as they reach a consensus over the dignity of their respective homes: they both have their own bed. We can hear it in Manny's move to confer dignity on his home in Terrace Gardens by invoking the markers of a "nice" home—spaciousness and big-screen TVs. In the everyday politics of belonging, Manny is not trying to "better" Huan, or simply "saving face" or managing stigma, as the earlier sociological interpretations of Erving Goffman (1963/1986) might have it. Manny is most importantly preserving his standing in the school and peer culture by making clear that he is cared for—that he is the deserving recipient of someone else's beneficence. The politics of belonging takes another form in Allison and Kendra's conversation as they plan a playdate to reject inherited social divisions and stigma about Terrace Gardens, instead jointly establishing their place as members of the same peer group.

Kendra revisits the politics of belonging again when she tells me about a photograph of a book, which she took to convey her love of reading (Figure 2.6).

Figure 2.6: My favorite book *Kendra, age 10*

I mentioned earlier that Kendra is generally soft-spoken and deliberate, but she becomes especially animated when telling the plot of the book, and I am suspended with the listening. *Sitting Pretty, True Blue* is a complex story about the demands of a teenage social world organized around shared values and longings—about being athletic, cool, savvy, popular, precocious (but not adult), blond ("strawberry blond doesn't count"), and most importantly "not poor." It is a story of three teenage girlfriends and the possible betrayal of the main character, Sam, whose new friend is wealthy and "very snobby." The plot is driven by the efforts of Trisha, the affluent girl, to "get in the middle" of Sam's friendships. Sam is conflicted, not sure where her allegiance lies, until the end.

As Kendra re-tells the story, I hear "Kendra-the-student" demonstrating her abilities—her reading-level, comprehension, and inference drawing. But I also hear "Kendra-the-person" voicing what she wonders and worries about. Kendra cares deeply about the risk Sam is taking if she is lured into Trisha's more "classy" world. Kendra worries whether Sam's friends will be able to forgive her and tells me she is greatly relieved when Sam's friendship circle is restored.

The drama of *Sitting Pretty, True Blue* parallels the drama among the children in their conversations about their photographs with their peers. Their discussions circle around freighted relationships, desires to belong, and attempts to uphold, reject, and circumvent social differences.[6] In the story, as in the conversations I witnessed among the children, there is much less concern about doing without consumer goods and "classy" experiences, and much greater concern with being *shut out* of social worlds in which young people travel. Indeed, Pugh found that most of the low-income parents she interviewed went to great lengths to protect their children from feeling excluded. In a culture that equates belonging with possessions and care with specific kinds of housing, provisions, and consumer experiences, dignity is not available to all—and this means that some children have to work harder than others to achieve it. Indeed, the emotional landscapes that children travel between home and school are far from equal.

## Cherished objects and stories of belonging

> Things tell us who we are, not in words, but by embodying our intentions. In our everyday traffic of existence, we can also learn about ourselves from objects, almost as much as from people. (Csikszentmihalyi & Rochberg-Halton, 1981: 91)

In a classic study of the meaning of household objects, Csikszentmihalyi & Rochberg-Halton (1981) argue that our homes contain our most special objects: "those that are selected by the person to attend to regularly or to have close at hand, that create permanence in the intimate life of a person, and therefore that are most involved in making up his or her identity" (1981: 17). Their study was based on a series of interviews with over 300 members of 82 families living in a "major metropolitan area." Interviews were conducted in the respondents' homes so the researchers could see and discuss the things that were part of people's everyday lives. The researchers spoke with three generations—children, parents, and grandparents—to discover the value and meanings attached to different objects.[7] They found that household objects that are tied to family traditions, continuity, and "signs of love" are the most meaningful objects in the home (1981: 143):

> Things tend to acquire meaning because they are signposts of family history, which help family members re-experience crucial events and relationships they share. In doing this the artifacts also preserve, vitalize and transmit to those who will come after, the goal of family and ethnic continuity that is an essential aspect of the identities of these people. (Csikszentmihalyi & Rochberg-Halton, 1981: 222–3)

These "signposts of family history" were abundant in the children's images, and the descriptions the young people shared in their interviews were often colored by a profound awareness of the complex significance of these objects. Eleven-year-old Sofia's accounts are exemplary in this regard. She came to the US from Albania in 2000 at the age of six with her parents and sister, leaving behind all her cousins, aunts, uncles, and grandparents. Of the following photograph (Figure 2.7) she says:

> "I took a picture of the Albanian flag because it represents our country. It is an important part of me because it represents my culture, and it is like sort of being different from everyone else and I like that because I don't really want to be the same as everyone else."

"How does being from Albania make you different?" I ask. Sofia pauses a moment, then replies, "Because of the way I talk or the way I think of things."

Later in the interview, Sofia expands on another aspect of her difference:

> "Because other people usually have their cousins, and uncles and aunts to, like, hang out with them. And, usually they get help with their homework or stuff like that from them. And, I don't really have that. So, it does feel sort of lonely."

Sofia tells a complicated and emotionally fraught story of belonging. For her, the Albanian flag symbolizes both the prospect of feeling different from other kids and the pride she feels for her homeland, her native culture, and her ties to others, especially her extended family. She identifies the flag picture as one of her favorites, along with pictures of photographs of her grandparents (Figure 2.8). "I knew for sure that I wanted to take pictures of my grandparents, because I really love them. And they took care of me when I was a little child when my mom and dad were at work.... These are the most important pictures out of the whole stack to me."[8]

Speaking about the teddy bears in Figure 2.9, she says, "I have memories for each and every one of them. Like, this one, I got for Christmas. And this one I got for my birthday by my sister's friend. And all of them have memories with me, and that's why I really love them." "So, it's not just because you like to collect stuffed animals,

Figure 2.7: An important part of me *Sofia, age 10*

but because each one reminds you of something?" I ask. "Yeah," Sofia replies and then continues:

> "But this boom box [Figure 2.10] is actually really important to me, because I got it as a present for my first year here in America. And, it's the same with the book. This was the very first book that I had in first grade. And, I used to love reading it all the time. I got the boom box my very first Christmas party here at school, which we used to have for the first and second graders, but I don't think we have it anymore. And, I remember sitting on Santa's lap and he gave me this present. But it doesn't work anymore now."

In further conversation with me, Sofia explains that she has carefully arranged these special objects. The boom box sits on her shelf as pictured, but Sofia has pulled out her most special book from the stack, "I just took it out for the picture."

Like Kendra, it is Sofia's hidden work (arranging the special objects in her room and then re-arranging them for the photograph) that brings her belongings to life; and her storytelling infuses the objects with meaning. It is not that she is a collector or enjoys snuggling with her stuffed animals, or that her boom box is even usable. Instead, these consumer objects commemorate her ties to family and friends and memorialize her transition from belonging in one world to

Figure 2.8: My grandparents *Sofia, age 10*

belonging in another. Serving as tangible manifestations of memories and relationships, these objects become "real" in interesting ways.

Sofia described the difficulties of her transition in school and what she learned as a result:

> "People didn't really know that I couldn't speak English. So when they would talk to me I wouldn't answer back. I didn't understand what they were saying. So they thought I was rude. And I had really short hair, so some people used to make fun of me and call me a boy."

"How did you feel?" I asked. Sofia didn't hesitate:

> "I felt sad because people shouldn't judge other people by how they look on the outside, but on how they are on the inside, how their attitude is, how they act, who they are. People make judgments about other people without even knowing them, which I don't think is right. I first get to know a person, and then if I don't like them, I leave them alone. And I don't really make judgments about them."

Alongside her feelings of being judged and training herself to reject others' disparaging judgments, Sofia also speaks of being "grateful" for the advantages she was afforded by her family's migration to the

Figure 2.9: Memories for each and every one *Sofia, age 10*

Figure 2.10: My boom box is really important to me *Sofia, age 10*

United States, which she explains through the following photograph (Figure 2.11):

> "I took this picture of my closet, because I'm grateful to have this many clothes, even though half of them are my sister's. Because, some people don't even have one piece

of clothing, and I have all of these, so I'm really grateful for that."

Figure 2.11: I'm grateful to have this many clothes *Sofia, age 10*

Figure 2.12: Albania was having a hard time *Sofia, age 10*

Being grateful is a recurring sentiment woven throughout Sofia's discussion of her photographs. She uses a photograph of a plaque commemorating her hometown and Albania's House of Commons (Figure 2.12) to tell the story of leaving her homeland:

> "If it wasn't for my mom entering the lottery, because in Albania, we have to win the lottery to apply for a green card and a passport. So my mom did that and she won it. She and my dad decided to come here for a better life because Albania was having a hard time then. They didn't have that much money and people were poor and they didn't know where to go and they didn't know what to do. So my parents thought it would be a better life for me and my sister to come here, and I am really grateful for them doing that. When I was really little I remember the moment when I would see the people, they would be walking around with no shoes, and ripped pants and a ripped sweatshirt and I would feel sorry for them. And it would make me just want to cry because of, because like, they kicked people out of their jobs. Like my mom owned a bakery, and they told her that she had to leave, because they had to sell it for, to someone else. And, I was really upset about that. And, I was mad, because I used to love going to that bakery and just smelling the warm air, and it was so nice. It was my place to relax, and I loved it there."

Sofia's cherished possessions evoke mixed emotions, carrying both comfort and reminders of the pain of her difference and loss of her homeland. To understand the unequal, hidden work of access and inclusion that marginalized and less advantaged children and youth are required to do in school, it is important to include the work of managing the heart, a process that sociologist Arlie Hochschild has called *emotion work*. Like any other cue given in a social encounter, emotions signal something about the kind of self an individual is claiming. And there is hidden work in bringing feelings into line with social expectations and norms. Hochschild describes these norms as "feeling rules," and the demands they place on social actors differ, requiring more work from some people than from others. Hochschild reminds us that feelings are socially produced as much as they are individually experienced. Anytime we ask ourselves or are asked by others (or imagine others asking us) "what am I feeling?" or "what should I feel?" or "why am I feeling this way?" we are in the presence of a feeling rule, and such rules depend upon our social status, class, race, and especially gender. For example, it is less socially acceptable (indeed, even life-threatening) for Black men to express anger or indignation in the face of (predominantly white) authority figures (such as police officers), thus Black men may feel pressure to "work" at maintaining deference at all costs, unlike their white male counterparts who have more social leeway. Similarly, it is less socially acceptable for women to express anger than it is for men, thus women must "work" at keeping their anger at bay or risk being viewed as "unfeminine."

In this case, Sofia is signaling something about the kind of self she claims to be, a self who feels grateful (not entitled) for what she has. She is grateful for her cultural difference, regardless of her loneliness or negative treatment. Listening to Sofia describe her special objects— from the wall plaque commemorating Albania, to her clothes, boom box, books, stuffed animals, photographs of her grandparents' pictures, and the Albanian flag—we can hear the multiple layers of identity work that she engages through objects, if not words. We can hear her work to preserve her ties to family, to establish her sense of belonging and identity (and to express its underlying difficulty), and to cope with her feelings of loss and longing, all forms of emotion work that constitute the everyday politics of belonging. Later, when Sofia at age 15 revisits her photographs taken during childhood and speaks about these prized possessions, she will reflect more abstractly upon her gratitude, cultural difference, and the work she was required to do as a young person to maintain her mother tongue and cultural heritage (see Chapter 5). But at this point in time, her cherished objects helped her establish who she is and how she wants to be seen.

Angeline, who migrated to the US from Kenya at the age of seven, provides another example. Angeline is part of a large, extended family with "lots of cousins … some are 'back home' [in Kenya], some live in Massachusetts, others are in Texas, Missouri, Atlanta, Canada. Like, they're all spread out." Reflecting on her transnational family circle, she says she is glad, "because then I have more culture in me…. Some parts of my family are, like, Kenyan culture and American culture. So, I have two cultures. I'm Black American, so, mostly Kenyan though." Like Sofia, Angeline values her dual cultures, and also like Sofia, Angeline photographs things for which she is grateful. Looking at a photograph she took of her apartment house, Angeline says, "Because my house means a lot to me, that's where I live. If I didn't live in a house I would be homeless, that's why I'm really appreciative [stumbles over this word, and gesticulates to her heart] that I have a house."

Angeline takes nothing for granted. This orientation—and underlying anxiety—about care and survival is a theme that cuts across the children's photographs and explanations of their homeplaces. They share an orientation toward care that emphasizes gratitude and, as I illustrate in Chapter 3, mutual obligation. But here I want to emphasize the alternative way of seeing consumer goods and children's participation in consumer culture. Angeline, like Sofia, took a photograph of the clothes in her closet, which could be read as signs of abundance and consumerism (Schor, 2004), as some teachers-in-training with whom I have worked have speculated. Angeline does say that she enjoys shopping and "dressing good," but more than this, her clothes signify that she is cared for, and serve as traces of the grandparents she has left behind in Kenya:

> "All my clothes mean a lot to me because if, when people buy them for me. Like, the ones I buy for myself and my grandparents buy for me are very special.... 'Cause my grandparents live all the way in Africa where I am from, so it's really special because that's something I can remember about them and when I wear them and look down at it I remember them. I picture them in my eye."

As she spoke, Angeline made a gentle gesture of cupping her hands over her face, as if she could not only see her beloved grandparents but could still feel their presence in her life.

Threads of childhood consumer culture weave family members together, and these threads could be heard across the interviews. The pictures Jeffrey took in his second year of participating in the project are a case in point. In sixth grade when Jeffrey and I meet again, he excitedly tells me that he has now become a "big brother." He has taken a photograph of his "household": his mother, his new baby brother, his mother's boyfriend, his mother's boyfriend's sister, and himself. He reminds me that because his mother had been sick during the time he had his camera in fifth grade he has "made up for it" this year. All but two pictures in his set of 27 are of his home and belongings, rich in color and textures and carefully composed.

Jeffrey's recent visit to Puerto Rico is commemorated by the shirt with the "rooster, the national symbol" on it (Figure 2.13). It was his first trip to meet extended family there, and he explains that the baseball jersey is a gift from his beloved aunt and uncle (Figure 2.14). "I am not a Yankees fan, but I couldn't give it away. I keep it close to me so I am close to them." He has also photographed another gift from the same aunt and uncle, a pair of sneakers and despite the fact they no longer fit, he keeps them to remind him of their absent presence (Figure 2.15).

Figure 2.13: The rooster is the national symbol *Jeffrey, age 10*

Figure 2.14: I keep it close to me so I am close to them *Jeffrey, age 10*

Figure 2.15: My special sneakers *Jeffrey, age 10*

Anthropologists have long explored the importance of gift exchange in stitching together the fabric of a society, where both the honor of giver and recipient are engaged and reciprocated (Mauss, 1990). Gift-giving, receiving, and reciprocating are emotionally freighted, serving to mark life transitions and maintain family connections, especially when faced with separation and loss.

Jeffrey also photographed the top of his dresser where, among some cherished objects, his babyhood is memorialized by his tiny sneakers placed carefully on a lace doily. The baby pictures above his bed also serve this purpose, as well as a reminder of family bonds and heritage—themes that resonate across the kids' visual narratives. Woven into Jeffrey's pictures of his belongings is a tenderness toward his mother, her family, and his childhood. His images and words convey a simple and crucial message: "I dwell in my family's world of care." This world comes into focus, as it does with so many other kids in the project, when they photograph and talk about their mothers, a theme we will address at length in Chapter 3.

Migration was not the only type of separation and loss experienced by the children, as ten-year-old Angel attests. Angel lives in Terrace Gardens with his mother and younger brother and sister. He took a photograph of his most cherished possession, a tattoo-art drawing that hangs on his bedroom wall (Figure 2.16).

Figure 2.16: This is something my dad made me *Angel, age 10*

He tells me:

> "This is something my dad made me when he was in jail. It says, 'Daddy's boys,' my name up here, and my brother's. And, he just made that with a pen. He, like, designs, and when he gets tattoos, he designs them himself and has somebody make it. My sister has one that says, 'Happy birthday.'"

The pride in Angel's voice was palpable, and I asked him to tell me more about his father. He explained that his dad has been in and out of prison over the years, so "it is not really surprising." Listening, I wonder if he says this to buffer what he imagines might be my surprise or judgment. He continues, "I just don't like it when he goes back. Like, right now he's back. I forgot what it was for, but, yeah, he's back in there."

"When you say it's not really surprising, what do you mean?" I ask. "Oh, like, because he usually goes there for bad stuff," Angel says unflinchingly. I repeat this phrase "Bad stuff" to give him an opening to tell me more if he wants to. "Yeah, so, I'm really used to it. But he wasn't always like that," Angel reflects. Then, picking up the photograph and holding it tenderly between his fingers he reiterates:

> "Yeah, I took this because it came from my dad, and I really love him. And, like, he's been with us a long [drawing out the word] time. And him and my mom been together since they were, like, 14 or something. Him and my mom never got along very good. Not arguing bad, but they would argue."

The layers of Angel's emotion work here reinforce the words of Csikszentmihalyi and Rochberg-Halton (1981) that open this section: "Things tell us who we are, not in words, but by embodying our intentions. In our everyday traffic of existence, we can also learn about ourselves from objects, almost as much as from people" (p. 91).[9] By his own intentional acts—hanging the art on his bedroom wall, taking a photograph of it, and claiming it as his favorite—Angel is telling himself, me, and any other imagined audience that whatever "bad stuff" his father has done, they remain bonded. His father's "bad stuff" does not alter the fact that he, his brother, and his sister are the focus of their dad's love and affection. While not idealizing his father, Angel is keeping alive the continuity of their connection and valuing the long-standing relationship between his parents and the family circle. He elaborates on his time together with his father, explaining:

> "I lived with my grandma once, my dad's mom, in Virginia. And when I was in kindergarten and first grade I got to see him more when we lived at [another public housing complex in Worcester]. He would come over and we used to always play video games together. I started playing games since, when I was like … maybe three years old."

Angel's emotion work is balancing the "bad stuff" with the good of his father—his father's talents, role in his life, history with his mother, and continuing presence. Whatever stigma is assigned to children of an incarcerated parent, Angel is holding this at bay. And against the structural impediments that the prison system puts in the way of preserving family ties and family time (Wakefield & Wildeman, 2014; Hollins, 2018), Angel is staking a claim to relational longevity, a key marker of the meaning of family.

Figures 2.17 & 2.18: I like collecting stuff, like action figures
*Angel, age 10*

Angel's attachment to two action figures that he has photographed (Figures 2.17 & 2.18) communicates another feature of his identity work.

Angel explains that he took the photographs:

> "to show that I like collecting stuff, like action figures. I keep them there on display. Like, that's on my wall, hung up with a nail. I just want to save them. My brother is begging me to open this GI Joe. But I'm trying to collect it. It comes with snowboard, a couple weapons. And, he has his little bag thing with the nightlight, a light to show in the dark, so that you don't have to put on the real one, so you can just sneak in. And he has a couple grenades there. You can see the top of this is broke a little, so I put it away."

"Does your brother collect them too?" I inquire. "No, he likes to open them. So he's begging me to open them. Even my sister is begging me. I saved those ever since Christmas," Angel says with pride in his voice.

Angel has set himself a goal that distinguishes him from his brother and sister. He is communicating something about himself and his desires that may be beyond words but is embodied by his relationship to the treasured collectibles he's "saved ever since Christmas" some three months before. By "saving" and "displaying" the action figures, does he mean to protect them? care for them? control their use? increase their value? ensure their future? individuate and differentiate from his siblings? identify with the qualities of a collector, or perhaps with those of the action figures? Whatever his intentions and desires may be, the point is that children's cherished belongings are a means to get to know them for who they are in the moment and how they want to be seen by others. But in the harsh light of the marketization of childhood and adult laments about children' consumption, it is all too easy to miss this way of seeing children's agency and identity work.

## The meaning of things: screens and the politics of belonging

The symbolic settings of home (in particular living rooms, bedrooms, and kitchens), as well as the same "ecology of signs" signifying domestic life and harmony found by Csikszentmihalyi & Rochberg-Halton (1981), recurred in the children's photographs. These included furniture, visual art, photographs, books, televisions, stereos (from "boom boxes" to iPods for music listening), sculptures, plants, and "plates" (a category that included eating and drinking utensils mentioned in connection with one's country of origin or ethnic background). When comparing the list of special objects most mentioned by the children in Csikszentmihalyi & Rochberg-Halton's study with those objects photographed by the PCS children and discussed in their interviews, I am struck by the similarity of object types, even if the percentage of kids mentioning a special object differs between the two groups (see Figure 2.19).

Certainly the introduction of new technology in communication tools (computers, laptops, iPhones, and so on) explains some of the differences in types of special objects mentioned by children in both studies, but the *meanings* that children gave for selecting objects as special were similar. For example, as in Csikszentmihalyi & Rochberg-Halton's study, children cherished things not because of their market value/cost or because of their material comforts, but rather for the

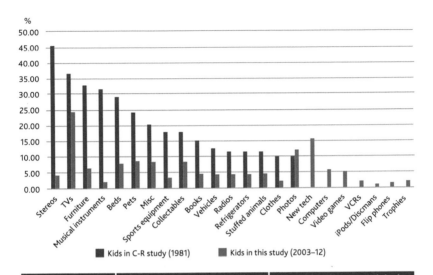

Figure 2.19: An ecology of signs

| Objects | Kids in C-R study (1981) (%) | PCS kids (2003–06) (%) |
|---|---|---|
| Stereos | 45.60 | 30.56 |
| TVs | 36.70 | 66.67 |
| Furniture | 32.90 | 38.89 |
| Musical instruments | 31.60 | 19.44 |
| Beds | 29.10 | 52.78 |
| Pets | 24.10 | 36.11 |
| Misc | 20.30 | 58.33 |
| Sports equipment | 17.70 | 36.11 |
| Collectibles | 17.70 | 19.44 |
| Books | 15.20 | 41.67 |
| Vehicles | 12.70 | 19.44 |
| Radios | 11.40 | 5.56 |
| Refrigerators | 11.40 | 8.33 |
| Stuffed animals | 11.40 | 36.11 |
| Clothes | 10.10 | 22.22 |
| Photos | 10.10 | 30.56 |
| Trophies | | 13.89 |
| Visual art | | 27.78 |
| Sculpture | | 8.33 |
| Plants | | 22.22 |
| Computers | | 41.67 |
| Video games | | 44.44 |
| VCRs | | 38.89 |
| iPods/Discmans | | 11.11 |
| Flip phones | | 5.56 |

information the objects communicated about the child and his or her ties to others (Csikszentmihalyi & Rochberg-Halton, 1981: 239).[10]

One household object deserves special scrutiny in light of childhood consumer culture and the everyday politics of belonging. What Csikszentmihalyi & Rochberg-Halton found to be the most controversial household object—television—remains laden with judgment as we listen to the children in this study. Once sources of family entertainment found exclusively in living rooms, television sets were ubiquitous in the children's photographs, pictured in kitchens and bedrooms as well as living rooms. Watching television after school, either while doing homework or after doing homework, was a shared experience in their accounts of everyday life. It was clear that the children understood that doing homework while watching television was frowned upon. Jeffrey drove this point home at the end of sixth grade during his exit interview. As we looked across all the photographs he had taken from the fifth and sixth grades, he picked up the photograph of the television in his bedroom. "What do I do after school? I watch TV. I do my homework watching television." He grins at me, then at the video camera, and back again at me, as if he is finally setting the record straight. Whispering between the lines of the children's relationship to television screens were voices from larger debates about consumer culture and how children should use their time.

In one sense, it seems that not much has changed since Csikszentmihalyi and Rochberg-Halton's observations about the guilty pleasures of television watching in 1981. As the authors reported, "often reasons given for appreciating TV sets are tinged by guilt, as if the respondent were talking about an addiction on which he or she has become dependent" (p. 74). They found that children cherished TV sets (37 percent) more than the oldest generation (23 percent), who talked about watching television to mitigate against loneliness or finding it easier to look at television than to read. The middle generation mentioned TV the least (11 percent), even as watching television was reported as the most frequent daily activity. Csikszentmihalyi and Rochberg-Halton concluded that what most stood out about TV sets as valued household objects was that they serve as a means for people to experience the present, but they were "not good vehicles for binding people to their own past or future, or for bringing them closer to others" (p. 76). The authors found that the socializing effect of TV watching was to provide "habitual, low-intensity experiences that are valued as ongoing enjoyment and release rather than as memorable occasions" (p. 76).

Indeed, in my study, the most common reason given for why a child photographed a television set was to explain what he or she did after school as a habitual experience. But the children also spoke of their television sets as embedded in webs of care—that is, as a means to differentiate, identify, and underscore their belonging.

So much has changed, and continues to change, in the marketplace of media and digital technology in which the meaning of television sets and television watching is now embedded. Fast-changing technology in home entertainment, including Xbox consoles and video game systems, the shift from VHS to DVD to TiVo players, and media streaming platforms like Netflix and YouTube, have transformed the reach of guilty pleasures, adding to the already charged debates from decades past. These changes could be noted in the children's photographs from the time the study began (2003) to the time it ended (2013). Looking through the archive of images, a whole new ecology of household screens and settings can be identified. "Big-screen" television sets, often surrounded by stereo and sound equipment, were mostly found in living rooms, while smaller television sets that also served as video game stations were found in bedrooms. Computer and laptop screens were photographed in varied household settings, from kitchen tables to computer desk units. Equally important for shaping new meanings and relationships to television sets is the rise of specialist cable channels, which regard children as a "niche market" and broadcast program-length commercials made by toy companies as a means to sell products. This increased commercial targeting of children—either as independent consumers in their own right, or as leverage to pressure adults into purchasing desired goods and services—is now a global stage upon which the politics of children's belonging is played out.

Children need access to specialized children's channels, such as the cable channel Nickelodeon, to gain the kinds of cultural knowledge required to join in peer conversations and relationships. Beyond owning coveted goods, what is important is *knowing about them* through watching children's television. Nickelodeon is a global brand that reportedly reaches 100 million households worldwide and offers children access to valuable information about the most recent electronic game systems, movies, music, "collectibles," dolls, clothing, character toys, and theme parks, to name a few (Buckingham, 2011: 196). Perhaps this explains why discussions among the children about each other's television sets so often focused on which households had cable and which did not. I overheard countless exchanges between the children about their families' cable bills. One child boasted to another that because she had improved her grades, her mother had promised to get cable; another proudly announced that since his mom had gotten a "better job" they would now be able to afford cable "in just one more month;" and still another group of children compared notes about how many cable channels they had access to. There was a lot going on in these conversations. The children spoke knowingly of "cable bills" with keen awareness of household expenditures and resource constraints. A cable bill expenditure was a sign of relative affluence, around which social ranking was more likely to happen than other tokens of value (for example, a new toy, bike, or video game). But at the same time, talk of the cable bill also forged a sense of community and joint excitement when cable access was secured—and, likewise, a shared sense of commiseration when cable was turned off due to a tightening family budget or job loss.

One example in particular made this community orientation clear. During one conversation about which photographs the children wished to appear in a public exhibition of their work, the following image of family photographs arranged around a cable receiver box raised some complications (Figure 2.20).

When the children were making selections for a public exhibition, I would ask them to explain their choices—what they liked about a chosen photograph, how it contributed to the exhibition, and what messages they thought it communicated to a public audience. Maureen, the child photographer, seemed pleased when her peers selected her photograph (Figure 2.20) for public display.[11] In this case, the reasons for its selection were especially varied—one child liked

Figure 2.20: They're really important to me *Maureen, age 10*

the colors, another the "arrangement of the photographs," another appreciated the subject matter (baby pictures), and still another said he liked the contrast between the two frames—one was "old fashioned" and the other was "cute and colorful." One boy in the group interjected, "We like it because it shows that we have cable." With that, the terms of the conversation shifted and the children began speaking over each other. "Well, we had cable last month, but now we don't"; "I didn't know you had cable, when did you get it?"; "If we don't all have cable then should we have a picture of it in the show?" I heard this remark and the conversation that followed as part of the kids' audience awareness; their sense that viewers might make assumptions or judgments about entire communities based on what they see in an individual photo. Their discussion pivoted around fundamental questions of "who WE are," and evidenced the children's struggle to forge community— to reach a consensus over how to represent themselves as equal members of the project group—despite their differences. In the end, the group put these differences aside and decided to keep the photograph in the exhibition, not because it showed something "true" about all of their lives, but because of aesthetic qualities in the picture they agreed were appealing.

Access to cable is an important vehicle of belonging for children and youth, especially in terms of gaining access to individualized programming for children of different ages.[12] Remember Manny, who used the coveted "big-screen" televisions that his mom's boyfriend had given his family as a means to deflect the negative perception of his Terrace Gardens home? There was more to his story. Manny also photographed the new placement of the older, smaller TV sets—one in his younger sister's room and the other in the room he shares with his brother. His delight was palpable as he told the interviewer that now his little sister could watch "her shows" (for example, *Rugrats*) and "I can watch mine" (live-action rather than "baby" animated cartoons). Having the television set in his room not only enabled him to watch his own shows, but to play his video games without having to negotiate with his sister.

Meanwhile, photographs of television sets and screens were the most highly charged household objects in terms of activating outsider judgments. The most common viewer reaction among teachers, teachers-in-training, and graduate students who have viewed the archive of children's photographs has tended to be hyper-awareness, if not criticism, of the preponderance of television sets photographed. Some viewers questioned the "priorities" of low-income families for spending money on large, wide-screen television sets with speakers.

Others questioned the wisdom of households filled with so many electronics, suggesting a concern that this might encourage "wasted" time spent in front of screens. At the same time, positive reactions to photographs of computer and laptop screens brought to light the deeply divided perceptions of "screens" as either "bad" (TVs, video games) or "good" (computers, laptops).

As reported elsewhere (Fontaine & Luttrell, 2015), one graduate student, Claire Fontaine, became aware of this dichotomy in her own viewing and elaborated on its multiple sources. She tied her way of seeing the screens to her "evaluative teacher identity"—a perspective that caused her to be critical of the dominance of television and video-gaming screens over computer and laptop screens. Her realization highlighted the ways that screens can function as symbolic scapegoats: too much exposure to the "wrong" kinds of screens or to the wrong uses is understood to degrade young people's brains, bodies, and educational trajectories (American Academy of Pediatrics, 2013). At the same time, the "right" kinds of screens and screen uses are understood to boost young people's life chances and upward mobility (Persell & Cookson, 1987) and to enhance human capital (Keeley, 2007), particularly for girls and women (American Association of University Women, 2000; Margolis & Fisher, 2002, quoted in Fontaine, 2015).[13] Similarly, within the ecology of television programming targeted specifically for children of distinct ages, some shows are considered "good" and others "bad," generating adult concern and activism (for example, the group Action for Children's Television, or ACT) around what is best for children to view. Nickelodeon bills itself as "good" television—that is, a network with educational value that provides a non-violent "safe space" for children (H. Jenkins, 2004 quoted in Buckingham, 2011: 197) through programs that promote diversity (for example, *Rugrats* featuring Jewish and Christian holiday specials), healthy eating, and caring for the environment (Hendershot, 2004). Thus, in addition to concerns about whether children are watching too much television or playing too many video games, there is also unease about whether children are watching the right kind of television or playing the right kind of video games.

I still remember my surprise upon viewing Mesha's fifth-grade gallery of images. Sixteen of her 23 total photographs captured what I thought were still images of a television show until I learned otherwise. Photographs like Figure 2.21 of a female character dominated the images, and I came to learn that the character is Yuna, the female protagonist, a practitioner of healing magic and one of the main playable characters in the role-playing video game *Final Fantasy X*. In keeping with expected scripts about best uses of time, Mesha assured me that she completed her homework before playing video games or watching movies. Initially, Mesha described her screen time as habitual, a "what-I-do-after-school" activity. Without knowledge of gaming and *Final Fantasy X*, I was ill prepared to understand its significance or to even ask the right questions. Mesha tried to explain the game for me.

"It is a game of adventure and the characters fly around the planet." "How do you play it?" I ask. Mesha seemed amused by my question and, with a slight laugh, said:

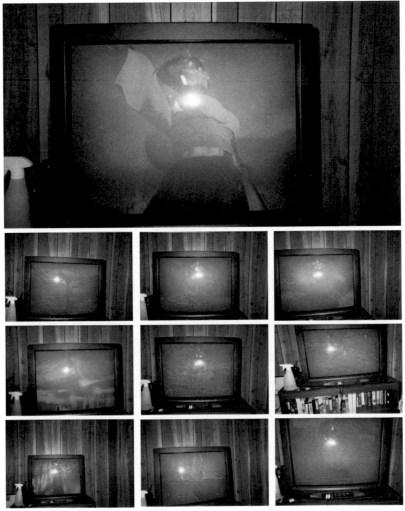

Figure 2.21: It is a game of adventure *Mesha, age 10*

"Well, you run around, you go inside that door, you see right there? [pointing to one of the screen shots.] And there's a little test you have to do. You have to pick up spears and all that stuff. They are fighting a battle. You have to run around and scream and act the part and fight in the battle. It starts easy and it gets harder and harder every time. It is fun because of the graphics. You can be any character you like and battle monsters. And you get to meet other people."

I asked about the female figure that Mesha has photographed multiple times, trying to cover for my ignorance of even the basics of a video role-playing game. Mesha is ever patient as she explains that Yuna is "doing something good for the people, the dead people. She is sending them to the Farplane." "There are dead people?" I must have sounded distressed as I asked because Mesha quickly assured me, "No, no, no, you don't understand it! It's just a game, and she's sending the people who died to their resting place. It is important to go to the Farplane so you get to see your parents or something like that."

Mesha was atypical in her singular photographic focus, and though this surprised me and concerned some of her teacher viewers, it captivated her peer viewers. To play the game requires a level of expertise not typically associated with a kid of Mesha's age and gender profile. Success requires mastering not only the instrumental controls, but being steeped in a complicated narrative with comprehensive knowledge of the *Spira* world (modeled on Southeast Asian rather than the mainly European-style mythical worlds founds in previous Final Fantasy games), including mythical figures, language, and characters. By featuring her ties to the game, Mesha was establishing her proficiencies—and perhaps offering a latent critique of the male-dominated gaming culture, as Claire Fontaine would later argue in her follow-up research with Mesha.[14]

My limited way of seeing Mesha's screenshots and my inability to grasp their relevance was further brought to my attention when I learned about how the game brought her closer to others, itself a form of care. Mesha talked longingly of past afternoons with her father, who was no longer available during the day because his work schedule had changed to night-shift hours. "He's so busy, we don't have that time to go play together anymore." Mesha also recounted taking pleasure in after-school gaming sessions with friends and described the rituals that framed these gatherings—cleaning up wires, organizing the controllers. When I first looked at her photos, I had imagined her gaming as a solitary activity—yet it was the social context of her gaming and the contours of care associated with it that Mesha wanted to communicate. Even Mesha's description of her favorite game speaks to these contours—the anxieties (and remedies) of family loss, separation, and heritage that are behind the motivation to get to the Farplane. Even in a fictional/fantasy setting Mesha is attuned to forms of care. My point is that the children's relationship to household television sets, screens, and video games was far more complex than current debates allow; and understanding that relationship requires an expanded way of seeing, listening to, and learning from children if we are to more fully grasp their childhood contexts, concerns, and economies of dignity.

## Ways of (not) seeing belonging

One important function of the children's photos was to inform teacher training, an aim from the earliest stages of the project. Offering these photos to educators for scrutiny and reflection opened new ways of approaching educators' perceptions of and responses to the images. In workshops and seminars, I asked teachers-in-training to follow sociologist Howard Becker's guidelines for working with images: "Don't stare and thus stop looking; look actively … you'll find it useful to take up the time by naming everything in the picture to yourself and writing up notes" (1986: 232). Then, after building up capacity for attention to detail, Becker encourages:

> a period of fantasy, telling yourself a story about the people and things in the picture. The story needn't be true, it's just a device for externalizing and making clear to yourself the emotion and mood the picture has evoked, both part of its statement. (1986: 232)

Using these two guidelines is a way to catalyze reflexivity about what the viewer sees and interprets and why one has come to this reading. I have learned that there are many lenses through which viewers "see" the homeplaces, activities, and mood of the children's photographs. It is an exercise that invites curiosity, as well as anxiety as some people worry about making negative judgments. All of these dynamics surfaced in discussions of the following photograph (Figure 2.22).

Kendra's own account of this photograph features her most preferred activity—"reading. I love to read." She handed her camera over to her brother with whom she shares a bedroom (along with her sister) and instructed him to "not mess it up." This is the photograph she selects as her favorite one to share with a public audience, perhaps because

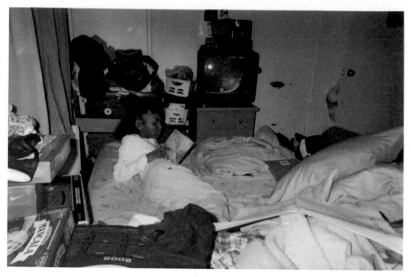

Figure 2.22: Don't mess it up *Kendra, age 10*

it provides the most intimate glimpse of how she dwells within her homeplace. In the inner sanctum of her bedroom, she is engaged in self-realization and surrounded by signs of care and comfort. She refers to this photograph as another image where she "feels respect," and I can feel the emotional weight of her words.

I have witnessed many adult viewers recalibrate their assessment of what they see—clutter, disorder, temporariness, multi-modality as Kendra reads with the television on—after hearing Kendra's own account of this snapshot of her self-realization and self-regard. I have also heard viewers worrying how photographic snapshots of their own homes and domestic order might be negatively received. One teacher remarked, "I cringe to think of anyone taking a picture of my teenage son's bedroom." I want viewers to be able to see Kendra's snapshot as an insight into how working-class children navigate the unequal terrain of childhood consumer culture, to hear the pride in her voice, and to consider what implicit assumptions they hold that might get in the way of recognizing the signs of comfort and care that Kendra holds dear.

In this chapter, I have argued that the children used their cameras in multiple ways: to traverse home and school cultures; to engage in the politics of belonging, both building and tearing down social divisions, including boundaries between public and private housing; and to manage difficult emotions and anxieties about care and belonging. There is no doubt that the photographs of household possessions reflect the reach and power of corporate marketing to children. It is evident, too, that the children relied on consumption to establish their claims to identity and status within their peer groups. Their photographs illuminate the value they placed on consumer goods, as well as their consumer desires—desires that critics say have been hijacked by a billion-dollar industry determined to turn a profit without regard for what may or may not be good for children and their development.[15] But I am suggesting that this framework eclipses what can be learned from and with children. Viewing the children's belongings through narrow lenses (for example, as good/bad; not enough/too much; affordable/unaffordable), or fixating on what "having things" or "not having things" signifies, ultimately sidelines children's own meaning making. As these children were keenly aware, household resources and constraints mediated their relationship to goods and services; as a result, there was hidden, extra work expended to secure their claims to inclusion and worthiness. And whether they were endeavoring to show themselves as the focal point of someone's care and attention, as knowledgeable about forms of social currency (video games, children's television programming, toy collections), as tied to a homeland and cultural heritage, or as secure in their difference, this work was accomplished through their belongings. It was not about what they had; it was about how cherished items brought them into significant relationship with others, enabling them to forge community around valuable tokens of care and belonging. Things were just not things and their homes were more than physical places. The small group discussions also revealed a common endeavor to become full members of a school community and culture, and they reminded us that individual experiences of that endeavor can differ widely: while school might feel "safe" and "fun" to those whose belonging is guaranteed, it can feel unpredictable, even threatening, to those whose dignity must be actively sought and defended (Pugh 2009: 82). In this context, the children's strategies for overcoming social differences, even if momentary and fleeting, suggest an alternative social ethos that rejects acquisitive individualism. Their willingness to challenge the social perceptions and divisions that interfered with their desires for connection and for recognition is at the core of their sociality and collectivity. The kids' powerful commitment to seeing and to being seen extends to their lives beyond the walls of the school, and it's this concern that I continue to explore in Chapter 3.

# 3

# Motherhood, childhood, and love labor in family choreographies of care

It is January, 2004. At 9:00 a.m., six-year-old Antonio stands in the doorway of the main office of PCS, where I am waiting to begin my first interview. He and his brother Cesar live in Terrace Gardens. Miss Corey, the school secretary, greets him with a smile: "Did you just get here?" Antonio nods his head yes. "Your mother didn't wake you up this morning?" Antonio rocks back and forth. "Did your brother already go to his classroom?" Antonio grins from ear to ear and nods his head yes. "Go ahead on, I won't write you up." Before Antonio is out the door Miss Corey remarks to me, "He's covering for his mother. It is a tough home situation, so tough. His mom has two jobs and works double shifts every other weekend at a nursing home. His older brother Cesar is in third grade and has been getting himself to school since kindergarten, and now he's responsible for getting Antonio to school too. They are late all the time."

School rules require a tardy notice and an eventual penalty of detention for repeated lateness, but Miss Corey is sympathetic to the predicament of the boys' single mom, an immigrant from the Dominican Republic who works tirelessly to provide for her children. Miss Corey feels it isn't fair to punish the boys because of their mother's work demands, so she reluctantly stretches the rules to accommodate the situation. Indeed, Miss Corey is herself a single mom, and she explains that her own children are on an early school schedule that makes it possible for her to drop them off on her way to work—if not for that, she says, she doesn't know how she would manage.

In this moment, I am reminded of the constellation of resources that my own children have had at their disposal and how these resources have enabled my "maternal visibility" (a phrase coined by sociologist Anita Garey, 2011) at their schools. Schools are where we are judged as parents—and especially as mothers—according to our apparent availability for our children. I hear this judgment laced into Miss Corey's remark that Antonio is "covering" for his mother. And I also hear Miss Corey identifying with Antonio's mom, a "there-but-for-the-grace-of-God-go-I" stance of recognition that she, too, could be negatively judged. It strikes me that Miss Corey's actions of bending school rules also serve as a "cover" for Antonio's mom. This momentary co-conspiracy reminds me of the countless numbers of teachers, workplace managers, and medical personnel Lisa Dodson (2011) interviewed. They also reported bending rules for the benefit of others. Among her participants, Dodson found a "moral underground" of middle-class people witnessing the effects of poverty wages and feeling compelled to do something to mitigate the risks and hardships imposed by an unfair economy.

I am especially curious about how Antonio hears Miss Corey's remark that he is "covering" for his mother. What messages about his family care is Antonio receiving—ones of stigma? Anxiety? Blame? And how about Cesar, the elder brother? How does he understand his own care-giving role? We know that children glean insight into their social position and value in society when they observe how authorities view their forms of family care. Using their ears as "tuning forks to gauge the emotional tenor of adult talk" (Hochschild, 2003: 172), children pay attention to what is said about their family care and find ways of making sense of it.[1] They learn early how to listen for and read signs of anxiety or stigma about their upbringings.[2] And what they hear is laced with moral messages about "good" and "bad" parenting, "good" and "bad" parents, "good" and "bad" care.

I draw attention to this incident because so much lies beneath its surface. In one sense, it reminds us that schools are powerful and enduring sites where motherhood is constructed and judged. It takes resources, as well as physical and emotional labor, to maintain the performance of the caring mother—the mother who has sufficient money, time, energy, transportation, flexibility in her job, and so on, to be "visible," and thus valued, by school personnel. Equally important is that schools are formative sites where childhood is constructed and children are judged. The effort that it takes to perform the cared-for and thus care-free, "school-ready" child is also dependent on resources that are not available to all children. By using the term performance, I do not mean to suggest actions that are in any way false or disingenuous.[3] The point is that when mothers and children "do school" in ways that fall outside the limits of normative rules or expectations, they are judged negatively, as this incident suggests.

How mothers and children "do school" rests on what I call choreographies of care—a concept meant to highlight the constellation of resources, people, rhythms shaped by different occupational demands and shifting schedules, feelings, and intimacies of family living. In this chapter I explore how the PCS children used their cameras to render this choreography visible and to acknowledge and affirm its value. Amidst prevailing deficit and stigmatizing portrayals of wage-poor households and working mothers' invisibility, I argue that the children's photographs and accounts accomplish two things: first, when given the opportunity, the children confirmed their mothers' care work, educational presence, and value; and second, the children, albeit differently for boys and girls, highlighted their own participation in choreographies of family care. I call the children's images and accounts counter-narratives of care because they offer an alternative way of seeing care as a concerted, collective activity, not as individualized or uni-directional (Luttrell, 2013). Through these interdependent activities (children and adults), the children's gendered identities are forged and emotional relations are structured.

## Maternal (in)visibility

In reviewing research written about family-school relationships, it is clear that gender, race, class, and culture play an important role in perceptions of what counts as parent involvement. Working-poor mothers, but especially Black and Latina mothers,[4] express frustration about how their educational presence and care is viewed within schools. Time and again, studies report that these mothers' inability to appear in school leads teachers to assume that they do not care or that they aren't responsible (David, 1993; Valdés, 1996, 2001; Moreno & Lopez, 1999; Valenzuela, 1999; Reay, 2000; Villenas, 2001; Hart, 2002; Cooper, 2003; Griffith & Smith, 2005; Zarate, 2007; Dodson, 2011; Dodson & Luttrell, 2011). "No-show" mothers, as they are sometimes known by school authorities, can feel judged and stigmatized for not living up to idealized, white, middle-class norms of parent involvement. What lies beyond sight is the skillful balancing of resources, people, and scheduling required of wage-poor, working mothers to enable their involvement in their children's education. In an interview with Camille Cooper (2009), one African American mother working two jobs characterized her school involvement as relying upon "the village kind of thing where you involve your whole family":

> And when I say "involved," that doesn't mean that you have to be at all the PTA meetings and be a member of all the groups and stuff, because I don't do that, I don't have the time. But you almost have to do it like the village kind of thing where you involve your whole family. You know my

sister and her son goes to the same school, so sometimes if she can make a meeting, and I just can't, then she'll bring me the information back, and she'll pick me up stuff. And if she sees something that's wrong, she speaks for me too. (2009: 389)

Traditional school-based models of parent involvement rarely account for the various and distinctive ways mothers can participate in their children's education and demonstrate care. These include strategies of "othermothering" and "motherwork" that African American women have historically used to assist, nurture, and care for others beyond the bounded family unit (Collins, 2000; Thompson, 2004; Naples, 1998; Hart, 2002; Stack, 1974). Latina mothers' strategies include laying a foundation at home and trusting that school will take care of the rest (Ada & Zubizarreta, 2001: 231). This foundation is built on transmitting important positive cultural values related to *respeto* (respect); *confianza* (trust and confidence); and by sharing *dichos* (cultural expressions) and *consejos* (advice) with their children about their experiences in school (De La Vega, 2007).

White, middle-class mothers, whether they are employed or "stay-at-home moms," constitute the majority of public school volunteers, and they most often govern the parent-teacher groups in schools (De Gaetano, 2007; Tutwiler, 2005). This public presence sets an unspoken standard for parental educational involvement that is shared by both educators and scholars. Research also suggests the presence and participation of middle-class, white parents wins them greater influence, status, appreciation, and value among educators (Abrams & Gibbs, 2002; Cooper, 2007; Evans, 2007; Henry, 1996; Lareau & Horvat, 1999). These benefits are then extended to many non-present white parents by way of positive association (Cooper, 2009: 381).

I join others who seek to critique racialized, deficit-based framings of parental involvement (Diamond & Gomez, 2004; Koonce & Harper, 2005; Lareau, 2003; Lewis & Forman, 2002; Smalley & Reyes-Blanes, 2001; Yan, 2000), but from a different angle. My aim is to appreciate young people's own perspectives about family-school relationships, including their implicit awareness that mothers are compelled to project—and they themselves must protect—an image of "good" parenting. This image depends on maternal visibility in school, itself dependent on scarce and unevenly distributed resources. As long as "invisible" low-wage, working mothers are judged by institutional authorities, teachers, and peers according to standards that do not account for their lives, stigma and blame will remain unchallenged.

But by contrast, children at PCS used photography to challenge the notion of their mothers' invisibility, rendering their unseen care work visible and publicly affirming its value.

## Moms in kitchens

Gina has just turned 11; she is wearing a bright pink sweatshirt and jeans. Throughout the interview she speaks with a buoyant confidence and humor, at times pulling her black, shoulder-length hair behind her ear in a familiar gesture of decorum that I often notice among a particular group of white girls at the school. Gina looks intently at her set of 27 photographs laid on the table and selects the following figure (Figure 3.1):

> "This is my mom, every night she makes coffee for my dad who won't get home until late at night 'cause he works the double shift and she gets up early to leave for work. We lead a pretty scheduled life."

This is an example of the most emblematic photograph of family care taken by the PCS children—what I came to call the "mom-in-kitchen" photograph—displaying a routine moment in the daily rhythms of working-class family-work life. Gina describes this life as "pretty scheduled," but not in the same terms as the "hurried childhoods" in many middle-class families where children are shuttled from one after-school activity/lesson to another as a means to enrich their competitive advantage—what sociologist Annette Lareau calls a concerted cultivation model of middle-class child rearing (2003).[5] Gina goes on to reflect:

> "My mom, she's very beautiful, I know that. She's also smart, even though she didn't go to college, but she's very, very smart. We love her very much. She loves us very much. She has a great personality. She has a good job. She mostly does all the work at her job. She goes to work an hour before everybody else, cause it's nice and quiet and she can get a lot of work done [she does clerical work at a law office].... She comes home at 5:30, so we don't really do much because she wants to eat dinner, have two glasses of milk. Then she lays down on the couch, watches some movies. Then we tell her about our day at school and she asks what papers she needs to sign."

Figure 3.1: We lead a pretty scheduled life *Gina, age 10*

Gina also mentions that her mom "is very good at baking. But she doesn't bake anymore because of work. So usually when we have a party in school, sometimes she bakes if she has the time, but most of the time she will buy something at the store."

Gina also describes the photograph she took of her dog (Figure 3.2) to show her habitual after-school routine. She and her sister come

Figure 3.2: After school *Gina, age 10*

home from school, attend to the dog, fix themselves a snack, complete their homework, and prepare dinner, while awaiting their mother's return from work. Gina portrays care work—her mother's, her sister's, and her own—as a practice of mutuality and interdependence. And along the way, she makes a point to emphasize facets of her mother's social value: her beauty; her smarts (even without a college degree); her personality; her competence at her job; her attention to school-based expectations and demands (that is, the "papers she needs to sign"); and her domestic role—whether she is preparing coffee, baking (if she has time), or buying food for school. School demands and values are foregrounded in Gina's admiration for her mother, as if to counter any misconceptions that her audience (the interviewer? her teachers?) might hold.

Time runs out during Gina's interview with the research assistant. When I next return to the school, she reminds me that she needs to finish talking about her photographs. Her emotions are almost palpable as she requests to speak to me, asking haltingly, "Can, can I talk to you about my mother?" "Sure," I reply, and she sifts through her pile of photographs to find the photograph of her mom in the kitchen. There is a faint smile on her face as she gazes on it, turning the photograph for me to see:

"I really like my mom because she's the one who mainly gave me life; my dad, with his help too. But she's the one that had, that had a lot of pain.[6] So, I'm really grateful for, to her."

There is an embodied sense of seeing and feeling in this moment as Gina tenderly holds the photograph, as if the picture carries the presence of her mom. It strikes me that care, gratitude, and pain are not only the themes of her photograph, but also the way she engages the photograph through touch, gestures, and intensity. I am reminded of Gillian Rose's (2004) article about the relationship between mothering and photography and its relevance for understanding the children's photographs of mothers in homeplaces. First, Rose suggests that to fully appreciate family photography, we must understand the everyday, embodied practices—the doing of things, like posing, developing, curating, framing, displaying, sharing with relatives, and so on, that are part of how family photographs are viewed and received, including the expectation that moms are primarily responsible for these practices documenting childhood and family life. Second, Rose suggests that the practice of taking family photographs, especially of young children, might serve to assuage mixed feelings—the strain, guilt, irritation as well as joys—that most mothers feel toward children, especially in a culture that valorizes what Sharon Hays (1996) has called "intensive mothering." Indeed, Rose notes that children are photographed most often during the time they are most demanding of their mothers, and thus when mothers are most likely to experience ambivalence. For the mothers she studied, "looking at photographs, then, may produce a proximal space in which the ambivalence of a certain kind of mothering can be encountered on its shifting ground" (2004: 561). Rose's article predates contemporary digital technology where with the click of a finger digital photographs can be curated into family albums and immediately shared with others. Still, her observation of the significance of both the picture taking and the picture looking as part of an expression of caring, relatedness, "togetherness" (to use Rose's terms) helps me make sense of what I am seeing in Gina's (and so many other of the children's) way of looking. How could these photographs of mothers serve as a means to assuage mixed feelings—the strains, discomfort, and reference to pain, as well as the admiration, gratitude, and pride associated with the demands placed upon their mothers, and by extension, themselves?

Gina continues talking about her mother's central role—how she "keeps the family going," and to lighten her mom's load, Gina is glad to do her part, including tidying up the sofa where her mother sleeps (Figure 3.3) and doing dishes (Figure 3.4).

Gina is making domestic work visible and explicitly placing value on it. This is interesting in and of itself, but even more important is *how* she values it. Gina's narrative features care-giving and care-receiving as reciprocal relations. Her love for her mother is expressed through the repetition in her account of the word "very," and in a language of

Figure 3.3: Tidying the sofa *Gina, age 10*

Figure 3.4: Doing dishes *Gina, age 10*

gratitude (it is not taken for granted) and reciprocity, including her obligation to be "helpful."

Ten-year-old Sebastian expresses the material and emotional parameters of his mother's homemaking. Sebastian is small for his age; he wears his dark hair cropped short, with a little sprig of cow-lick standing up at the front of his forehead. His grin is infectious. Sebastian speaks softly and smiles at the end of almost every sentence. He has just finished telling the interviewer about how his family watches television in the living room: "But not my mom, she's really busy. Sometimes on Saturdays if she has nothin' to do she will sit with us, my whole family, we all like to talk around commercial breaks. But mostly she is working." He giggles, "I do my homework in front of the TV," furtively glancing at the video camera as if to say, "I know that isn't the best way." Holding up the next photograph of his mother (Figure 3.5) he says, with reverence in his voice,

"I admire her. I like her, she's nice. My mom, she was a Grade A student in Colombia. She cooks good food; rice, beans, chicken. She cooks soup on Sunday mornings called *caldo*." He continued, describing weekly meals with extended family members:[7]

> "My uncle comes for food, 'cause usually he just gets home late from work and my aunt, she comes really, really late, like, after him. And when they both get home my mom calls them to offer if they want some food because it would mean a lot. So they come over and eat."

Sebastian uses glowing terms to describe his mother, who migrated to the United States from Colombia; he explains that she comes from a "long line of intelligence." Like Gina, Sebastian highlights his mother's role in feeding the family, speaking not only about her skill as a good cook, but how her cooking provides sustenance for those who have limited time to cook because of work schedules. Sebastian identifies the choreography of care—its weekly rhythm on Sunday mornings that also establishes connection and sociability with extended family members. Also like Gina, Sebastian mentions his mother's educational value, "a grade A student" in Colombia regardless of her educational credentials in the United States. He says he doesn't know how she manages—"it is tough with her job and all she has to do," but she is "always there for us." She has worked hard since she arrived in the United States, providing for her three children. Sebastian describes his own weekly chores—washing dishes, taking out the trash, helping with the laundry, cleaning his room—and adds, "It is family rules. My mom helps me so I have to help her."

Gina and Sebastian both project positive images of their mothers, extolling their mothers' virtues. They both express an awareness of the many challenges their mothers have had to face—childbirth, migration, over-work, tiredness. They hold their mothers' hard work and fortitude

Figure 3.5: I admire her *Sebastian, age 10*

in high regard and establish their mother's active presence ("always there for us") alongside time constraints. Their explicit sense of gratitude comes through not only in their words, but in their deeds, as they too engage in care work for the sake of others.

Gabriel also praised his mom (Figure 3.6) "'cause she's creative with food. You can tell because the cupcakes are there. She's baking cupcakes for the cupcake sale. They were gone quick."

Gabriel is taller and looks older than others his age, with his buzz-cut hairstyle, black sweatshirt, and St. Joseph silver-chained necklace. But the high-pitched tenor of his voice confirms his ten-year-old-ness. He regaled the interviewer with descriptions of his mother's cooking, including his favorite dish: "White meat that has no bones and also red skin with a lot of pepper, I like hot stuff." When he is asked whether he helps his mother cook, he says, "only on cook days."

The interviewer is curious, wanting to know about cook days. Gabriel explains with vigor:

> "On cook days we make breakfast, dinner, and dessert, which we did. I made chicken wings, and the stuff, I made it tender, I put wine in it [gesturing as if he is pouring the wine] and it makes it delicious [squeezing his fingers like a professional chef]. I learned that trick from my mom."

Figure 3.6: She's creative with food *Gabriel, age 10*

Gabriel picks up the photograph, caresses its edges, and continues, "I love her so much, I could explode from too much. That's why I love her very much because she helps me with a lot of things." The interviewer seems to be holding back a smile. "What else does she help you with?" Gabriel engages her question. "She helps me with my homework, and [pausing] mostly, she helps me with being a child." Still probing, the interviewer asks, "How does she do that?" Gabriel laughs. "It is the same mother's rules," and then shifting into a directive tone of voice, "clean up your room, fix your bed." Gabriel concludes in a softened voice, "But I like it when she does that, it's really nice."

Gabriel's unselfconscious expression of explosive love for his mother is a statement that pulls at the heartstrings. Aside from its tenderness, I hear in Gabriel's words and in his affect an awareness that mothers' care work is unlike other kinds of labor. Indeed, sociologist Kathleen Lynch (2007) refers to mothers' care work as "love labour," a useful term for thinking about the multiple dimensions of the young people's orientations toward care:

> Because [love labour relations] have an other-centred dimension to their character, they cannot be entirely marketised without undermining their care or solidarity purposes. One of the distinguishing features of love labour relations is that they are not commodifiable. (2007: 563)

I want to highlight the other-centered emotional relations that resonate in Gabriel's account and reverberate in Gina's and Sebastian's as well. Gabriel's mom's "creativity with food," her teaching culinary "tricks," her help with homework, and her "rules" are not simply about (re) producing a child in instrumental ways (that is, a child "ready for school"), but a child who is expressively loving and oriented toward the needs of the other ("she helps me so I have to help her"). I am also struck that Gabriel sees his mom as helping him with "being a child" (not "becoming an adult") and that he stakes a claim of appreciation for "the same mother's rules, clean up your room, fix your bed"— spoken as if these are shared or commonly held relations between mother and child.

A main feature of the children's photographs is the central positioning of women's love labor. Sometimes, but not always, the subject turns to engage the photographer (rarely with a smile) or poses with one hand on her hip while gazing directly at the camera. These images clearly depict the kitchen as a woman's domain, a space in which she is in charge. In them, I see the importance of food and cooking, of kitchens as the family hearth, and of women's central role in "feeding the family" (DeVault, 1991). In her classic sociological account, DeVault examines the invisible labor involved in housework, addressing how its gendered organization leaves women with disproportionate responsibility for that labor (whether they do the work themselves or arrange for others to do it), and how class status and material conditions effect how women perform and experience their efforts to create a sense of family and be "good" wives/mothers. I use DeVault's work to interpret not only what I see in the photographs, but also what the children told me about why they had taken them and what the images meant for them: "I took this picture of my mom. I admire her. She's creative in the kitchen." The children speak about the work of sociability (the term DeVault uses) and their moms' attentiveness to their own and others' food preferences (including, as will soon be evident, teachers who asked their moms to prepare particular favorites for school events, like spring rolls and tres leches cakes). The children identify their moms' cooking as a means to sustain family heritage and family ties (including religious festivals and birthday celebrations), sometimes training their camera lens on specific foods. And most importantly, they speak of gratitude and reciprocity.

Digital Interlude #2: Feeding the Family is meant to communicate the intimacies of mothers' love labor—its settings, objects, relationships, movements, gestures, and postures. Here I wish to address my decision to blur the faces of the moms as a way to conceptually convey the sense of the mothers' always-in-motion-activity, the DOING of feeding the family and home making that the children spoke of and honored. To blur the mothers' faces is also a means to deal with ethical issues I discuss more in the Postlude as well as reference to the work of artist Ramiro Gomez discussed in Chapter 6. Digital Interlude #2: Feeding the Family is meant to challenge maternal invisibility while at the same time suggest that wage-poor working moms are not fully seen or recognized for their pivotal role in their children's education.

## *Digital Interlude #2: Feeding the Family*

 childrenframingchildhoods.com/digital-interludes/feeding-the-family

Mothers' work "feeding the family"—and the ways it established and sustained family connections and an orientation toward the needs of others—extended beyond kitchen walls and into children's sense of belonging and value in school. Gabriel's conversation with his peers about his mom-in-kitchen photograph illustrated this connection. Gabriel's eyes gleamed when the children in his small group discussion all agreed that his mom's cupcakes were "the best," which secured him a valued place in school culture. As previously described, these discussions were informal and child-directed as the participants examined each others' five favorite photographs and talked about what they "noticed." As various small groups of children spoke about the moms-in-kitchen photographs, I could hear the outlines of a larger story about how different mothers measured up or not in regards to this aspect of school culture. One particular moment stood out. Nalanie, whose family migrated from Laos, spoke about her mom-in-kitchen photograph (Figure 3.7).

Nalanie told the interviewer that her mom was preparing spring rolls for the school and described how they are made. But during the small group discussion with her peers, Nalanie said that while she wished her mother would bake cookies for school: "All the teachers love them [the spring rolls] so much, so now she has to keep making them, and making them, and making them" [spoken in a mother's voice of endless toil]. Braided into Nalanie's playful performance in front of her classmates is a dual recognition that is worth noting. In the first instance, Nalanie seems to be acknowledging her mother's investment (time and energy) in school culture and its facilitation of Nalanie's sense of belonging. At the same time, whereas Nalanie's mother's efforts seemingly earned her a special regard from her teachers, it was from her *peers* that she also sought recognition. Cupcakes and

Figure 3.7: Making spring rolls *Nalanie, age 10*

other home-made sweets were more valuable tokens, as Pugh might argue, than spring rolls.

The children took an array of images of food that was prepared (or bought) by mothers, aunts, and grandmothers that signified sociability and belonging beyond school culture. They photographed open refrigerators stocked with groceries, and documented food tied to special occasions—(store-bought) birthday cakes being a quintessential sign that they were the subject of their mother's love and attention. Others photographed food made for parties and religious holidays and food specifically associated with their homelands (Figures 3.9 & 3.10). In describing her photograph of the red, white, and blue ices (Figure 3.8), Camila commended her grandmother's "secret recipe from Puerto Rico. Nobody knows the recipe, not even my mother. But when I grow up she is going to teach me so I will know and can make them for everyone on the block." Here Camila is showcasing a

Figure 3.8: My grandma's ices *Camila, age 11*

sign of her grandmother's "funds of knowledge" (Moll et al, 1992) or community cultural wealth (Yossa 2005); and she is also signaling that she is the recipient of her grandmother's attention. At the same time, she is orienting herself toward a future in which she will continue the tradition and provide food "for everyone on the block."

 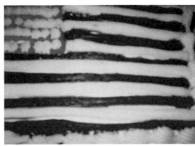

Figure 3.9: Holiday food
*Nadia, age 11*

Figure 3.10: My mom's special cake
*Nia, age 12*

In a variation of this same theme, Tina took a photograph of food that she helped her mother prepare (Figure 3.11).

Tina, who migrated from Vietnam with her parents, animated the story behind her photograph, play-acting her own and her mother's role in cooking. She started with an expert rendition of the proper preparation for frying the fish that she had learned from her mother, explaining that she most likes the salty, crispy taste of the fish tail. "I tried to cook it, but it almost got burned, and I yelled, 'Mommy, mommy help me!'" Tina demonstrated her mother's swift rescue of the burning dish with a quick flip of the pan. With wonder in her voice she asked, as if speaking directly to her mother, "How did you do that?" Then, returning to address the interviewer, Tina admitted in a less animated tone of voice, "Mostly I make rice." She again described her preparation technique and summed it up: "it is easy and mostly we eat rice." Like Gabriel, Tina performed pride in her mother's expertise and in her role as her mother's child and apprentice.

Of course, not all photographs referencing mothers' care work were set in kitchens or related to food. Capturing an iconic image of family literacy, Allison (who, readers will remember from the previous chapter, voiced her mother's concern about the safety of Terrace Gardens) asked her sister to take a photograph of her and her mom snuggling on the couch together:

> "This is me and my mom, reading together. That's my favorite book, cause our teacher reads it to us every day. I

Figure 3.11: Helping my mom *Tina, age 10*

love to read with my mom, she's a really good reader, cause
she used to read a lot when she was a little kid."

Praising their mothers' love of reading was a common thread in the
children's discussions. Kendra showed a snapshot of her mother standing
in front of the bathroom mirror, stating proudly, "I admire my mother."
In answer to my question about what she admires about her mother,
Kendra listed three attributes: "She's 33, married, and loves to read,
I know that."[8]

Kendra was not the only child who wanted me to know that her
mother is married and that her mother loves to read. In an interesting
twist on this theme about reading, Natalia spoke about a photograph
that she had taken of a vacuum cleaner. Aside from making her mother's
domestic labor visible, Natalia's account features her mother's love of
reading. She explained: "My aunt watches TV while she's vacuuming,
but my mom reads a book. She must read 30 books a week!" Natalia's
economy of dignity, to use Pugh's phrase, translates the worth of her
mother's domestic work into educational value. Again I think it is worth
asking, who is the audience for staking these claims to dignity? Is it me
and the interviewers? Their teachers? Classmates? Their own selves,
as daughters of mothers who identify as readers (not TV watchers)?

To summarize, the PCS children used their cameras to establish their
mother's goodness, nurturance, value, and presence. As if to counteract
negative evaluations, the children positioned their mothers as praise-
worthy in the school domain—as involved (by providing food); as

"intelligent"/"very smart," even without a college diploma; as lovers of reading/promoters of literacy; as a source of help with homework; and as an effective "teacher" of "how to be a child." The children also used their cameras to photograph their own roles in choreographies of family care, rendering visible and audible a structuring of emotional relations—love, gratitude, reciprocity, obligation, pride, pain, and some ambivalence. It was as if, when speaking with/performing regard for their mothers, the children were also speaking with/performing regard for themselves.

In the next section, I elaborate more on the complex factors shaping the children's own participation in choreographies of care.

## Making a living

The majority of PCS children's parents worked in the low-wage sector of the economy (for example, service work, retail, home health care, landscaping), with each occupation imposing distinctive rhythms and routines. These rhythms and routines also depended on (extended) family composition and a constellation of resources, including housing and access to transportation.[9] There were some exceptions. Ling's family owned a restaurant, which was atypical, and yet her account highlights the kinds of patterned family care-work routines and webs of meaning found across the children's representations.

Ling's family immigrated to the United States in the mid-1990s from the rural Chinese province of Fujian, located on the southeast coast of China, when she was a year old. Her parents joined other family members to work in a Chinese restaurant, the site of many of Ling's photographs. She begins her interview by telling me a complicated story about the family business: "My cousin's dad and him and his brother and his mom used to own it with my dad and my family," but the restaurant had come to be owned solely by her parents once the extended family members left town. "Now they [her parents] don't have time because when the restaurant is all theirs, you know how they have to take care of it all the time."

Explaining a photograph of her house, Ling describes her parents' arrangements for their Fujianese employees, who are offered housing and meals as part of their compensation package, a common arrangement among Fujianese restaurant owners (Coe, 2009 in Fontaine, 2015: 56).[10] Living in a house "with workers in the restaurant," Ling explains, "they get rooms, and bathrooms, a refrigerator, and all that." Ling's photographs serve as windows into the way she participates in and navigates two worlds: her school world (she took photographs of classroom rules, friends, homework, and her report card), and her family's work world (with photographs inside and outside her home and the restaurant).

Ling describes her after-school routine with some embarrassment. Since her family moved to a new home to accommodate the restaurant workers, Ling is now supposed to join the line of students who are escorted by teachers to board school buses at the end of the day. But Ling's mother prefers that she walk directly to the restaurant, located a short distance from the school. Thus Ling explains, "So that's why I wait, waiting for the teachers to pass. And then I go across the street, go to the restaurant and eat, and then I do my homework around five or six." Sometimes, if the restaurant gets busy, Ling is asked to pitch in, ringing up customers on the cash register. She expresses mixed emotions about this, on the one hand saying it is "boring and when there are no customers I fall asleep," but also delighting in her proficiency. She is "good" at the task and notes that she is better than her much older brother. Ling believes the customers "don't really trust" her and "are like, 'Oh, you're so young!'" After long, busy nights at the restaurant, she reports that her mother and brother carry her home if she has fallen asleep. "So I'm alright." Meanwhile, Ling relishes her relationships with the restaurant workers and regular customers and takes numerous photographs of them. She receives gifts and Valentine's cards, and she photographs a stuffed animal passed down to her from one of the customers:

> "'cause they like me a lot and I draw pictures for them. So, they gave me it 'cause they clean, like, this person's house, the neighbor's, and they have a lot of stuff that they don't want, so they gave it to me."

This integration of family and work life has both benefits and limitations, and Ling makes a point to assure me of this on several occasion, by saying, "I'm alright," or "it is okay." A year later, when I speak with her again in sixth grade, Ling lingers on a blurry photograph of her report card that she has taken, saying with satisfaction, "I am the only person in the class who got all As, no Bs." This accomplishment "make[s] my mom and dad proud because they want a good child like me." She says she didn't actually get to share her report card with her parents, "'Cause they usually come home at 11, and I go to bed at 10:30. But it's okay." Instead, she says, she asked her older brother to sign it ("because he is 20, he could sign it"). Perhaps she is assuring me that it is okay according to school rules that her parents didn't sign her report card, or perhaps she is acknowledging her parents' preoccupation with the restaurant and its demands (or both). If Ling is reading signs of stigma or anxiety about her parents' school involvement or her upbringing, she is navigating information and her self-presentation skillfully.

Ling's reference to food and nurturance was also especially telling. In both fifth and sixth grade, she photographed the buffet table at the restaurant explaining that this is where she eats. But in sixth grade she elaborated on the array of choices. "You get the noodles and the chicken and the broccoli. The second row is the soup and some fried stuff. And the third row is supposed to be seafood. And the side is fruits. And the back is drinks." Then she remarked, "I'm sick of the food." "You're sick of the food?" I repeat her words. "Why?" "Eating there every day. I think I've been there for at least five years, I think. So, everybody would be sick of it," Ling replies.

Ling's complaint about the food did not go unaddressed, as she tells me in the next moment:

> "I don't eat there often anymore 'cause my mom cooks at home and there's this soup that I like. It has rice in it and my mom cooks it and leaves it in this pot for me. I had it for breakfast today with a cookie. She makes a big pot so when I don't want to eat the buffet food, I can just go home and eat the soup. Sometimes, when my brother has time, he goes to Wendy's for me and buys something."

Again we hear the salience placed on mothers' roles in "feeding the family." While her mother's labor in the restaurant produces food as a commodity, it is her mother's cooking labor at *home* that ensures that Ling feels loved and cared for. Ling's appreciation for the time her brother occasionally takes from work to indulge her desires for fast food highlights another form of care that relates to belonging.

Ling's family choreography of care was unique for its merging of family and work time. While this meant her parents' attentions were almost always divided, it also meant that she spent more time with her parents than most children with two working parents, and within an extended care network of family, employees, and customers. This more extended circle of care notwithstanding, Ling still reported that it was her mother who addressed her daughter's needs, whether by preparing her favorite soup, directing Ling's activities after school, or integrating her into the work routines of the restaurant.

Angeline's family choreography of care is shaped by a different rhythm of work. Readers will remember Angeline from the previous chapter, as the appreciative daughter of parents who migrated from Kenya, who photographed the clothes in her closet as a reminder of her beloved grandparents. Angeline went to great lengths to photograph her mother and then her parents together (Figures 3.12 & 3.13), rising early in the morning, before her mom's departure for back-to-back shifts as a home health care assistant. "She goes to work 7 a.m. to 11 p.m., on Saturdays 7 a.m. to 3 p.m. Most of the time she goes at 7 a.m. to 11p.m. and my dad goes at 3 a.m. to 11 a.m." Angeline explains. "So you took a picture of your parents and you wanted to show..." As I pause, Angeline interjects. "To show that I admire my parents, I love them because they born me into this world, with the help of God [smiles], yeah."

I am drawn in by the lyrical cadence of Angeline's voice, her mesmerizing storytelling style, and her cherubic smile. Her take-nothing-for-granted stance toward life punctuates her remarks about family and school life. "Your family is always there for you more than anybody else. Family is the one who takes care of you when you was growing up...." But she cautions, "Not everybody—kids can be born with their family but their parents don't want them. So, the kids don't even know that much about their parents." As mentioned in the previous chapter, Angeline is aware of the precarity of care, and she uses her photographs to express gratitude for all of the things that others have provided for her—clothing, shelter ("If I didn't live in a house I would be homeless, that's why I'm really appreciative"), and life itself ("with the help of God").

Angeline photographed an empty, and strikingly tidy kitchen (Figure 3.14)—the stage upon which she narrated to her listener her own role in the family choreography of care. "That's the kitchen. I wash the dishes a lot, that's where I do most of my chores, most of my chores [are] in there," Angeline explains. I ask, "Do you have weekly chores?" Angeline nods her head. "Yes; cooking, cleaning up the house. This is where I wash the dishes. I like cooking a lot. That's where I do my chores, most of the time on the weekends, that's what I do. I love cooking." I am curious to know more. "So do you cook for your whole family, too?" Angeline pauses. "Sometimes, but sometimes my mom has to do that because I'm still learning how to cook a lot of things. She's been teaching me."

Here, too, akin to Tina's and Gabriel's accounts, cooking is learned by way of an apprenticeship of sorts.[11] Part of this apprenticeship includes the necessary complementary "emotional labor" of appearing

Figure 3.12: My mom *Angeline, age 10*

Figure 3.13: I admire my parents *Angeline, age 10*

happy about the work: "I like cooking a lot ... I love cooking". Arlie Hochschild defines this as "labor [that] requires one to induce or suppress feeling in order to sustain the outward countenance that produces the proper state of mind in others" (1983: 7). And, as she writes, "big emotion workers tend to raise little ones" (1983: 156).

As Angeline is learning to cook, she also speaks of her father's cooking:

Figure 3.14: That's the kitchen *Angeline, age 10*

"Sometimes when my mom goes to work and she has to leave early, and she doesn't have time to cook, then if it's the weekend and I'm not going to school and I need something to eat, then I ask my dad if he can cook for me and then he cooks. He's a good cook, *for a man*." [She emphasizes this last phrase as she smiles first at the video camera and then at me.]

Angeline's nod to the conditions under which her father cooks (when her mother can't) and her valuing of his cooking as good (*despite* his being a man), encapsulates the gendered logic that weds care work with "women's work." This logic permeated the PCS children's accounts, which I will elaborate on in the next section.[12]

Looking closely at Angeline's photograph of her parents (Figures 3.12 & 3.13) and listening to her narration of it sheds more light on the invisible emotional labor that is part of women's care work:

"My dad had just woken up. He had to take my mom into work. He's so grumpy when he wakes up. He looks kind of mad, he doesn't have a smile. Okay, this is my mom [who is smiling]. She was going to work, that's why she has her work clothes and her jacket."

The photograph reveals Angeline's mom's support of her husband and his presence. She is gripping his wrist and putting her arm around his waist, as they both stand stiffly in front of the front door. Angeline's mom is orchestrating the moment, satisfying her daughter's request for a photograph in spite of the early hour and her husband's "grumpy" mood, captured by his refusal to smile (despite Angeline's instruction to do so, as she tells me). Her mother, on the other hand, manages a smile in spite of a set of quite challenging circumstances: the very early hour, the need to leave for the first of two work shifts, Angeline's request for a photograph at an inconvenient time, and her husband's grumpiness. Once again, the gendered emotional work that has gone into the creation of this photographic artifact—and the moment it depicts—might remain unseen, if not for the lucid narration that Angeline provides.

## Picturing care as gendered

Again and again, the children chose to photograph their mothers, making their care work visible and highlighting their mothers' goodness, nurturance, value, and presence. The visibility of mothers and their nurturance was in sharp contrast to the relative invisibility of fathers, an observation routinely made by viewers of the visual archive. Where are the fathers? This vexing question was sometimes laced with deficit assumptions about single-mother households lacking "male role models." But it is also a question that I could hear the children addressing in both indirect and direct ways. Some children made their fathers' presence known despite their physical absence, as Angel did through the tattoo art he photographed (and keeps displayed in his bedroom). One child photographed a gift she had been given by her father, still in its box; another documented a makeshift memorial commemorating her father's death; and two other children took photographs of their fathers' workplaces. Even when fathers were "not home," many children took pains to show that they were very much "still here" in their families' lives.

In this section I want to draw attention to the complex and nuanced ways that the children pictured care, and its gendered organization. For children growing up in single-mother as well as two-parent families, photographs of women at home—mothers, aunts, grandmothers—predominated. Overall, pictures of men at home—fathers, uncles, grandfathers—were few and far between. And when men did appear in person, they were not found in kitchens (except for one photograph, where it appears that a man is carrying food out of the kitchen). Men appeared in dining rooms being served food (by women), in living rooms reclining on sofas, or posing at a child's request (as in Angeline's photograph). While women were all photographed inside the home, men were photographed out and about (in shopping malls, going to church, in front of cars). Junior's photographs and accounts of his mother and father serve as an interesting case to explore the gendered picturing of care.

Junior, as readers will remember from Chapter 1, described himself as "Haitian." He made a point to tell me that his language of Creole and knowledge of Haiti made him "creative." He took several different photographs to represent and reference his mother's love and care. In the first one (Figure 3.15), his mother sits composed, hands neatly clasped, on the arm of the living room sofa.

He said he took her photograph because he "admires her," and is grateful for "how hard she works." He also explained his multiple efforts to secure her photograph:

> "I asked her if I could take her picture but she said, 'Not right now.' And then she forgot about it. And then I just told her when she was on her way to work, and then she said, 'Okay. But take my picture later.' And then when she got home from work in the morning I told her, 'just relax, I am going to take your picture,' and she goes, 'You want me in my uniform? Let me go get ready.' I go, 'No, I'll just take it now,' and she goes, 'Okay.'"

Figure 3.15: She works hard *Junior, age 10*

This reported negotiation between mother and son highlights Junior's effort to produce maternal visibility despite his mother's demanding work schedule (and, perhaps, despite her own resistance). His mother clearly preferred to be photographed when she considered herself "ready"—in different clothes, possibly with her hair styled and make-up applied. But she relented, perhaps out of tiredness after returning home from her 12-hour shift as a CNA, or perhaps out of a sense of duty to oblige her son's request for a school-related activity. Whatever her feelings, like Angeline's mother, she offered a slight smile, meeting her responsibilities to "manage" her own emotions (Hochschild, 1983) in order to address the feelings of her child.

Still, Junior was not finished with his task. He took two other photographs to speak about his relationship to his mom. The first was picture of his mom (Figure 3.16), prominently displayed in the living room that she called, "my mom's teen self."

Mounted on a wooden plaque with "1988" engraved on the side, Junior's mother looks glamorous, wearing a pink, off-the-shoulder gown, gold necklace, and a shoulder-length, prom-like hairstyle. Junior also photographed a teddy bear that he had bought for his mother when he was four:

> "I bought this for my mom for Valentine's Day. It was taller
> than me and my dad had to help me pick it up. And, then,
> I just gave it to my mom for Valentine's Day. She cried.
> She gave me a hug and all that."

Junior used his camera to illuminate a mother-son relationship inside a homeplace with signposts of love, care, affection, and attachment. These photographs, like so many others taken by the children, are themselves documentations of care. They can be read as forms of intimacy, as acts of love and caring that join the children and their mothers into relation. As I mentioned previously, Roland Barthes writes metaphorically of a photograph serving as an as "umbilical cord" of light that joins viewer and viewed into relation (1981: 81). This metaphor is useful for what I have been describing throughout this chapter as the children seek to portray the salience of their relationships with mothers. There is a formality to Junior's pictures that signifies his mother's worthiness—her beauty, dignity, and respectability in the past and in the present. He also chooses to photograph the gift that symbolizes their mutual affection. The stuffed bear on the wicker chair with its bright red bow has pride of place in the living room, signaling its value to both mother and son (and indirectly to dad, who helped).

Figure 3.16: My mom's teen self *Junior, age 10*

Junior chose yet another photograph (Figure 3.17) to be part of a public exhibition.

It is a formal studio portrait that can be read as a stereotypical depiction of the relationship between mother and child. It is an iconic, mother Madonna-style image—mother and child at the center, arms protectively wrapped around a child in her lap (Junior) while another child standing to the left (Junior's twin brother) lays his arm around their mother's shoulder. It is a stylized pose: mother and children gaze directly at the professional photographer with intention, eyes alert, no smiles, relaxed facial expressions. The angle from which Junior takes this photograph makes it clear that the family portrait sits perched on a shelf above his height and reach. The flash on Junior's camera casts a glistening, white light in the lower left corner that picks up a silvery, shimmering tint to the background, bathing the subjects in radiant light. Junior selected this photograph to share with his peers and as they discussed it, the children agreed that it belonged in the public exhibition because it "glows" and is "like a painting." Junior titled it, "My People."

Both within his entire set of 27 photographs and in his curated contribution to the exhibition, Junior chose to make his mother most visible; to do so, he drew on a prototypical mother-child portrayal of love and care. His father's role in family care is also documented, but expressed through different means. For example, Junior took this photograph (Figure 3.18) to speak about his father's strategies of care, which include making sure that he and his twin brother don't "fight

Figure 3.17: My people *Junior, age 10*

too much" and are "well behaved." Junior explains his dad's strategy to the interviewer:

> "My dad, he puts some glass stuff just in case we start wrestling. So, then he knows if we do. So, we don't break it. Like, this one, he said that he wanted that furniture right there. He's always telling us we shouldn't fight. One day he's gonna put a camera and not tell us. Mostly he says, 'You keep my back, I get your back.'"

"How do you keep his back?" the interviewer inquires. Junior replies, "Like, if I leave my room clean. And, then, like, sometimes I help him out, like, when he's outside and he's fixing the car, sometimes I help. Or, sometimes when he's cooking, I sometimes help."

In his account, Junior not only identifies his father's contributions to family care: working outside and fixing the car as well as cooking,

Figure 3.18: Glass stuff *Junior, age 10*

typically defined as women's work, but also his own participation and how he is being apprenticed into an interdependent, reciprocal framing of care in which "You keep my back, I get your back."

Just as the children pictured their mothers and fathers according to gendered conventions, they also represented themselves in the same way. Whereas girls showed themselves at home doing domestic chores, boys more often photographed themselves engaged in leisure activities (video-gaming, sports, watching television). Boys typically referenced their domestic labor as chores and "rules of the house," but these were not tasks the boys showed themselves performing. Sebastian was the one exception to this rule. He described a photograph he had asked his brother to take by saying "These are my hands washing the dishes" to show that he helps his mom because she helps him. By contrast, several girls featured themselves doing the work, either in staged scenes with props (with vacuum cleaners, holding children, folding laundry, washing dishes) or in self-portraits, speaking with mixed emotions.

Allison proudly posed with a smile in front of her completed domestic work and asked her younger sister to take a picture. She said:

> "And this is me going to fold the laundry, *all* the laundry [emphasis hers]. I usually do that every day of the week. When she [her mom] picks us up [at her aunt's house where Allison, Allison's sister, and her cousins organize their own leisure activities] she's usually tired so I do this to help her out."

Others, like Gina mentioned previously, also photographed themselves with completed tasks, such as tidied-up beds or closets, or neatly arranged groceries. Tina, who photographed the fish and expressed pride in her role as her mother's apprentice cook, photographed a twenty-dollar bill and used the image to narrate her recruitment into housework:

> "Make my bed, clean the computer, sweep the house, do
> my homework, and laundry. That is my important-est job
> because every single day I see if the laundry basket is full. If
> it is not full I don't need to do it, but if it is, then I do it."

She explained that "every single morning" her job is to fold and "choose out" clothes that she takes to her four brothers (she is the only girl). This task is directed by her mother, who "tells me how to divide, like sort clothes …" [gesturing her hands as if she is sorting clothes into piles]. "She gives me a list, so that is my job, to take them their clothes." I do not detect any sense of resentment or complaint in her voice; she simply notes that if she doesn't complete the laundry, then she only gets $15.00 for the week. When asked how she uses her money, Tina explains that she is not allowed to use it; it is deposited in a savings account for her to attend college.

Nia, the oldest of four girls in her family, speaks with the most mixed emotions about her domestic labor. Something about Nia's deportment, the straightness of her back, makes me think of a ballet dancer. Her pitch-black ponytail and caramel-brown skin are highlighted by the bright white sweater she wears. She described herself as "responsible" and "from the Dominican Republic." Fourteen of Nia's 16 photographs were related to her participation in her family care world. Of the photograph she took of the house telephone (Figure 3.19), she remarked:

"When my cousins call on the weekend, I say, maybe I'll come over later after I'm finished with all the cleaning." She continued:

> "I'm always helping around the house, because it's always a
> mess. Ebony [her sister], she always says, 'I want to be like
> you.' And I say, 'No, you don't,' and she says, 'I'm going
> to help you clean today.' And I go, 'You are? Really?' And
> she's like, 'Yeah.' So she tries. I thank her, even if she doesn't
> help much, cause she wants to help."

Told as a dialogue between older and younger sister, Nia's story places value on her little sister's desire to "help" and expresses gratitude that her sister does not take her work for granted. But even as she warned her sister that she shouldn't wish to be in Nia's shoes, Nia's pride about serving as an example was unmistakable. She took a self-portrait

Figure 3.19: When I'm finished cleaning *Nia, age 11*

(Figure 3.20), holding the camera at arm's length and beaming into the camera (a "selfie" before there was a word for it), "to show that I am a role model for my sisters."

Mixed emotions punctuated Nia's description: her pride in her family, the respect she gets from her sisters, the responsibility for their welfare that she shoulders (for example, accompanying her sister to a birthday party at her parents' request because they are at work, which at least provides her "a little break"), and her belief that her sisters should not aspire to be "just like me."[13]

In contrast, the boys tend to speak about their domestic responsibilities as routine "chores" or direct requests ("take your sister out to the playground," or "clear the table") or as "rules" made by mothers, like Gabriel mentioned earlier ("do this, do that, clean up your room"). Jeffrey describes a picture he took (Figure 3.21) that I anticipated was going to be about his television, which, as readers will remember from the Prelude, Jeffrey explained he was "lucky" if not "spoiled" to have. But instead, the photograph represents what he "hates most"—"Sunday is the cleaning day for my house. I clean my bed, organize my bureau, clean the floor, organize my clothes."

Making sure to express his dislike for housekeeping, Jeffrey establishes himself as a good son and "manly" helper compared with Nia, who positively identifies with her domestic responsibilities, even if they are burdensome—a familiar trope of motherhood and women's work in general.

Figure 3.20: A role model *Nia, age 11*

Insofar as domestic labor is understood to be "women's work," when it is done by girls, it is tied to who they are and who they are becoming. Nia's "selfie" is a quintessential example. When similar work is done by boys, it is understood as a way to "help" the women in the household, which may in its own way be an expression of their manliness. Alanzo offered an interesting illustration of this. All but four of his fifth- and sixth-grade photographs were taken inside his Terrace Gardens apartment and feature his sports equipment, video game equipment, and the toys he prizes, as well as images of himself and his friends playing video games. In his sixth-grade exit interview, talking about his experiences with the project, I asked him, as I asked all the kids, to fill in the blanks: "What I know about myself is _____; what people don't know about me is _____." His answer surprised me. "That I like sports. What people don't know is that I clean my house." I want to know more. "Is that something that you do because your mom asks you to?" Alanzo reflects. "No, sometimes I just like do it myself, when my mom's out of the house. Since my dad is not here I have to be the man of the house and help her out." So while Alanzo doesn't "show" himself cleaning, he does take pride in his care work as an extension of his manliness.

This version of manliness that reframes the doing of "women's work" into "helping women out" resonates with research about working-class vs. middle-class husbands' and wives' views about the division of labor and gender ideologies. In *The Second Shift*, (1989/2003) Arlie Hochschild found that despite an espoused egalitarian ideology about

Figure 3.21: What I hate most *Jeffrey, age 10*

sharing housework among the middle-class couples she interviewed, the middle-class men actually did less housework than their working-class male counterparts, who identified as traditionalists but nevertheless routinely pitched in to help their wives out. In both cases, the preservation of the sexual division of labor and women's over-work was maintained, but through different means. Research documents the privileges that continue to accrue to men as a result of women's unpaid labor (like more leisure time and sleep). And despite increased numbers of women in the paid labor force, they continue to do or manage the care work in the home in what Arlie Hoschschild (1989/2003) has called the "second shift." As of 2014, women in households with children under age 18 on average spent 75 percent more time doing household activities and 86 percent more time caring for household members than men did.[14]

This broader context for understanding the children's photographs is useful and perhaps helps to explain what the boys and girls considered "picture-worthy" in relationship to domestic labor. Insofar as their photographs tell us something about the sort of household labor activities they chose to be identified with, traditional gender-role expectations seem to be held in place.

## Un-covering care

Both boys and girls used their cameras to "regard care." They featured the primacy of mothers (including the lessons of care taught to them by their mothers), and they took pains to express their gratitude for their mothers' care, as well as a sense of obligation to be caring in return. Boys and girls also elaborated on their pictures to describe the complex choreography of family routines and rhythms in which they played a major role—not as passive recipients of care, but as active care providers. They reported helping out on adult job sites; accompanying young siblings to and from school; going to neighbors before school to eat breakfast and pack their lunch; organizing themselves into groups to travel to after-school destinations that changed daily; and coming to school early and staying late "hanging out" with school personnel to accommodate parent work schedules. They also showed themselves in pictures "hanging out" after school and on weekends with siblings and cousins generating their own leisure activities (watching TV, playing video games) or completing domestic chores. And finally, their pictures and accounts are only part of the evidence in which the theme of care predominates. We get this sense through other means as well. Care resonates in the methods and purposes of the photo-taking, too: in their determined and careful efforts to achieve a particular photo or capture a particular subject, their creative ways of presenting the traces of people no longer physically in their lives, their concern for tidying things up before a photo, and, in several cases, their decisions to frame photographs and give them as gifts to their moms. The theme of care can even be seen in the kids' tender gestures and ways of looking, touching, and holding the photographs, regarding them as if to say to their subject, "I see you and value what you do for me."

Remember that Miss Corey worried that Antonio was "covering" for his mother, meaning that he was covering for his mom's failure to meet the norms of care. I have argued that the kids used their cameras to document the complex evidence of family care, zooming in on their mothers' centrality within those care relationships, and emphasizing their mothers' social and educational value and goodness. And through their images, they are allowing their audiences (me and my research team, their teachers, their classmates) into family care worlds that are working, albeit through asymmetrical gendered relations. In contrast to Miss Corey's "covering for" Antonio, and Antonio's "covering for" his mother—choices that might be seen as a chained commitment to hide something from view to preclude negative judgment—we can see the kids' images and accounts as concerted efforts to uncover care work.

I have referred to the kids' images and accounts as counter-narratives of care because they challenge deficit perspectives about working-class upbringings and parents who are judged by their invisibility in school. Indeed, in the evidence the kids share from their lives, they forcefully dispute that invisibility, insisting instead that their families' efforts—and especially their mothers'—be seen as valuable, sustaining, and important. Theirs are mothers who teach how to fry a fish and season a sauce, who read 30 books while vacuuming floors, who take time out after a day of exhausting and often underpaid labor to sit for a photo or cuddle on a couch, prepare meals for family members with no time to cook, make cupcakes and spring rolls for school, and, on very special occasions like birthdays, purchase fancy store-bought cakes. These images of mothers are vivid, full of detail, color, sound, and feeling—anything but invisible. And though their fathers are less prominently featured in the photographs, they are certainly present. Theirs are hardworking fathers who "get your back" and insist on good behavior, pitch in with the chores and the cooking, keep the car running, carry the kids, give treasured gifts. Their siblings look out for each other and share responsibilities for family well-being. The kids are highlighting a trove of skills, orientations, knowledge, cultural wealth, and commitments that make care work in their homes, communities, and lives, and they resolutely affirm—indeed, celebrate—the value of those assets.

They also picture care as a collective effort, not an individual responsibility, and in this sense, too, their images and accounts are "counter-narratives." According to capitalist logic, domestic labor is not as valuable as wage labor. The activities of care and its choreography—feeding the family, nurturing social ties, having each others' back, feelings of mutual regard that arise—are all hidden from view and devalued according to the reckoning devices of a capitalist society. The kids' resistance to this is remarkable in its conviction and its effectiveness. By uncovering the choreographies of care that operate in their lives, often out of the view of institutions and policy makers, the PCS kids are helping to ensure that their families are afforded some measure of the visibility and value that they deserve.

# 4

# School choreographies of care: being seen, safe, and believed

We met Gina in the previous chapter, as she was telling her interviewer about her mother's beauty ("My mom, she's very beautiful, I know that"), her intelligence ("She's also smart, even though she didn't go to college, but she's very, very smart"), their mother-daughter bond ("We love her very much. She loves us very much"), her "great personality" and her "good," if tiring, job. Now she slowly scans across the photographs laying before her on the table and picks up the following photograph (Figure 4.1).

"That's Mrs. Hart," she says, pointing to the woman in the white sweater, "the main teacher, and this is Mrs. Doyle." She points to the woman in the black jacket. "She is young and beautiful." The interviewer laughs, and Gina leans over to whisper in her ear: "She knows I think she is beautiful. But Mrs. Hart doesn't mind being old, she knows that. She has three children, ages two, ten, and nine, so she knows what she is doing. My teachers are nice—I like all my teachers, but especially Mrs. Hart and Mrs. Doyle."

Figure 4.1: My teachers are nice *Gina, age 10*

I hear Gina link Mrs. Hart's skills and knowledge of teaching to her mothering, as if this were a given—an equation that seemed to occur to many other students, too. And at the same time, Gina references traditional feminine qualities to praise her teachers, just as she did with her mother. The outlines of Gina's positive identification with her teachers resonate with my own memories—I still remember very clearly my own long-ago crush on the beautiful young woman who was my third-grade teacher. I am reminded, too, that my identification as a white girl with a white teacher was itself a form of learning privilege, and that even today too few kids of color see themselves reflected in the teachers who stand at the front of their classrooms.

This chapter explores how the children portrayed the hub of classroom life, the web of adult female caregivers in their "schoolplaces". The choreographies of classroom care that the kids describe are both similar to and different from the depictions of their homeplaces. I begin with the children's perceptions of their teachers as caring, devoted, altruistic, and loving, and as "pretty," "kind," "calm," and "nice." These traits, prototypically valued for women, are a window into larger cultural perceptions of gender and care, especially about what kind of work is fit for women, what kind of role women play in child development, and what kind of "care" is needed, acknowledged, and appreciated. But beyond these familiar gendered ideologies, I reflect on what is revealed about learning as a relational and collective activity through the stories the children tell about their female adult caregivers. Just as they used their cameras to highlight their mothers as loving, caring, and present, and to portray themselves as active participants in their own family choreographies of care, they also used them to render visible the care work taking place in their elementary school. Their images and accounts depicted a school choreography of care that was similarly intentional and relational, and also influenced by gendered and racialized undercurrents.

From the children's perspective, schools are "affective enterprises" (Lynch & Lodge, 2002: 11) in which both teaching and learning are deeply intertwined with relational, ethical, and affective dimensions of care and interdependence in ways that challenge an individualized and uni-directional concept of care. These dimensions are made apparent in many of the children's photographs of classroom settings, including those that do not show teachers but instead feature children in their learning groups. I argue that the children express a critical awareness that learning goes beyond student-teacher relationships. Even when teachers are perceived as "nice" and "caring" and children's educational needs are met, students also recognize that they themselves are playing an active role in this dynamic—they are helping each other to make learning happen. Understanding learning as a joint effort and a shared responsibility is a corollary of seeing care as "other-centered and solidarity-oriented" (Lynch, 2007).

## Love, not money

Ten-year-old Claire is slight and soft-spoken. Her straight, light brown hair is streaked with natural blond highlights, and her bright blue eyes are framed by wired-rimmed glasses that make her appear serious and self-conscious—until she smiles and swivels playfully in her chair. She explains why she took a picture of her teacher (Figure 4.2). "She's nice, she doesn't have a bad attitude. I like her because she works not just to get paid, but to help us."

Claire's comment highlights a common cultural framework for understanding women's care work as motivated by love, not money; and by altruism, not self-interest (Glenn, 2010). This is an assumption that the female-dominated teaching profession has had to wrestle with in its effort to gain legitimacy and respect (Acker, 1999; Biklen, 1995; Weiner, 2002; Weber & Mitchell, 1995).[1] The care work of female teachers, like that of mothers, is naturalized, seen as instinctual and innate rather than as depending on practiced skills and hard-won knowledge (Collins, 1998; Grumet, 1988; Fisher, 2001; McBride & Grieshaber, 2001). Moreover, as Arlie Hochschild reminds us, being

Figure 4.2: My teacher *Claire, age 10*

"nice" *is* work—though when skillfully done, the "work" of niceness is invisible, a hidden piece of emotional labor that underpins women's successful care work:

> Niceness is the necessary lubricant to any social exchange … beyond the smaller niceties are the larger ones of doing a favor, offering a service. Finally, there is the moral or spiritual sense of being seriously nice, in which we embrace the needs of another as more important than our own. (1983: 167–8)

Claire's classmate Cheryl is also quick to make a connection between teaching and motherhood. Looking at a photo she took of her teacher (Figure 4.3), she remarks: "What impresses me about my school is that teachers are working to teach us a lot of *hard* stuff, like fractions … She is our helper teacher" [a school designation for a student-teacher]. I wait a moment, sensing that she has more to say. In a hushed voice Cheryl continues, "I really like her, she is nice. You can tell she loves teaching because she loves kids and she doesn't have kids of her own." As Cheryl and Claire both suggest, teachers are perceived as being good at teaching in relationship to mothering—whether they have their own children, and thus "know what they are doing" (as in the earlier example), or because their students stand in for the children they might otherwise have.

Figure 4.3: Our helper teacher *Cheryl, age 10*

The conflation of teaching and mothering has a long history, dating back to the mid-19th century. The refashioning of teaching as "women's work"—also known as the feminization of teaching—is a complicated story, tied to processes of industrialization, population growth associated with new waves of immigration, the use of schools to Americanize the children of immigrants and "equalize" society, and the need to pay teachers cheaper salaries in order to staff the expansion of compulsory education. Men, who had previously dominated the teaching profession, often combining teaching with seasonal agricultural labor, were drawn into manufacturing jobs with higher wages (Strober & Tyack, 1980). Women moved into their place, where they were typically paid one half to one third of male teachers' salaries (Apple, 1986 quoted in Restler, 2017). At the same time, industrialization ushered in new gendered ideologies that associated men and manhood with the public sphere and thus positioned men as best equipped to handle the ruthlessness of work outside the home. In contrast, women and womanhood were associated with family life within the home, which was viewed as a site of virtuousness, a "haven from a heartless world" (Lasch, 1995). Known as the "cult of true womanhood," this ideology set the stage for a rising white middle class whose version of family life centered around a male breadwinner and a stay-at-home mother raising children. This ideology also fueled class and race distinctions between women who could achieve the feminine idealized version of purity, virtue, and moral superiority, and those who couldn't—specifically women of color, immigrants, working-class and poor women.

If there was a "good" place for white, middle- and upper-middle-class women outside the home, schools came the closest. And if there were children needing acculturation into middle-class ways of being, it was assumed that women, as mothers, were constitutionally best suited for this primarily moral task. In an examination of the history of teaching as a female profession, Nancy Hoffman shares a mid-19th-century assessment of the expectations of the job, in which "'the Christian female teacher will quietly take her station, collecting the ignorant children around her, teaching them habits of neatness, order, and thrift; opening the book of knowledge, inspiring the principles of morality, and awakening the hope of immortality'" (1981: 51). This formulation fed two birds with one seed, so to speak; it served to keep white, middle-class women in their place, while at the same time socializing those perceived as "other people's children" (working-class, poor, immigrant children, children of color) into their place.[2] Teaching construed as "women's work" could be seen as a calling rather than a professional desire or pursuit (or, for that matter, a political activity). And it was a safe activity for women outside the home because it could operate as a training ground for women's supposed main purpose in life: to marry and raise children.

Female teachers in the early 20th century were advised to "treat each child as if he were your own," guidance that historian Carolyn Steedman (1985) attributes to the influential British educator, Margaret McMillan. But models of teaching and learning that pivot around the mother-child bond have always been inherently problematic for poor and working-class children. Steedman points out the fundamental impossibility woven into McMillan's maxim:

> The reality cannot match the prescription because it is impossible for women as teachers to mother working-class children. The prescribed act of identification with the children implies a further and harder one, with the children's mother, that 'dark young woman with touzled hair and glittering eyes', playing out a travesty of motherhood in her cellar dwelling. (1985: 159)

Nor does "treating each child as if s/he were your own" fit easily into the strictures of school schedules, standardization and regimes of power. Rather than enabling teachers to really know and care about each child, schools label and sort children, and substitute rules for relationships. Framing education as a patriarchal institution, feminist philosopher of education and curriculum theorist Madeline Grumet (1988) argued that through the normalizing rituals of schooling, women are required to repress their own knowledge and maternal power. From Grumet's perspective, the feminization of teaching has at once "promoted and sabotaged the interests of women in our culture" (1998: 32).

## Seeing women's emotional labor

Looking through the children's photographs of their teachers, it is hard not to notice the ubiquitous smiles on teachers' faces. The children's pictures offer a portrait not just of their own devotion and admiration, but also of the enjoyment and delight their teachers project—the core piece of invisible work, or "emotional labor," required of women working in a range of caring professions (Figures 4.4–4.6).

Figure 4.4: My teacher *Emily, age 10*

Figure 4.5: My teachers making learning fun *Claire, age 10*

Arlie Hochschild would interpret these teachers' smiles as a requirement of their job, manifestations of an obligation to convey enjoyment. In writing about flight attendants' invisible emotional labor at work, she described the smile as a commercially valuable asset:

> The workers I talked to often spoke of their smiles as being *on* them but not *of* them. They were seen as an extension

Figure 4.6: My teacher is nice *Angeline, age 10*

of the make-up, the uniform … For the flight attendant, the smiles are a *part of her work*, a part that requires her to coordinate self and feeling so the work seems to be effortless. To show that the enjoyment takes effort is to do the work poorly. (1983: 8, emphasis in original)

The same could be said of teachers and the female-dominated teaching profession. The children's photographs resonate with the characterizations of primary school teaching that applied at the beginning of the 20th century. As Carolyn Steedman reviewed accounts written by sociologists of the time, she included the following 1911 description of primary schoolteachers by Alexander Paterson, who wrote that teachers' faces:

reflect no discontent, no weariness of spirit or monotony of work. They seem born to the task … The relation of teacher and child is happy and natural because the teacher is absorbed in the human interest of her work.

Moreover, this happy relation "is so much more natural to the woman's nature" (Paterson, 1911: 58, quoted in Steedman, 1985: 159).

The female school staff are photographed not only smiling, but also engaged with children in affectionate ways, arms wrapped around bodies in loving, cuddling poses. Such displays are not simply reflections of inevitably gendered characteristics ("a woman's nature"), but need to be understood as "signs of a social work that women *do*—the work of affirming, enhancing, and celebrating the well-being and status of others" (Hochschild, 1983: 165, emphasis in original).[3]

If there was a phrase that rivaled "nice" in the young people's descriptions of their female teachers, it was that they "make learning fun." Angeline joined Sofia in making a clear distinction between the "fun kind" of teachers (all females), and their one male teacher, Mr. Hopper, who "pushes us" (Angeline) and "is all about concentrating really, really, really, really, really hard on the work and pushing us" (Sofia). As Angeline explained, "I'm really glad he pushes us, 'cause then he will get us into college." By contrast, her other teacher, shown earlier (Figure 4.6) "helps me learn new things, and if I don't know what to do, she explains it to me and helps me understand it, and I appreciate her very much. She makes learning fun, not hard." Angeline perceives both teachers positively, with a small caveat about Mr. Hopper ("he annoys me sometimes when he won't let me talk so I can understand things better"), but she speaks about the two teachers through different discourses. Her talk of the male teacher is rooted in an economic and social mobility discourse of education, in which the goal of learning is to get into college. By contrast, Angeline's talk of her female teacher seems more grounded in the relationality or affect of learning. Angeline offered a similar gendered account of the distinctive carework provided by her mother compared to her father. She described her mother as encouraging "all the things I want to do," while her father encourages "math" and her ability to perform on the state's high-stakes test.[4] There is a contrast between the language of *understanding* the girls associated with their female teachers, and the language of *pushing* they used to characterize the male teacher, and perhaps this sheds some light on the role of women's emotional labor. The "fun kind" of teacher displays the enjoyment of teaching and learning, as if it were effortless; whereas the "pushing" kind of teacher need not take on the extra labor it requires to make children happy.

There may well be differences in how male and female teachers approach their jobs, but my interest here is in the children's discourse— how they attached gendered associations to teachers' activities and talked about the web of female school staff in gendered ways, including taking up the language of love, care, and mothering, and hinting at the salience of emotion work.[5]

The cultural conflation of teaching and mothering can also lead teachers to assume extraordinary responsibility for teaching and caring for "other people's children," whom they may see through deficit lenses

(James, 2010). A well-intentioned feeling of responsibility can be tied to a (white) "savior" orientation toward children who are defined by what they are lacking, rather than for their assets, or are seen as the victims of uncaring families and communities whose needs must be filled by the school or teachers. When (predominantly white and middle-class) teachers assume a motherly role, they may assume that they can intuit their students' needs, even when they are culturally very different from them. "A mothering discourse," James concludes, "precludes the need to listen closely to students as it privatizes the classroom space and puts the teacher in the position of moral authority over children" (James, 2012: 172). Concepts of care are not benign; if teachers project their own preconceptions of caring onto students, assuming that what they know about care can map neatly onto students' lives and experiences they can do more harm than good.

Though popularized by numerous recent movie and literary depictions, Steedman (1985) notes that the roots of the teachers as savior orientation have been in place for some time: "By the end of the nineteenth century, the school saw itself as a place where working-class children might be compensated for belonging to working-class families" (p. 159). Indeed, during the first wave of immigration at the turn of the 20th century, a politics of maternalism (sometimes called "social motherhood") was based on a conviction that white women reformers should function in a motherly role toward the poor and promote a middle-class morality. As several scholars have noted, these politics were riddled with "race anxiety" directed toward immigrant populations (Mink, 1996).

By the 21st century, scholars and educators have come to recognize the racial as well as class undertones of how teachers convey their "care" and protection. School spaces are still bastions of white privilege, and implicit racial bias and coercion flourish even amid the best of intentions of individual teachers. The most stark example of this is a systemic corrosive violence rather than care, found in the formation of what has been called the "school-to-prison pipeline", where disciplinary policies push disproportionate numbers of students of color out of school and into the criminal justice system (Wald & Losen, 2003; Wallace et al, 2008). The reach of this "pipeline" has been documented to start as early as preschool. According to a US Government Accountability Office report, Black students accounted for 19 percent of preschool students in public schools but represented 47 percent of students suspended from preschool (Strauss, 2018). Kindergarten students are being suspended or expelled from schools under zero-tolerance policies, which began in the late 1980s and mandated specific and harsh punishments for the violation of school rules, including minor infractions like "insubordination."[6] The rigidity of these policies has elevated penalties and increased the involvement of law enforcement.

In the face of well-documented manifestations of systemic racism, concepts of care in education and the relationship between teaching and mothering have been scrutinized for their implicit racism (Siddle & Tompkins, 2004). Whether named "critical care" (Antrop-González, R. & De Jesús, A. 2006; DeNicolo et al, 2017; Rolón-Dow, 2005), "culturally responsive caring" (Gay, 2010), "culturally relevant care" (Jackson et al, 2014), or "teaching to restore Black boys' childhood" (Ladson Billings, 2011), there is a shared consensus: care begins by acknowledging the role that race/ethnicity has and continues to play in defining the sociocultural and political conditions under which children of color are schooled. In the lives of Black and Brown children, school has been a site of neglect, discrimination, cultural/linguistic erasure, forced deportation, and boarding schools (Lomawaima & McCarty, 2006). Thus, teachers' care must extend to being concerned about and advocating for racial justice, including the sustenance and protection of communities of color within which children grow up. In simplest terms, when defining the parameters of care for poor and working-class children of color in schools, "nice is not enough" (Nieto, 2008).

## *Digital Interlude #3: Nice...?*

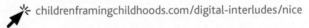 childrenframingchildhoods.com/digital-interludes/nice

Thinking more broadly, the parameters of care should reach beyond securing children's *inclusion* into schools and instead, focus on their *liberation* from the logics of white supremacy and settler colonialism that have defined schooling from the outset (Patel, 2015; Glenn, 2015). As bell hooks has put it, education must be experienced as a "practice of freedom" (hooks, 1994). This same shift in emphasis is suggested by calls for "culturally sustaining" pedagogies (Paris & Alim 2014).

There is much more to say about teaching as women's work, dependent on hidden emotional labor; about teaching as mothering, especially in elementary education; about heteronormative expectations of teachers; and about how these enduring prescriptions to (predominantly white, middle-class) women teachers cannot adequately address the task of educating children in a structurally unequal and racially unjust society.

My focus here is a modest but, I think, an essential one: I want to emphasize the importance of listening to diverse children in order to learn from their own perspectives about what caring in school looks and feels like. Research on these themes to date has been tilted more toward teenagers' perceptions of teachers' care and has indicated that while there is some agreement about what constitutes caring behavior (for example, fairness), students from varying cultural backgrounds hold different perspectives about what counts as a teacher's caring (Alder, 2002; McCamey, 2011; Rolón-Dow, 2005; Tosolt, 2010). Younger children have important insights to share, too, as the PCS kids' counter-narratives of care demonstrate.

Of particular interest, given the racial landscape of PCS's student population and its staff, is that the whiteness and femaleness of the school staff went unmarked by the children. But what *was* marked was a greater stated appreciation on the part of Black and Latinx children than their white and Asian American peers that their teachers believed them and trusted their goodness, especially around the issue of "trouble-making" and fighting. One way to see and listen to these difference is in terms of a system of racialization that pivots around a white-Black binary, with Latinx kids (in this case Puerto Ricans and Dominicans) being part of what sociologist Eduardo Bonilla-Silva (1997) calls the "collective Black" and Asian American kids (Chinese in particular) holding honorary white status (that is, model minorities). But my intention here is to lift up the kids' varying insights about the nuanced contours of care in school—its ethics, activities, and gendered and racial inflections—in an effort to deepen discussions about what a robust, feminist intersectional theory of care and affective justice in school might entail.

In the next section of this chapter, I consider what can be culled from what the children chose to photograph and how they chose to describe those pictures as emblematic of "care." In particular, I examine what the Black and Brown children had to say about the importance they placed on relationships of care that confirmed their believability, trustworthiness, and goodness. Crucially, they repeatedly emphasize that these relationships of care were bi-directional: if a teacher/principal trusted a child, then a child could trust the teacher's/principal's care.

## Care as trust and believability

Crystal seems to delight in being video-taped and interviewed. "It is like being a celebrity," she giggles. Indeed, she looks celebrity-like, with her black, zippered Ecko brand sweatshirt and black stretch pants, her reddish-brown hair pulled back into a ponytail, and her oversized silver hoop earrings that brush the bottom of her jaw. As I hand her the envelope with her photographs in it, Crystal suddenly pulls her hands over her eyes and peeks through her fingers, pausing before opening it. We both start laughing. As she flips through her pictures, she keeps stopping to remark, "I don't remember this one ... or this one ... or this one.... Oh, I see!" She laughs at a picture of herself dancing. "My mom must have taken pictures at the birthday party we had this weekend for my aunt."

When I ask Crystal to describe herself, she does so in the third person: "So, Crystal is a person who thinks it's very important to be honest. She's good in math. She has the goals to become a dance teacher and to get awards for that. And she has family and friends who are hard-working. And she's Dominican." She describes a string of photographs of her home in Terrace Gardens, her family members, and her baby cousins with whom she spends her weekends.

One of the few photographs she has taken in school is of her "favorite teacher." Crystal has asked her friend to photograph the two of them side by side, arms wrapped around each other in an affectionate embrace:

> "I've known her since I have been here since first grade, but I had her in fourth grade. She's always there for me. She's always by my side. And, when, when I'm down, she brings me up. If I'm sad, she'll always cheer me up telling me jokes and stuff if I'm just dopin' around. She always gives me advice. Like if I get in trouble and go to the principal's office, she'll say, 'If you didn't do it, then look her straight in the eye and tell her that you never did it.' Cause every time I get in trouble, she helps me. She'll say, 'Tell me the problem first, and if it's a big deal, I'll tell Dr. G. [the principal] but you won't get in trouble.'"

Crystal's characterization of care—its relationality and affect—is layered. She makes a point to say that her teacher took an interest in her and has been "by her side", even before becoming formally responsible for her as her teacher. Their relationship is grounded in time (how long she has known her teacher), consistency (emphasized by her multiple use of the term "always" and "every time"), presence ("she's there for me"; "by my side"), responsiveness (gives advice when it is needed, makes jokes when needed), and acknowledgment of Crystal's trustworthiness ("if you didn't do it, then look her straight in the eye and tell her that you never did it"). Her teacher's care is not only about solving practical dilemmas ("like if I get in trouble and go to the principal's office"), but believing in Crystal's word.

This contour of caring—trust and believability—is not a given in adult-child relationships within adult-controlled institutions. Heidi Pitzer, who conducted research in a range of under-resourced urban schools, identified a default assumption among teachers and administrators that students had to prove they could be trusted. Rather than beginning a relationship assuming a student was trustworthy, these educators expressed wariness, more or less taking a "guilty-until-proven-innocent" stance, rather than the other way around. Meanwhile, the sixth-grade students (ages 11 & 12) Pitzer interviewed thought that most teachers and adults in their schools usually did not believe them in specific situations, unless: (1) an adult corroborated what they said, or (2) they had a reputation as a "good kid" or were a teacher's favorite and therefore seen as trustworthy (2015: 4).[7]

Echoes of these same dynamics could be heard across the children's stories, especially related to "kids with problems" or "kids in trouble." In the previous chapter we met Sebastian, who was extolling the sacrifices made by his mother, an immigrant from Colombia. Sebastian's brother, Christopher, photographed the school principal and offered the following version of care:

> "She is really nice and cares for all the students. She won't, like, yell at the students to tell 'em what to do, she's just, she's really nice and with a calm voice, not every principal is that calm. She really wants to help students so that's why I took her picture."

"How does she help you?" I ask. Christopher explains:

> "Well, one time my mom wrote a complaint about some kids who were making fun of another boy in the class. It was, like, a long time ago, not in this class, and they were making fun of him so I told my mom and she wrote a letter … So all the boys that were involved, she [the principal] talked to us to help solve the problem … Like, she would talk to us and we would be able to tell our own part of the story. And then she would tell us that we would have to talk to each other and say we're sorry. When we were walking back to class, I don't know how, but when we got

back to the class, we're already friends and we're already discussing something else."

Christopher's narrative, told half in the past and half in the present tense, signals his sense of the ongoing attention (by his mother and the principal) it takes to foster social relationships. He also elaborates on the meaning of "niceness" as more than a necessary lubricant to social exchanges. He highlights the fact that his principal doesn't yell and that this should not be taken for granted—"not every principal is that calm." Instead, Dr. G. brings kids together to talk to each other and offer apologies rather than doling out punishments, tying "niceness" as an alternative response to school discipline.[8]

Alanzo, whose parents are from Puerto Rico and lives next door to Crystal in Terrace Gardens, also photographed the principal. He offered a variation on the same theme in his discussion:

> "She's a very good principal, the nicest principal I ever met. She likes being nice to *all* [emphasis his] the students, no matter what. Instead of giving them a bad punishment she thinks of ways of calming them down."

Setting himself apart from "them," Alanzo appreciates the principal's calm and equal treatment of children, including those who have misbehaved. He elevates "niceness" to a serious sense of fairness ("to *all* the students, no matter what") and a "calming" form of discipline.

Alanzo continued to provide examples of how the principal helps kids "resolve problems," including offering an after-school program called Steps to Respect.[9] Alanzo described the program in the following terms:

> "After school on Wednesdays, we have a program called Steps to Respect to teach us how to be respectful, and ways to stay out of fights, and gang violence, and all that stuff. We get to learn new ways to get out of fighting. One of them was, like we would play telephone, and sometimes if the words get mixed up, she [the teacher] says, 'Well, that's how life is.' If someone says something to someone else, they might think it is something else, and they might misinterpret, and that's when a problem could start. And, then she would say, 'if that ever happens, just go to the person and ask them what really happened, just don't start a fight.'"

Crystal spoke about her own experience drawing on this approach:

> "Once, I got in trouble 'cause this boy talked about this other boy's mom. And, I told the other boy that the boy was talking about his mom. Dr. G. said that I should have never told the other boy. I should have just stayed out of it. But, I just told him, 'cause I really felt bad for him. She didn't yell at me or suspend me. She knows I don't want to get into fights."

Again, Crystal describes Dr. G.'s approach as being grounded in a belief of Crystal's goodness—"she knows I don't want to get into fights." Put differently, Dr. G. sees her in the same way Crystal sees herself—not as a troublemaker who wants to get into fights, but as someone voicing empathy for the boy who was being mistreated.

Manny, a cousin of Alanzo's and also a resident of Terrace Gardens, spoke of his own "troubles" in school. He took a series of photographs of his teachers, past and present, and one of the principal, vaguely referencing the fact that he had spent time in another school and returned to PCS to repeat fifth grade. Manny handed his camera to a friend so that he could pose with his "all-time favorite" teacher. Manny and Mrs. M. stand closely together, almost, but not quite, embracing like Crystal and her favorite teacher. "I really love this one, of me and Mrs. M. She is the *best* teacher *ever* [emphasis his]. She's nice and helps me out when she knows I have troubles. She knows I am a good kid."

In their own view of themselves and in their perceptions of their teachers' views, I hear the children's words in dialogue with racialized punitive systems of discipline and punishment that are predicated on stereotypes of brown- and black-skinned children, but especially boys, as troublemakers.[10] I hear the residents of Terrace Gardens—all children of color—highlighting the ever-present need to "answer back" to discourses about "good" vs. "bad" kids, searching for a way to position themselves against problematic categories even in the face of "caring" and "nice" teachers. I take notice that they speak about the principal being "calm" and "not yelling" as exceptional rather than given, and this gives me pause about what they have been primed to expect about school discipline and discipline in general (in their communities, from police, and so on). I hear the imperatives of trust, consistency, time, and the affective ("nice") or, some might say, racially and socially "just" demeanor required of a teacher or principal so that *all* children (whether they are "good" or "bad") feel secure.

What was so striking to me was how much trust these children put in their school to make them feel cared for—not just for themselves but for their peers—and how tenuous this trust could feel. They seemed aware that care was linked to one's social standing and worthiness, that belief in a child's goodness was not automatic. This was Crystal's point when describing her favorite teacher. What she cherished about her teacher was her unconditional care, her teacher's steadfast trust in her word. Crystal's understanding of her teachers' care went beyond solving a problem (getting in trouble); teachers' care was non-punitive, relational, and justice-orientation, speaking truth to power: "if you didn't do it, then look her straight in the eye and tell her that you never did it."

Junior's reflections are the exception that proves the rule about the tenuousness of feeling trusted in school. He confessed that he "worries" about getting in trouble because "they got so many teachers there watching you." As readers will recall from Chapter 1, Junior described himself as Haitian and as a "good kid, I pay attention more than my [twin] brother." At age ten Junior mentioned his anger—"some people say I have anger issues"—and spoke about the role his father plays in disciplining him and his brother (described in Chapter 3), including the importance of care as a reciprocal "having each other's back." Indeed, this is what most distinguishes his friendship with Angel:

> "Like, if I'm in trouble or something, he gots me, like he'll find out the truth and stuff like that. If I get into a fight and someone hops in, he gots me. My brother would probably do that too, but I don't know if he would win."

In his exit interview at the end of sixth grade, Junior's self-identification continues to pivot around being "good" and "bad." When asked about how he had changed since the project began, he remarked:

> "Like, I used to, like, be bad, and then, like, sometimes be a little bit good, but not more good than bad. Like, now I don't start to fight with my brother as much. Like, I try to calm down. Or, I don't yell that much at people who yell at me."

The interviewer wonders, "How did you learn to do that?" and Junior is quick to answer. "Step Respect. Like, they teach us things about what you do in different types of situations. And, then, like, what happens in stuff like conflicts, and things like we probably did or we know the meaning of it, and, like, what's wrong, what's bad." "Oh, can you give me an example?" Junior becomes more animated as he explains:

> "Like, um, if someone's following you, if you're going, if you're, if someone's following you, and you don't let them get too close, you go to a public place. And, if you pass by your house, you don't even look at it, don't pay attention. You don't run to your house. You go to a public place and ask somebody for the phone and be like, "I think I'm being followed." And they told us about, um, some ways of how when you get anger, like, count to ten slowly, or just think of happy things, or just, like, hold it in, or, or, like, just think of you doing something good instead of doing something bad. And, so you don't get in trouble."

I hear Junior's apprehensions about his safety (being followed), conflict, fighting, whose truth matters, and who "gots" him (a group that does not necessarily, from his perspective, include teachers). His desire to stay out of trouble hinges on the axis of "goodness" and "badness" that are embedded not only in larger discourses about criminalization and the dangers of Black boyhood, but also by an illusion of racelessness that is embedded in school norms and expectations for success. As researchers Stoll and Embrick (2013) found, the way schooling frames "good" versus "bad" choices are encoded with racial ideals (pp 85–106). Insofar as "good" choices align with white norms and expectations, a painful dynamic is established for Black children to perform within. Black parents also recognize that adopting a non-threatening stance means appropriating certain white norms required to reject Black stereotypes (p. 112). I hear Junior wrestling within this affective bind when "you get anger"—from counting to ten slowly, or thinking of "happy things," or "holding it in," or "doing something good, instead of doing something bad." As Junior frames it, the goal is not so much to resolve his feelings of anger (itself a result of being caught in a bind) but mostly importantly to avoid getting in trouble.

## Provisions of care

The PCS principal, Dr. G., figured prominently in the children's images; her presence was documented in an array of school settings— in her office, in classrooms, in hallways, in the gym/auditorium with her walkie-talkie in hand, wearing a wig on "funny hat day." Her involvement was repeatedly described as something that inspired pride among the students. As Jeffrey put it, "I took this picture of what makes me proud of my school. It is the principal. She really cares about us. And I took it because she helps manage the school and she gives us, she gets us a lot of stuff for our school." His words resonated with other children's accounts framing their principal's care in terms of securing valued school resources, from new textbooks to a new computer lab to much-anticipated play equipment in the now-empty schoolyard. "She makes sure we have everything we need to learn and to have fun," explained Camila. Sonya remarked, "Dr. G. is like an idol to us." Nalanie described her as:

> "the role model for everybody. And she's the boss of all the teachers and she does a really good job with it. She's nice, and she's always willing to do something fun so we can play. Like she signed up for stuff like Nickelodeon and she wants to get some new equipment for the playground. She lets us do regular activities like seeing the Polar Express or stuff like that."

The students consistently commended the principal for her leadership ("she brings the teachers and the students together to make this a wonderful place"). Especially striking to me were the children's repeated references to Dr. G.'s provision of resources that would enable children to "have fun," "play," and have access to Nickelodeon, a television channel that provides a coveted means for belonging and participating in childhood culture, as noted in Chapter 2. Sebastian followed up his appreciation for Dr. G. with praise for her request that sixth-graders "take a survey every year" about how to improve the school. "We couldn't tell each other our answers. But what I said was, better lunches and a much safer environment. Sometimes people start fights outside in the schoolyard, and I get scared."

The children's perceptions of their principal as manager, boss, idol, and role model locate her in the in-between space of elementary school, part homeplace, part workplace, and part fun/play place. The principal is at once a caregiver and care manager, mobilizing resources and organizing the daily activities of students and teachers. Akin to how the children described their mothers' caregiving and care managing roles, the children did not take Dr. G.'s work for granted. Her investment in and provision of the basic necessities of childhood (food, safety, protection, and fun), including the "special" things like the computer lab, signaled to the children that they were seen as having social worth and educational value. The children linked

Dr. G.'s care to her interest in their voices—whether that meant eliciting a child's version of what led them to get in trouble ("telling our own part of the story"), soliciting sixth-graders' thoughts about school improvements, or encouraging children to "talk to each other," sort out their differences and apologize. Again, the relationship between Dr. G. and her student charges is described as grounded in mutual regard: she cares for students, and students care for her as their "idol" and "role model."

## The rules of care

The children repeatedly associated Dr. G. with the school's most official sign of school care, its motto: "Be Here; Be Ready; Be Safe; Be Respectful; Be Responsible" ("The 5 Bs"). As Huan put it, "I took a picture of the principal to show that she cares—she makes the rules and teaches us to follow them." Riva, a Yemeni student who was new to the school, was one of many children who photographed the bright yellow laminated posters hanging throughout the school building, in classrooms, bathrooms, and hallways (Figures 4.7–4.9). Riva explained:

> "These are the 5 Bs—Be Here; Be Ready; Be Safe; Be Respectful; Be Responsible. Without them the school would be a mess. And people would be running around and could hurt themselves. It shows that we care for each other."

Figure 4.7: It shows we care for each other *Riva, age 10*

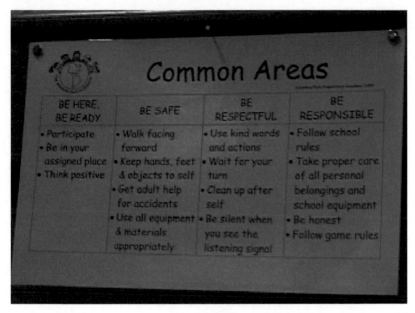

Figure 4.8: What our school is about *Sofia, age 10*

Sofia also photographed the 5 Bs (Figure 4.8):

> "I really love this one because it represents what our school is *about*, really, that we *care*. These are the rules that we have to follow every day that we go to school here. And, this is what keeps our school, like, organized."

As Ling described her own photograph of the 5 Bs (not shown here), she offered some specifics:

> "'Be Here' is when you are here. 'Be Ready' is when you go to gym, you have to have sneakers. 'Be Safe' is keep hands and feet to yourself. 'Be Respectful,' you be kind to people. 'Be Responsible,' you have to be responsible, like, staying in school and keeping your promise and making good choices."

Claire gave an especially thick description when speaking about her photograph of the 5 Bs (Figure 4.9), saying:

> "The 5 Bs show we always follow the rules, without talking. The 5 Bs remind us to keep to the listening signal, to keep your hands by your side, facing front, and telling other

Figure 4.9: The 5 Bs show we always follow the rules *Claire, age 10*

people to be quiet if they're talking so everybody stays silent. Be here and be ready is be quick in the bathroom, keep the bathroom clean, use soap and water, keep your feet on the floor, knock on the stall, give people privacy, use quiet voices, sign out before going, flush after use, return to classroom promptly."

I ask Claire what is important about the rules and she replies, "Because if somebody gets hurt or something, the teachers know."

If this all sounds scripted, it is. Like Steps to Respect, The 5 Bs is part of a guidance curriculum marketed to schools that promote school safety and positive youth development. My interest here is less about how the children repeated the script, and more about their perception of these posters as signposts of care and as representing collective, not individual, efforts (as signaled by Claire's use of "we" and "us," not "I" and "me"). The children are fully aware that it is the people of the school (teachers, staff, and children themselves) and their concerted actions that ensure that a curriculum is successful. They understand their learning and their success as a school community depend on how children and school staff together interpret and give life to the concepts of cooperation, respect, responsibility, and affirmation. Their photos and their words show their appreciation of how people, rules, activities, and routines enable their school to run smoothly. Through collective efforts, expectations are communicated, guidance is provided, and the daily work of learning is achieved.

Alongside the teachers and the principal, the school nurse was an important figure in the world of caring adults at PCS. Mesha, whose fifth-grade photographs featured the video game *Final Fantasy*, re-trained her camera lens in sixth grade to focus on friends, family members, and caring adults at her church, school, and most importantly, the school nurse. Mesha explained: "She helps me set life goals for the year, and how to avoid trouble and gangs." Mesha, who is Black, echoes the concerns voiced again and again by children of color about the dangers of violence and of being perceived as troublemakers. Like many others, Mesha takes note of the need to "avoid trouble and gangs." I noticed that these anxieties—and their photographic representations—seemed to increase in the sixth grade. Several Black and Brown children in the exit interviews at the end of sixth grade confessed that they feared leaving PCS to attend junior high because of safety issues. Crystal explained that she had shared her worries with the school nurse, even though she was confident that "my cousin is going to protect me." She added that the school nurse had told her that "gangs of girls avoid people, who, um, girls that work. So I am going to work hard."

Jeffrey also associated care with protection when speaking about his photograph of the school nurse: "I took it to show that she makes sure kids are safe and taken care of." Jeffrey had explicitly expressed

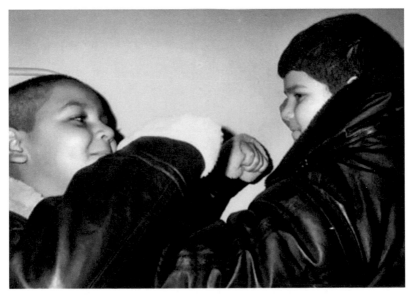

Figure 4.10: What concerns me most about my community—fighting *Jeffrey, age 11*

143

his concerns with violence and safety when he had taken Figure 4.10, which he said represents, "What concerns me about my community—fighting. Basically they weren't really fighting, I made them pose like that"—and here he gestured playfully, miming a punch pose—"like they were going to start a fight." Jeffrey laughed at this, but then grew serious. He spoke haltingly, carefully considering each word. "I am concerned about that because I never know if like … because fighting can hurt a lot of people." He turned to make eye contact with me, then returned his gaze to the photograph. "And like, I don't want to be like one of them that gets in a fight." He turned again to meet my eyes, and there was another long pause, as if he was searching for the right words. "Basically, I just really don't want to get into a fight, that's it."

I hear Jeffrey's 11-year-old concerns expressed through multiple channels, as if there were distinctive voices and discourses participating in our conversation. There is his uncertainty ("I never know if"); his concern for his community ("fighting can hurt a lot of people"); his determination to not be seen as "one of them"; his fear for his own safety; his skillful claims to boy-ness that plays with the trope of fighting while also expressing caring. As I listen, I detect a palpable sense of anxiety, vulnerability, and danger from which he is trying to extricate himself. His sense of vulnerability calls to mind Christine Sharpe's (2016) characterization of racism as the normalization of premature death among Black people, especially Black men, as well as Ruthie Gilmore's (2007) assertion that "structural genocide" is accomplished, in part, by the social and spatial containment of Black and Brown boys and men growing up in urban neighborhoods where "intentional and accidental violence, lead[s] to premature death from a variety of causes" (2007: 74).

The extent of the apprehensions expressed by PCS students of color—their yearnings for care, trust, and protection—is notable. The fact that they look to school staff to prepare them to face life's dangers, fears, and anxieties is sobering. It makes evident the enormous expectation placed in schools—not only by these individual children and their families, but also by a society in which a sense of safety and security is unequally distributed. This affective inequality (who can feel safe and cared for) is tied to racism and anti-Blackness. This affective inequality is the ground upon which schools are built and from which students, parents, teachers, and staff must address the contours of care. From a critical childhood perspective, we could say that the children used their cameras to exercise their rights to care, protection, and goodness—an especially poignant form of agency in an institutional setting that is known for its harsh policies of discipline and punishment directed toward Black and Brown students.

## "Helping out": care and reciprocity

While discussing photographs of a web of female caregivers in their school, the children often spoke about their own desire to "help out" those who cared for them. Alanzo photographed the school secretary, explaining:

> "She is really nice. She gives me a lot of stuff and she helps me out when I have a problem in class. I stay with her in the morning before school starts [because his mother drops him off early to get to work on time]. So I work in the office to help her out."

Angeline described her photograph of Sue, the "lunch lady":

> "That's Sue the lunch lady, she's really nice. I like her because she's very nice. I help her a lot with her work. Because sometimes I like doing kitchen work and she is really nice, she is really kind. The main reason I help her is because she's really nice and I like helping her clean the tables."

"Why was it important to take her picture?" I ask. Angeline answers with dramatic flare, "If we didn't have her we would be starving, starving—and we won't be able to learn." "Why?" I am drawn in to her telling. Angeline's hands gesture as if pleading. "How can we learn without no breakfast, no lunch, how can we learn like that? Our stomachs will be going, 'Give us some food!'"

Angeline and Alanzo used their cameras to pay tribute to the vital, if easily overlooked, role school staff play in children's learning and growth. In both cases, the children are reading these signs of care as grounds for reciprocity, and both indicated a sense of personal satisfaction through being "helpers." The importance of reciprocity resonated with what we heard the children say in Chapter 3 about helping their mothers, upon whose nurturance they depend. Similar gendered patterns toward caring behavior and identity are apparent here, too—I take note that Angeline's appreciation for Sue's "niceness" goes a step further than Alanzo's. Angeline presents her own work as effortless and enjoyable—"I like kitchen work. I like helping her clean the tables." It is more likely that Angeline likes Sue than the kitchen work itself—but in keeping with the cultural prescriptions for women doing service work, there is a blurred line between love and labor.

Jeffrey also took a photograph of "helping out" during his "Free Friday" time—one period during the week when PCS students are allowed to select an activity of their choice:

> "I took a picture of a classroom helping the teacher in a class in the basement because she is busy with the other kids and I go down and help them. Like a girl who was missing her mom and I told her that school was almost over so not to cry because she would see her mom soon. Fridays are free days, so I go help some kids who need help."

Jeffrey explained that part of this motivation for "helping out" is because the teacher is "busy with the other kids." In establishing his helper identity at school, Jeffrey seems to extend and expand upon the vision of himself we saw him present in the last chapter. At home, despite the fact that he "hates" Sunday cleaning, he nonetheless wants to document that he meets his household obligations. A consistent element in these "helping out" narratives is Jeffrey's awareness of someone else's needs: his mother's, a busy teacher's, a homesick little girl's. In all three cases, his desire to help is relational, responsive, and other-centered.

## "Helping each other learn": the value of interdependence

It would be a lopsided picture if my analysis featured the kids' pictures of teachers only. Indeed, the posed and candid photographs of kids in classrooms without teachers far outnumbered those with teachers (Figures 4.11–4.13). More significant than the number of these classroom scenes, however, are the complex meanings the children attached to these pictures of "helping each other" learn. The relational orientation they adopt in their accounts adds another layer of understanding of care as "other-centered and solidarity-oriented" (Lynch, 2007).

Allison offers a simple assessment of how her group shares resources to help each other learn when she explains to me, "I took this picture to show how we help each other learn in class." "How do you do that?" I ask. Allison replies as if the answer were obvious. "So, we come together if somebody doesn't have a book, you just don't leave them. You help each other out."

Expressing an ethic of care ("you just don't leave them") is one cornerstone of learning in groups. Sonya emphasized other reasons her group matters to her:

> "I took a picture of my desk in my group [Figure 4.12] because I do my work there, and I like to, I like that group because I can really work with them. And I'm not afraid to

Figure 4.11: Kids helping each other *Emily, age 10*

Figure 4.12: Not afraid to ask for help *Sonya, age 10*

ask for help. Because you have your friends there and they can help you and make you understand. It is important to show because sometimes schools don't have kids working together and in groups and stuff, and I wanted to show that it's okay to have groups because you learn better and it is more fun."

Underlying fears and anxieties about learning, as well as desires about belonging, reverberated across the children's discussions of their groups. Sonya values learning in groups because it eases her anxiety associated with not knowing or sitting on the edge of understanding ("I'm not afraid to ask for help"). Sonya's shift from speaking about herself and her personal feelings ("I'm not afraid," "I can really work"), to speaking more generally about how anyone benefits from a group ("you have your friends"; "you learn better and it is more fun") is telling. Her focus on "having groups" is about an embrace of a relational model of learning. This model includes the connection between belonging and learning ("you have your friends there and they can help you and make you understand") and the realization that learning is "fun" (not in the entertaining sense but in the enjoyment sense). I notice that Sonya seems aware that learning in groups may not be the norm ("sometimes schools don't have kids working together") and that it might be negatively judged ("I wanted to show that it's okay to have groups").

A similar caution is expressed in Christopher's description of his photograph. "This is a picture of my reading group, and how we work hard in our groups, instead of by ourselves. I think that's why I work so hard at school, 'cause we work in groups." The interviewer asks him to tell her more about working in groups. "Well, people can help you out, like checking your answers, like, if you say, 'I got this, but I still need help on this question.' And, then, they can help you on that question *without telling you the answer*" [emphasis his].

Christopher makes sure to point out that helping each other doesn't mean being given answers, and his emphasis is delivered as if in dialogue with someone who might think otherwise. Christopher adds another feature to the benefits of learning in groups: the relational motivation to work "so hard."

Emily begins her explanation of the photograph she took (Figure 4.11) by confessing to her interviewer that the photograph, which appeared to be a candid shot, was actually posed:

"So this is kids helping each other. It is in my classroom. This is during our practice book center time. We finally finished that one and now we have a whole other one to do. The funny thing was, my group, they were actually kind of talking a lot, but I was like [laughing], 'Hey, can you guys *pretend* you're helping each other out?'"

"Why did you want to show kids helping each other?" the interviewer asks. Emily replies sounding perplexed by the question:

"Because why would anyone want to come to PCS if people didn't help each other out? Like, we were pretending that we had a cousin coming to the fifth grade? So, I wanted them, if I did have a cousin, to like welcome her and see this as a good school to go to and that it won't be too hard here."

I hear the intersecting elements of care, belonging, and learning (and its underlying anxieties) expressed in Emily's account. A "good" school makes children feel welcomed, nurtures a sense of camaraderie, and instills confidence that people can and will help each other out. Her association of what makes a school "good" is affective and relational, not instrumental and individual achievement-oriented. And while Emily values group learning, she doesn't idealize it, as her admission indicates. Asked more about how kids help each other, she states unapologetically and without bragging:

"Well, I'm usually the one helping them. But, just, um, getting them to finish their work. Sometimes I look at the directions and I say, 'No, wait for the teacher.' But here they were pretending, like, Aya doesn't get something, so, Maureen is helping her and showing her what to do. And Vivian has a lot of trouble, so Sonya will help her and she'll explain to her what you have to do to get the work done. That is usually how it works."

In her account the individuals within the group are not simply lumped together; Emily presents each individual player with her/his own needs and tendencies. Her attentiveness to group dynamics of reciprocity—that some people may be the givers and others the receivers of care or help—is noteworthy. I heard this awareness expressed across the children's accounts. They highlighted dynamic collaboration that facilitates, clarifies, and redirects ("No, wait for the teacher"), and that is explicit about not doing the work for others.

In one sense, this kind of support by group members is a way to foster cooperation, mutual regard, and solidarity. It values the success of the team or group (the family, the clinic, the business, the class) over the competitive advantage of the individual. At the same time, there were some children who chose to honor an individual member of their group, as Yanira did: "This is Maureen and she makes sure that I don't get confused multiplying negative numbers, so I wanted to show how she helps me learn." Even in identifying particular helpers, the children shined a light on the value they placed on relationality and interdependence. It is interesting to note how Yanira frames her comment, emphasizing the mutual obligation of reciprocal caring and explicitly connecting that recognition to visibility: Because she supports me in math, I want to "show" how she helps me learn.

Claire, too, is aware of complex dynamics of care and learning. She unselfconsciously describes herself as a receiver of help as she points to the photograph she took of two adjacent groups:

> "This is the group I usually sit at. But I moved. And there's Gabbie, Kristin, Caroline, and Tina. Those are the people that help me in, like, math and stuff. They help me with directions and help me to understand it better. Because they know how to put it into simpler words better than the teacher. They're actually the smarter people and they are sympathetic. Also, they're nice and kind. They care."

"What do you mean they are the smarter ones?" I ask. Claire ponders my question, then says:

> "Like, they, like, they're more advanced. Like, they get it right away. Like, some other kids like me and my group now don't get it right away. Like, we don't really get it. Like, most of the things we do, but some things we don't really get at the time. And they can do work faster."

I ask, "What do you do when you don't get it?" "Well, I either ask the teacher or ask my parents or ask [my group]. Or my other friends." There is much to learn from Claire's insights about groups, learning, and the loop of support. Unlike most of the children, Claire sensed that the groups were based on levels of readiness or ability-based (a view expressed by only three of the 36 children). Some groups have "smarter people," which Claire equates with speed and efficiency ("they get it right away" and "they can do work faster"). She backs away from the idea that she and her group members lack basic comprehension; indeed, they grasp most things—they just need more time. Ann Arnett Ferguson has observed a similar awareness among youth, who understand that "it is the timetable, the form, not the content of the curriculum, [that] is the significant element in their education" (Ferguson, 2000: 166).

Claire also senses that the groups (and thus learning) are fluid and influenced by social interactions, not innate capabilities:

> "We change groups every semester. Or we change every once in a while because some people talk. Like, if we are talking in a good way ... like if we are getting to know other people in the classroom so they can help us, that's okay. But if we are talking and not getting work done, that's not okay."

Claire seems to understand that groups have regulatory effects designed to ensure that everyone completes their work. She easily distinguishes between the types of social interactions that accomplish this goal and those that do not: talking in a "good" way promotes relationships as a means for learning, or at least "getting work done." But interactions that distract or are not related to getting work done can result in group changes. I am especially struck by Claire's portrayal of her own agency in this process. First, she says, "we change groups every semester," as if the children are the agents of change—even though it is the teachers who organize the groups. Moreover, despite being assigned to one group, she says "I moved" to get help from kids who, she believes, are not only "smarter," but "sympathetic," "nice," and "kind," highlighting again how learning and teaching are deeply affective and variously concerned with connection and interdependence.

At the same time, it is important to note that group work and the giving and receiving of help was not romanticized or presented as flawless, as Nalanie's description of her learning-group photograph illustrates. She explains, "This [Figure 4.13] is a group of kids who was helping each other. This is the purple group. But before it was the red group. I took the picture to show people helping each other." I ask, "Why is that important?" Nalanie's explanation is telling:

> "Well, people help each other because they get to learn from each other and because then you get to know that person more better. Most kids help each other. But there

Figure 4.13: The purple group *Nalanie, age 10*

are some kids in a group where they wouldn't help each other, they would, like, talk and sometimes just pretend when the teacher walks by. [Pointing] This is Michael, he's funny, he gets into trouble a lot. He distracts me. He doesn't really get his work done, but sometimes he does. The funny thing is—this is the third time we've changed groups. He was in the red group the first time, the second time he was in the red group, and the third time he was in the red group. So I have only been in his group once."

Nalanie is aware that some kids "pretend" to be working and helping others, but overall "most kids" embrace the norms where "work really gets done." She also senses that groups are organized around social relations rather than ability.[11] She has an inkling ("the funny thing is") that children move in and out of Michael's group in search for the right social combination. Given the earlier discussion about strategies used by the teachers and principal with kids who "get into trouble," it is also worth noting that Michael is not excluded from the group, but rather placed with a new configuration of students. This form of classroom management sends a powerful message to Nalanie and the rest of the class, namely that the best way to "help each other" is in community, not in isolation. Importantly, this regulatory technique maintains an environment of connection that is at odds with typical strategies of discipline through exclusion that are embedded in the institution and culture of schooling. Perhaps this is also part of the "funny thing" that

Nalanie is addressing: that despite Michael's transgressions, there is a determined effort to maintain his place within the group.

What ties all of the kids' accounts of group work together is a shared value placed on relational learning and interdependence. The details of their accounts reveal the "hows" and "whys" of group learning that may not be obvious to an observer. Again, the children have taken pains to document with their cameras and to spell out through their accounts the otherwise invisible ties between caring (helping each other), interdependence and learning.

The notion that children learn through the process of teaching other children is well established, dating back at least to the 1960s and the development and widespread implementation of Learning Through Teaching (LTT). As Herbert Thelen put it:

> The idea of students learning through helping each other is a very promising alternative to the traditional system of learning through competing with each other. It also makes the acquisition of knowledge and skills valuable, not in the service of competition for grades but as a means for personally significant interaction with others. (Thelen, 1967, quoted in Gartner et al, 1971: 6)

In writing about the rise of LTT, the authors made a point to tie LTT to larger educational and social trends of the time. The rise of self-help and the human potential movements, coupled with a greater emphasis on participatory processes of governance, were challenging top-down approaches within social service work. Meanwhile, an anti-poverty focus in education (including the inception of Head Start) sought to address the failure in traditional school curricula to meet the needs of "disadvantaged" youth (Thelen, 1967, quoted in Gartner et al, 1971: 5), and LTT offered an alternative. Perhaps LTT's most important contribution was its challenge to the "banking" model of education, which conceives of children as empty vessels into which teachers deposit knowledge. The highly influential writings of Paulo Freire provided a useful distinction between the transmission of knowledge from teacher to student (that is, learning as memorization), to the problem-posing model of education that leverages students' own knowledge and experience to actively solve problems and declines to treat the teacher as the sole repository of knowledge. Versions of the problem-posing model of teaching and learning persist, but the social context of schooling and reform measures have changed dramatically in the face of today's accountability culture (Taubman, 2009). The meaning of group learning—its hows and whys —are now tied to performance-based measures for what counts as success, which by 2003 focused specifically on high-stakes standardized testing. The PCS children reported these tests as a persistent and looming feature of school life.

## "A big deal at this school"

The stress, anxiety, and performance pressure associated with standardized testing was palpable in the children's stories and voices. Sofia's account is emblematic of the dread many children described and dramatized:

> "MCAS [Massachusetts Comprehension Assessment System] is a big deal at this school, it's really big. We don't get the best scores all the time ... especially for the fourth graders because they have to write an essay. We have to take the tests every year, third [grade] through sixth. I get nervous, so nervous that I'm sick to my stomach. It is coming up in a week and a half again. It is tough and my teacher keeps on saying, 'Don't worry about it.'"

Sofia took a deep breath and sighed before she continued, "Sometimes I feel it's gonna be boring and sometimes I feel it's gonna be tough. We have to split our desks up for it. And then, we do our work and the teachers are walking around trying to help but they can't help as much 'cause it's the MCAS." She sighed deeply again. "It's tough for the teachers 'cause they don't know what to say, because they want to help us get it, but they can't give too much information as part of the question."

Listening to the children's accounts of test-taking, I was struck by the consistency of their reports about teacher responses —"breathe deep," "don't worry," "relax," and "it will be over before you know it," advice often offered to kids bracing for their dreaded immunizations. These ritualized responses signal a teacher's concern for how a child is feeling over how the child will score on the test. Note, for instance, that teachers were not quoted as offering advice on strategy or optimizing performance ("just do your best," "keep trying," "pace yourself," "check your work," and so on). Put differently, within what has become called school's "testing culture," the children seem to be situating their teachers in a discourse of caring rather than a discourse of performance. But Sofia's view goes a step further by pointing out the problematic effects of testing culture on teachers, not only students, forcing an interruption in care relations of learning (and imposing limits on teacher agency) as teachers "try to help but can't." Equally striking to me is that Sofia is consciously aware that test-taking individualizes students, requiring them "to split up our desks," shifting from their collaborative working groups—which, as we have just seen, are so strongly associated with their sense of themselves as successful, interdependent learners who learn from each other. The test-taking routines not only interrupt group work, but also affect the type of person a student and teacher can be (someone who can or can't "help").

Others have written about the changing routines and relationships that high-stakes testing has introduced in classrooms, where students become "treated like objects for testing rather than as students being cared for by their teachers" (Löfgren & Löfgren, 2017: 405).[12] The specific concerns associated with standardized high-stakes testing are manifold. Primary among them are that students are learning more about how to take tests than they are about content, and that teachers are teaching more to the test, narrowing and simplifying important subject matter. Equally important, the testing culture has narrowed curricular content to tested subjects, and subject-area knowledge has become fragmented into test-related pieces. Finally, teacher-centered pedagogies are coming to dominate classroom practices and curriculum, and highly structured "teacher-proof" curricula are marketed as a means for achieving universally consistent results.[13] Whereas standardized testing is supposed to ensure efficiency and equity in learning outcomes on a national level, critics have pointed out that testing is in fact being used to manage, market, and control schools rather than to assess student learning and growth (for example, Ball, 2003).

When schooling prioritizes test-taking, the effects are not lost on students, as the comments of PCS children make clear. The intensification of test-taking pressures can be heard in more recent studies about children's experiences. For example, Löfgren and Löfgren (2017) reported that students in Sweden regard test-taking as an experience akin to the gruesomely competitive spectacle described in the post-apocalyptic novel *The Hunger Games*:

> It feels like they're making this a real big thing, the size of a Hunger Game. "It is like this, folks: now it is time for the national testing, you must be prepared wa, wa, wa!" (2017: 402)

Sjoberg et al (2015), also from Sweden, studied testing situations from children's perspectives. They found that nine- and ten-year-old students taking high-stakes national tests invoked discourses of competition to describe themselves as either "winners" or "losers." And they perceived their teachers as being more concerned about their performance and competitiveness than their well-being. In other words, the focus on performance was perceived as eclipsing any focus on care.

Children at PCS acknowledged their teachers' tendency toward care and sympathy, even when facing the difficult challenges and pressures of standardized testing. But their worries about testing highlight the degree to which relational models of learning are undercut by these trends toward individual, quantitative, summative assessments. Care theorist Nel Noddings (2005a, 2005b) would agree that standardized testing —"largely a product of separation and lack of trust"—gets in the way of a fundamental regard for the expressed needs of students (as opposed to the needs that adults determine for them). She notes:

> First, as we listen to our students, we gain their trust and, in an on-going relation of care and trust, it is more likely that students will accept what we try to teach. They will not see our efforts as "interference" but, rather, as cooperative work proceeding from the integrity of the relation. Second, as we engage our students in dialogue, we learn about their needs, working habits, interests, and talents. We gain important ideas from them about how to build our lessons and plan for their individual progress. Finally, as we acquire knowledge about our students' needs and realize how much more than the standard curriculum is needed, we are inspired to increase our own competence. (Noddings, 2005a, n.p.)

I appreciate two things about Noddings' remarks about caring relations. The first is her acknowledgment that care has mutual benefit—for students, who are cared for and are listened to, as well as for teachers, whose exercise of care strengthens their own knowledge, competence, and self-regard. Second, Noddings sees caring as a means to develop and sustain classroom relations *and* learning outcomes, reminding us that these need not be mutually exclusive (Noddings 1984, 1992, 2002).

Nonetheless, the practices and routines of standardized testing are a key means by which the "ideal schooled subject" is produced—a type of person who is characterized by "competitiveness, independence and self regulation" (Link et al, 2017: 835). To illustrate how the "ideal" student is molded in school, ethnographic researchers Holly Link,

Sarah Gallo, and Stanton Wortham conducted longitudinal research in a public, Title I elementary school, focusing on how specific children became certain types of students (that is, "struggling vs. successful") from kindergarten to fourth grade. The researchers examined changing disciplinary and regulatory techniques used by teachers over the course of time, especially around test-taking. Starting in second grade, test-taking rituals served to normalize the characteristics of what makes a "good" student—working silently, independently, and seeing oneself in competition or at least in comparison to others based on test scores. Test-taking routines created an environment of competition and comparison rather than collaboration, which had been valued in kindergarten and first grade. One compelling example from their study illustrates what Sofia described as having to "split our desks up" for test-taking. In it, a teacher gives a set of instructions for "the testing way to sit at your desk," which involved students "separating their desks, shielding their papers from one another, not looking at each other's answers, remaining silent, and sticking with the exact pacing of teacher instruction as she read aloud, question by question, from sample tests." (Link et al, 2017: 853).

The researchers report that over time, this "testing way" undermined cooperative learning among children and increased (teacher-centered) surveillance as well as regulation of self and others. It effectively re-defined the kind of learner that their school expected. One girl, Abi, evidenced this shift. Abi began kindergarten having recently arrived from Mexico. While kindergarten was a challenge for her, especially during whole-group instructional time conducted in English, Abi thrived in small-group interactions where she could draw on both Spanish and English. Throughout kindergarten and first grade it was clear that Abi was a "helper": she was clearly oriented toward collaboration, which the researchers described as stemming from "an authentic desire to help a classmate learn, not to show off her expertise or exercise power over others." Abi's skills and desires had been valued characteristics in her early school years, but they were soon to be undervalued (Link et al, 2017: 848). In second grade, Abi learned to take on the self-regulating posture of test-taking, including hiding her answers from other students as they were all being instructed to do. It seemed that Abi was absorbing the imperative to be a more autonomous and independent student and thus was positioned by the teacher as a model student.

In third grade this began to change. Despite the fact that Abi excelled in a small-group setting for English as a Second Language (ESL) support and continued to serve as a helper in support of others, because of her low test scores in reading and writing (but not in math where she scored well), she was positioned and began to self-identify as a "struggling" student compared to others. By fourth grade, the classroom environment had shifted to a primary focus on individual work and testing, with little opportunity for Abi to interact with her peers or for students to learn from each other, an area that had been her particular strength. Abi was observed reaching out to other students, who often ignored her. Rather than being seen and appreciated for her efforts to engage others in learning, as she was so skilled at doing, Abi's position as a "struggling" student became more fixed. "She finished fourth grade positioned as a low performer and continued to experience exclusion and rejection from many of the children she had played, taught, and learned with in earlier grades" (Link et al, 2017: 860). Regrettably, argue the researchers, Abi's investment in relational learning and interdependence was not supported in school, and this played out to her detriment. If schooling acknowledged ways of learning that encouraged interdependence and ways of being that supported collaboration, it could have been otherwise.

The fifth- and sixth-grade classrooms at PCS had not yet foreclosed on the salience and value of relational learning, even as students were encouraged to regulate themselves and each other through the "groups" as a means to get work completed. What remains most compelling to me about the PCS kids' focus on "helping each other" and interdependence was how it merged with their sense of mutual regard for each other, their teachers, and school staff. Even when Sofia described her deep anxiety about the state standardized test, she took care to relay her concern for her teachers: "It's tough for the teachers 'cause they don't know what to say, because they want to help us get it, but they can't give too much information as part of the question." I am struck by Sofia's awareness of limitations that get in the way of her teachers' ability to care and undermine the collaboration she and her peers value. More specifically, Sofia has come to understand that this intrusion comes from an outside force—in this case, the power of state policy (embodied in the standardized MCAS exam). She and her peers are seeing firsthand that adults—even in an adult-controlled institution—are unable to change or challenge policy that disrupts and undermines classroom collaboration. Given the children's sharply perceptive attention to care and trust in adult-child school relationships, this lesson in adult powerlessness is profound.

Viewed against a backdrop of an instrumental model of education measured by individual achievement, the PCS children's insights suggest new possibilities for how we conceive of the purpose of schooling, the means of learning and teaching, and what the "ideal schooled child" should be. What makes the kids' accounts "counter-narratives" is the value they are placing on being "caring," interdependent, and connected over and above being independent and competitive.

## Choreographies of caring at home and school

In the past two chapters I have highlighted the reciprocal pieces of caregiving and care receiving that are lifted up in the kids' images and accounts of home and school: love, trust, believing-in and being-believed-by, mutual regard, gratitude, and reciprocity. Again and again, the children show that they perceive care relationships to be essential for learning; and crucially, they do not take these elements of care for granted. Across both domains, the children acknowledge that how children and adults "do school" rests on a choreography of care and constellation of resources. What is useful about this metaphor of choreography is that it allows for an understanding of children's development, learning, and care as an interplay of what is seen and what is not, what is frontstage and backstage, what is present and absent, what is close, near, and far. For example, what can be seen are teachers' smiles and hugs; what is not seen is women's emotional labor and the patriarchal and heteronormative expectations that make these demands. What is frontstage are provisions (food, textbooks, technology, soon-to-be acquired playground equipment, things that make learning fun); what lies backstage are the joint efforts of the principal, teachers, and staff school to secure these things. What is present is "niceness," "calm," and inclusion; what is absent is yelling, harsh punishment, and suspension/exclusion. What is close are classmates and friends "helping each other"; what is near are teachers; and what is far are state requirements.

By using their cameras as a means to regard care at home and at school, the PCS kids have rendered visible the labor of women, as mothers and teachers, and asserted their appreciation for that labor. Their photographs bring viewers into spaces that we immediately recognize as the hubs and hearths of childhood, family, and school life: kitchens and classrooms. The parallels between these spaces are significant: both kitchens and classrooms are meeting places where "private" lives and "public" matters collide: information is exchanged, stories are told, histories and values are transmitted, and children are apprenticed into family, school, community, and national cultures. Both are spaces where children are "helped with being a child," to use Gabriel's terms from Chapter 3. And both kitchens and classrooms are prototypically arranged, maintained, and managed by women (mothers, sisters, aunts, grandmothers, teachers, and school staff)—and serve as sites of children's development. They are places where dwellings are made possible through women's invisible labor.[14]

We can see the evidence of this labor in the children's photographs of kitchens, where windows are adorned with floral-laced curtains and matching floral-patterned canisters displayed on countertops. Windowsills are lined with small figurines, knick-knacks, flower pots. Picture frames holding family photographs hang at eye-level above sinks or on refrigerators, as if celebrating the family unity and sociability made possible through women's work. The children's snapshots of kitchen walls, countertops, tables, and refrigerators show signs of family activities and the coordination of daily life (calendars, grocery lists, and so on) that indicate kitchens are "command centers" of family life (Arnold et al, 2012). The kids proudly showcased their moms' care in kitchens, where they worked to sustain family ties and cultural heritage through "feeding the family," and through apprenticing their daughters (and some sons) to maintain these ties. Mothers also worked to solidify social ties in school, where children's sense of belonging and status at school was secured by a mother's "creativity with food," as Gabriel proudly put it.

The PCS students' pictures of teachers in classrooms also evidenced the labors of dwelling-making. Classroom decorations—bright posters and bulletin boards, letters, and numbers hung like wallpaper borders above blackboards, posted rules, and motivational messages—are carefully chosen artifacts that serve to organize and guide daily activities. Amid the markers of institutional life—painted brick, exposed pipes, harsh florescent lights—there are also signs of the comforts of home: lace curtains, lamps, plants, coffee mugs, hand cream, collectibles, and children's artwork on display. These adornments are selected and arranged, set in place by teachers' hands to create for their students a sense of comfort and belonging.

The children's affirming, appreciative way of seeing care work and dwelling-making at home and at school stands in stark contrast to public narratives that regularly position teachers as inept, unqualified, poorly trained, overpaid, inept, self-interested, lazy, and easily replaced (Gabriel, 2011; Kumashiro, 2012). This discourse is not accidental. As Berliner and Glass (2014) point out in their book *Fifty Myths and Lies that Threaten America's Public Schools*, it serves to advance corporate interests and buttress the legislative agenda of those who seek to privatize education and capitalize on reforms. At the same time, the thicket of public disinvestment that surrounds the poor and working-class children attending PCS is woven into a complex racial landscape. The children's images highlight the evidence of that landscape in the juxtaposition of all-white, all-female adult figures with racially diverse figures of children. These images raise vexing questions about the "whiteness" of school care, highlighting the need for an interrogation of whose definition of care predominates and what creates a sense of "home" within classrooms from the perspective of diverse students.

As the PCS kids know well, the work of care in school takes time and attention, just as it does at home; it is accomplished, in part, through school routines, rituals, rules, and relationships that foster collaboration, safety, and conflict resolution against potential threats (violence, gangs). Care—whether undertaken by teachers or peer group members—allows for joy in the learning process, even against the looming anxieties of school: not knowing, being slower, confronting dreaded high-stakes testing. In school, as at home, the children are alert witnesses to the ways that care is choreographed. It does not lie in the hands or bodies of individuals; rather, it is coordinated and distributed across social units, including family members and friends and various adults in school. Relations of care can also be interrupted by external forces, whether demands of low-wage workplaces or state-imposed high-stakes testing. The children also recognize that the goal of care is not just about providing a feeling of comfort. It is also about succeeding together. In their images and accounts of school and home, the kids emphasize that individual success is possible *because* of the distributed and shared work of care. Students cooperate with each other, teachers make learning fun, parents encourage and support, lunch ladies supply nourishment, nurses offer advice and counsel, custodians provide a clean learning environment. The work of many people supports the learning of each student. And as much as the children may subscribe to an achievement ideology, they also locate that achievement within a facilitative network of relationships, mutual obligations, skillful collaborations, and cooperative supports.

# 5

# That's (not) me now: development, identity, and being in time

It is mid fall, 2011. I am sitting with 17-year-old Juan in the lunchroom of the vocational high school where he is now enrolled in a welding program. We are looking through the photos he took as a fifth- and sixth-grader, which he'd used to position himself as a grateful son and as a valued member in school and in his youth ministry. Readers will remember him as Gabriel, whose photo of his mom in the kitchen sparked a declaration of his explosive love for her. He praised her help "with being a child" and noted the ways her "creativity" in the kitchen earned him a special place in his school culture. Like some of the other participants in the study, "Juan" chose a new pseudonym to fit his present self, and as he reflects on his past self, figured in the photos before him, he periodically chuckles and asks, with a slight tone of embarrassment, "What was I thinking back then? I must have thought I was so cool."

"Back then," in our last interview at the end of sixth grade, we had talked at great length about his "gangsta style" change from fifth to sixth grade, which he attributed to his older friends at church. "I'm like, 'Yo, why do you wear white tees under your shirts and all that?' ''Cause that's gangsta style,' they said." At the time, he relished his time with the "older kids" who accepted him, and he wanted to adopt their style. He also confessed he was trying harder to "make my mom happy."

These past sentiments don't seem to occur to him now as he looks through his old photographs; he can't remember why he would have taken them. But as we conclude our interview, his parting words shine a light on how the photography project related to his sixth-grade self at the time. He says:

> "You made us look good and gave us attention. It was good, and I had some negative qualities, my attitude, 'cause when I got angry, I gave everyone attitude. People talked trash about me, like bad stuff. But you know, times change. That's not me now."

163

Juan was unable to participate in the follow-up photography and video component of the project because he had no time. In addition to his vocational schoolwork, he was working two jobs after school and on the weekends to help his mom pay the bills—as he told me, "My mom and sister depend on me." But despite the absence of his images from the last phase of the project, Juan's parting words highlight my argument thus far: that the kids used their cameras with an awareness of the partial views of others, often counteracting or holding at bay potential negative views they believed others might have ("people talked trash about me"). We have heard this awareness referenced again and again in comments like "my mother is very, very smart, even if she didn't go to college," and "this is the safest place I have ever lived," and "this school makes me proud." Whether they were staking claims to the dignity of their upbringings against a perceived stigma or warding against a view of their school as lacking, they were using photography to do more than just document or describe. They were using it to redress *how others see*. They were mindful that others' vision is incomplete, so they used their own vision/(in)sight to enable their audiences to see more completely. And part of that more complete picture had to do with recognizing how other members of their community (mothers, teachers, friends, classmates, family members, and research team members, including me) endowed them with a sense of value and self-regard.

By highlighting the kids' ways of seeing and self-conscious positioning, I have argued that their insights push us to consider a broader definition of development that rests on choreographies of care at home and in school, and that understands care and caring as a collective, not individual activity—a social good, not an individual achievement. The kids' vision of care and caring is nested, distributed across family members, friends, school staff, kids and adults, girls/women and boys/men. The experience of being cared for and caring for others is at once anxiety-ridden and stressful, and the source of love, gratitude, reciprocity, solidarity, and pride.

In this chapter, I consider how the young people, now in their late teens, returned to their childhood photographs and reflected upon their past selves. For those who were able to participate in the creation of an additional set of still and video images—a subset of 18 young people—I examine how they used their cameras to represent their present lives and "what matters most." I identify their ongoing commitment to redress how others see and to stake claims to their valued activities and identities. This chapter weaves together an array of visual and textual material: childhood photographs and individual interviews about them; contemporary photographs, videos, and "VoiceThreads" produced by the participants (described further on); and small-group discussions during the screenings of the videos they made.

In one sense, inviting the young people to reflect upon their childhood photographs resonates with my own experience as an ethnographer—revisiting the field to face the daunting task of crafting a meaningful, intelligible, shared narrative about "growing up" from a wealth of diverse and sometimes conflicting materials.

I have immersed myself in these materials, looking, listening, re-looking, and re-listening, sifting through the evidence of how the young people encountered their selves in the past and fashioned their selves in the present. I found that they often, but not always, cast themselves in light of an aspirational future, or in the glow of a nostalgic past. Particularly striking are what these materials suggest about different ways of inhabiting time and how, as the boy who was once Gabriel and later became Juan put it, times and selves change. Paying attention to the young people's subjective experiences of time allows us to see their stakes in and claims to their own development, as active subjects rather than objects of socialization.

## Digital Interlude #4: Being in Time

childrenframingchildhoods.com/digital-interludes/being-in-time

It is hard to convey my feelings as I began reconnecting with the PCS youth in 2011—a mixture of excitement, anticipation, and wonder. I was curious to know how the young people's lives had unfolded in the five to seven years since we had last met. How would they respond to their childhood photographs? What would they think of the password-protected website that now housed their digitized photographs and videotaped interviews? Would I recognize them?

I was able to track down 26 of the original 36 participants who were attending seven different high schools in Worcester.[1] After I contacted the principals of each school, they kindly made the initial contact with each student to discern her/his interest in participating in a follow-up project. All agreed to be interviewed about their childhood photographs, although four did not return their consent forms and thus weren't interviewed. Of these 22, 18 were able and willing to participate in the photography and video portion. Those who didn't participate, like Juan, all gave time constraints as their reason. This dimension of time—its limits and unequal distribution—was an early alert to what would become a central topic.

I can still remember the flood of feelings as I sat with each young person, seeing and remembering them as children. Together we were coming into contact with the visual markers of "growing up" and "growing older." I remember feeling dwarfed by Juan's tallness and his full stature. I was awed by the glamorous looks of some of the girls, now young women. The young people all remarked in one way or another on the passage of time, and they shared an array of reactions to the ways they appeared, acted, and spoke as children. Some kids took delight in, others puzzled over or lamented what they were thinking or doing at the time. Still others, like Juan, disclaimed his past self, raising the question of why some kids perceived their selves as less continuous than others. What I didn't expect was how these conversations made me tune into different frequencies or scales of time, including "physical aging, personal maturation, life course, biographical, historical, and generational" (Thorne, 2009: 327)—as well as the experiential sense that we all shared of time having passed since our last encounter.[2]

In our culture it seems almost impossible to reflect on individual lives without invoking notions of progress and decline, understood in developmental terms (Zerubavel, 2003). We expect that an individual will "mature" with the passage of time, transitioning from childhood innocence and youthful folly to settled adulthood and elderly wisdom. We anticipate that personal trajectories will unfold in a linear fashion, driven more or less by cause and effect. These causes and effects are sometimes cast as psychological (that is, the determining effects of early childhood) or as social (that is, the defining effects of class, race/ethnicity, and gender). Moreover, life's "disruptions" (for example, illness, divorce) are cast this way precisely because we anticipate a more steady, straight-line journey. Indeed, this perspective on time is embedded in longitudinal research that searches for explanations about how people end up in the lives they lead. In my case, I was interested in how the young people would reflect on and represent their lives over time—how would they say they and their lives had changed? But I would learn that this notion of a linear path is not the only way of being-in-time that would be salient, and this discovery stretched my understanding of time and development, as well as their relationship to choreographies of care. These themes form the central focus of this chapter.

After reconnecting with the young people and interviewing them about their childhood images, I gave each participant a disposable, analog camera and asked them, just as I'd done years earlier, to take pictures of "what matters most." Since 2003, technological advances had made digital photographs commonplace, and disposable film cameras were now a relic of the past—a marker of historical time that the kids commented on. Many (but not all) of the young people now had cell phones with cameras and regularly posted photos on Facebook. But because not everyone had a phone with a camera (or an accompanying data plan), I decided to use disposable cameras again. I planned a gathering in Worcester to bring all the participants together to reconnect, meet the current members of my research team,[3] view their own and each other's new photographs, and to learn how to use VoiceThread (described further on). I had also raised funds to support a final gathering at the Graduate Center, City University of New York, where I am a faculty member. On this "field trip" the young people screened and discussed their videos.

The software program VoiceThread allows users to upload photographs and create audio and text-based commentaries or stories within a secure collaborative network. These "threads" then can be shared with a community of "friends," who are also free to contribute comments or ask questions. Since the young people were dispersed across multiple high schools, using VoiceThread made it possible for them to connect, ask questions, offer commentary, express their ideas, and present their own "takes" on the meaning and significance of their own and each other's images. This format also helped kids participate "on their own time"—late at night, after homework, after their jobs—rather than planning multiple group gatherings, which were hard to schedule.

VoiceThread is a format that resonates with other digitally mediated youth-cultural practices, or what Glynda Hull (2003) has called "new literacies for new times." She writes of these new literacies, "The most obvious thing to say about digital stories and other kinds of signification that are mediated by new information technologies is that they offer distinctive contrasts to the primarily alphabetic texts and the forms of textual reasoning that predominate in schools and universities" (p. 230). Indeed, the young people in the project proved to be proficient users and consumers of digital media, turning notions of expertise and authority on their heads (Ito et al, 2009: 2). Far from being introduced to new skills and technology through the research project, the young people were quick to instruct us, the researchers. They took the lead, whether it was helping me get past school internet blocks to access the archive housing their childhood images, or helping each other use VoiceThread, or setting up the Facebook page that would be our group's primary mode of communication.

To supplement the "old-time" analog camera technology with new digital media, I also gave each participant a FlipCamcorder to "make a short video about you, your world, or your life." Video was, as one participant put it, the medium of his generation. In addition, many expressed special excitement about receiving the FlipCamcorders and repeatedly asked how much the cameras had cost and whether they were theirs to keep. (They were.) For most of the young people it was their first personal video camera (a few mentioned that their parents owned video cameras). They expressed a similar concern about caring for the video cameras as they had for the disposable cameras when they were children. What would happen if the video cameras broke? Would they receive a replacement? Would they need to pay for a new one? This may sound odd now, as it was only a short matter of time before cell phones would include affordable, high-quality video cameras, turning Flip video recorders into technological relics. It is hard to convey the reverence with which the young people received access to this now-commonplace technological capacity.

Like VoiceThread, making videos was already part of some (but not all) of the young people's digital media practice. All were familiar viewers/consumers of multi-media compositional strategies—for example, the addition of music for humorous or ironic effect or re-contextualizing images—but not all of the young people had produced their own videos.

As I listened to the young people discuss videos and video-making as their "generational" medium, I observed two things that would shape my approach to analyzing the images, sounds, and sensibilities of what they produced as teenagers. The first was a shift in gaze—what some scholars have characterized as a move from "a familial gaze" to a "youth-culture gaze," where young people can produce narratives that may be inaccessible to adults (Schwarz, 2009). The second was a tendency for the young people to self-consciously position themselves straddling different systems of value: the banal and the singular; the familial and the youth-cultural; the "interesting" and the "boring"; the ordinary ("normal") and extraordinary aspects of their working-class and racialized lives and identities.

Both of these patterns—a shift in gaze and a straddling of value systems—constitute what social theorist Michel Foucault (1988) called "technologies of self." He used the term to describe a range of activities individuals engage in to refashion themselves, re-orient or maneuver emotions, re-shape values, and feel "agentic" in their lives.[4]

This is why Schwarz (2009) refers to the production, exchange, and consuming of digital media as "*new* technologies of self," which, in the case of teenagers, can allow them to stretch beyond adult regulation and comprehension of meaning. These new technologies of self also serve as a means of transforming the value young people attach to their everyday activities. One of the participants, Danny, put it this way: "Well, you have to understand, you're looking at a guy who grew up watching thousands of YouTube videos. So when I got a camera—this was my first camera—I just thought well, I guess I'll do what I saw. I didn't just want to show my normal life because it's pretty boring." Danny's statement is emblematic of how the young people used their cameras to shift and sometimes interrupt dominant gazes and to affirm their lives. Their alternative, if not confrontational, practices of visibility (that is, not showing themselves or their lives as "boring") are a subject of this chapter. And as they created their own materials and responded to each other's creations, we can hear how contingent, value-laden, and conflicted are the kinds of time that the young people inhabit.

## Multiple lives, multiple identities

I immediately recognize Danny when he appears in the school office. Though his voice has grown deep, his smile is unmistakable, as are the quickly shifting facial expressions that he used to entertain his peers, the research team, and me in the first stage of the project. As he glances through the archive of his fifth- and sixth-grade images, he says wryly, "I'm still short."

Danny's video, entitled *Danny who?*, opens with a close-up shot of his face smiling and his voice saying, "Let's see all the nice things people have to say about me ..."[5] The video cuts to several quick clips in interview format, each with a different boy. A white teenage boy with close-cropped hair says, "Danny? Danny who?" Another boy with dark hair and darker skin looks quizzically into the camera and deadpans, "Danny? You mean that little Spanish kid?" In this beginning sequence of Danny's video, three male teenagers hurl insults (with a gleam in their eyes): "Danny is a jerk!" "Danny's ugly." "Danny's not funny." But in fact, Danny is very funny, and he has brought a witty, self-deprecating sense of humor to interviews, group meetings, and to his visual narratives since he was a ten-year-old.

Danny's video accomplishes the task he says he set out to do—that is, to make his life look "interesting."[6] He projected two orientations toward his self, an "interesting," youth-culture-oriented persona (playing at an arcade, playing video games, shopping, driving outside of town, as I will describe more later on), set alongside an everyday, ordinary persona oriented toward family and toward his role in its choreography of care.

His familial-oriented self comes through in the tender, playful portrayal of his relationship with his younger sister, whom he says he has "taken care of since she was a baby and sometime more than our parents because they weren't around during the day." She appears in the video several times: At the arcade we see him (and his girlfriend) pose with her for a digital photo-booth picture, leaning his head into hers and squeezing her cheeks; later she and Danny play video games together at home and when she wins, she joyfully bounces around in her *Beauty and the Beast* pajamas and makes faces at the camera, shouting, "No one can beat me, huh? Huh? Huh?" The expression that Danny adopts for the camera is not the look of a competitive older brother embarrassed to lose or annoyed by his little sister's silliness, but the look of a proud care-giver who is enjoying the glow of her accomplishment. While screening his video, Danny set aside his comic sensibility and spoke earnestly: "Family is the most important thing to me. And I love my whole family, but I would say my sister most of all. We're really close."

Danny's self-presentation is fluid as he experiments with creative re-appropriations of cultural codes around gender and ethnicity. He cleverly plays with masculine gender codes throughout the video, both taking up and spoofing "manly-man" conventions. He poses before a mirror wearing a pair of slick dark sunglasses in the lingerie department of a TJ Maxx store. As he spans the camera across his face, he zooms in for a close-up, whips off his shades, and whispers. "It's cold ... as ice." Here he imitates a pivotal moment, akin to the sound-bite scene found in movie trailers, presenting himself like an action hero caught out of place in the fluorescent-lit bra department of a discount store. "The moment is funny for its blurring of contexts: consumer culture, intimate feminine wear, and masculine action hero" (Luttrell et al, 2012: 172). In another scene that plays with cultural forms of masculinity, Danny films himself driving in the slow-moving traffic of downtown Worcester, turning to the camera and narrating with a sly smile, "A very slow car chase" (Figure 5. 1).

Danny plays with the boundaries of ethnicity and cultural codes of "Asian-ness" throughout the video as well. One striking example is the way he situates his friend's joking query at the beginning of the video: "Danny? You mean that little Spanish kid?" His friend may well have made the comment on his own, playfully mocking their shared familiarity (his friend is, of course, well aware of Danny's Vietnamese

Figure 5.1: (Video still) A very slow car chase *Danny, age 17*

Figure 5.2: (Video still) A big Chinese gate ... A big Asian gate *Danny, age 17*

heritage). Importantly, though, it was Danny who chose to put that comment front and center, and in doing so, he offers a caricature of ethnic classification and identification. His video also draws on the sentimental, synthesizer-heavy genre of Korean pop music ("K-pop"), which is layered over scenes of a flashy video arcade, rides, and food (including a two-second clip scanning pastries and custard tarts (labeled in English and Chinese characters). His music choice conveys a familiarity with, if not a spoofing of, an Asian/Asian American subculture, a web of engagement that extends beyond mainstream American pop-culture.[7] At the same time, he's able to recruit this global

171

media form to create a scene reminiscent of a romantic musical montage from a movie—the couple out on a date, being silly, having fun. These romantic sentiments and sensibilities of global media imbue Danny's playful way of poking holes in stereotypical versions of heterosexual masculinity—whether it is a male romantic lead, superhero action figure, or loving brother and family man.

Danny's video plays with references to Chinese culture, including a well-known marker of the Chinatown community in Boston—its traditional *paifang* gate, erected in 1982. "Danny stands several hundred yards from the neighborhood's border, training his video camera lens on the elaborate entrance way [Figure 5.2]. He says, 'This is how you know you're in Chinatown. There is a big gate ... A big Chinese gate ... A big Asian gate'" (Luttrell et al, 2012: 170).

Perhaps, because there is little in the way of Vietnamese/Vietnamese-American popular culture and visual markers in and around Worcester and Boston, he selected symbols of Chinese and Korean culture as the closest available next-best thing.[8] Or perhaps Danny's use of these symbols is more strategic, just like the opening line about "the little Spanish kid." By *playing with* Asian-ness and its ambiguities, he is not just being funny, but being critical and wise, identifying a chain of problematic semiotic relationships in which "Asian things"—for example, Korean music, Chinese gates, Chinatown—come to be seen as equally suited to represent any particular Asian. Just as he does with representations of masculinity, Danny uses his camera and his humor to poke holes in the stereotyped frames of identity that constrain him.[9]

Danny's video showcases the landscapes, both local and global, of his belonging. He uses transnational trends, styles, music, and imagery in ways that open up broader, more fluid boundaries within which he can fashion his identity. And insofar as Danny is utilizing new literacies and repurposing these transnational elements in his own "creative universe and social world" in Worcester, he is exercising "very powerful authorial agency" (Hull, 2003: 231).

Challenging identity boundaries is part of a politics of belonging, and this was a thematic undercurrent across the young people's images, sounds, sensibilities, and practices of visibility. An affirmation of multiple points of belonging was common, as Danny did in referencing his family, community of friends, his Vietnamese and greater Asian American community (including his "second family" at his Buddhist temple youth group), and his connection to a larger global youth media culture. Part of his craft, so to speak, was to point out how these identities are perceived by others through tropes, stereotypes, and problematic semiotic chains.

This way of seeing and representing is also featured in his VoiceThread presentation, titled *My Five Lives*, which included a reflection on what he calls the "ironies" of his life. Danny photographed a corner of his bedroom and wrote the following commentary to accompany it (Figure 5.3):

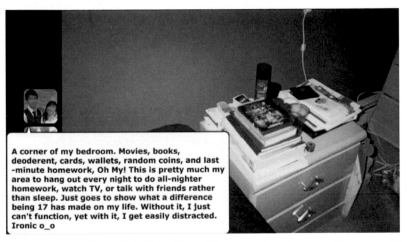

A corner of my bedroom. Movies, books, deoderent, cards, wallets, random coins, and last-minute homework, Oh My! This is pretty much my area to hang out every night to do all-nighter homework, watch TV, or talk with friends rather than sleep. Just goes to show what a difference being 17 has made on my life. Without it, I just can't function, yet with it, I get easily distracted. Ironic o_o

Figure 5.3: (VoiceThread) A corner of my bedroom *Danny, age 17*

Danny positions himself as straddling the demands of two systems of value: his commitment to homework and books signals that he is cultivating his value in educational and achievement terms, and his engagement with friends and media signals the value of belonging and camaraderie—which is greater, apparently, than the value of sleep. The language of "functionality" and "distraction" suggests his concern that he must account for what he is doing to improve himself—that is, just "hanging out" is not sufficient. In the context of the project, I hear him asserting/affirming his grown-ness, his development. He highlights being 17, making his own decisions, having some economic independence (a wallet); watching R rated movies (shown on his dresser), using deodorant. But he also expresses a sense of surprised *irony* ("Ironic o_o") about the corner of his bedroom, and he experiences his being-in-time through a sense of simultaneity and contradiction rather than as a linear shift from one state to the next (functioning, then distracted).

Danny's sense of irony further reminds me of phenomenological philosopher Merleau-Ponty's reflections of time as a river that "flows from the past towards the present and the future" (1995/1962: 411 quoted in Conrad, 2012: 204). And as critical childhood scholar Rachel

Conrad points out, our ways of thinking about time and childhood have originated from the perspective of the adult standing in the river. To the adult, the young person comes from "upstream in the past and is changing toward the future downstream, whereas for a child herself, she is a living presence." (2012: 205). Perhaps Danny's irony about his subjective experience of time surpasses adultist conceptualizations.[10]

Sofia provides a different variation on these same themes of identity, development, and time. Readers will remember that she migrated with her family from Albania as a young child (Chapter 2). The images she made as a fifth-grader highlighted her close ties to faraway family members, as well as her celebration of her own perceived linguistic and cultural "difference" at PCS.

The first words out of 15-year-old Sofia's mouth when we meet in the teachers' lounge of her high school were ones of amazement: "I can't believe you found me, just like you promised!" I would hear this refrain of surprise over and over again from the young people, as if they had not expected my return. Sofia's long dark hair and piercing eyes were immediately recognizable to me, but her demeanor was changed. No longer reserved and soft-spoken, Sofia bounced into the room full of energy and expressiveness. As she clicked on the photographs in her gallery of images, she laughed at times, asking the perennial rhetorical question, "What was I thinking?" and then confessed, "To be honest, I don't know what I wanted to show people back in fifth and sixth grade." She didn't mention her changing appearance but focused more on her "girly" possessions. She reminisced about the gift of her Barbie boom box, a photograph she had taken in the fifth grade and chosen as one of her favorites. "It was my first Christmas in America, my first present. I got it at school. I don't know where it is anymore. That's sad."

Sofia was quick to offer her thoughts about how she would use her video camera, which led to the following conversation. "I want to show my interests, and my friendships are part of how I am seen by others, and how I am labeled." "How do you think you are labeled?" I ask. I am struck by the force of Sofia's response:

"I am an immigrant, but it is weird to refer to yourself like that because it seems like people use that as such a negative word. That's why I'm not an immigrant. I'm a foreigner. I say 'foreigner' because it doesn't sound as bad. A foreigner sounds classy, whereas as an immigrant, is like, 'You are not allowed here, you don't belong in this country, blah,

blah, blah.' A foreigner is, like, you come from somewhere else. That's it."

When I heard Sofia refuse the label of immigrant, I was taken with the urgency in her voice. She didn't just say the words, she dramatized them, changing the register of her voice and using direct speech—"you are not allowed here, you don't belong in this country"—as if she were being reprimanded by a US Immigration and Naturalization Service agent. She muted the force of the reprimand with "blah, blah, blah," but the sting of the admonition was clear in her presentation. I heard Sofia's words in dialogue with a moment in history where political controversies about immigration policy in the United States were powerful shaping forces, and she was struggling to construct an identity around these debates. (Hearing her words and experiences now in 2018, as I write in the grip of a more divisive and dangerous moment in history for immigrants in the US, I am reminded of the ineffectuality of universalizing "immigrant childhood" outside of historical context.)

Sofia's choice to define herself as a "foreigner" and not as an "immigrant" strikes me as her way to affirm her value.[11] The resolve in her voice highlighted the demanding, ever-present task of answering to others' negative judgments, if not outright attacks—a reality so many immigrant youth must contended with. Sofia's choice of responses indicates the powerful role that race, class, and citizenship status play in how she is able to answer back. Sofia prefers the label "foreigner," which she understands to add value and distinction ("classiness") to her identity. This isn't how I heard the word "foreigner"; in my experience, calling someone a "foreigner" would be used to exclude, if not "other" them.[12] Meanwhile, whether she was aware of it or not, Sofia's sense of value and belonging is influenced by her relative advantage within the hierarchical order of immigrant status. As a documented, white-skinned Christian from eastern Europe, she can "come from somewhere else" and expect to be accepted, with less cause to fear the racism, Islamophobia, and risk of deportation that vex so many other immigrants.

To summarize her sense of self, Sofia explained:

"Looking back, I think that being born in a different country and spending the first four years of my life there has had a greater effect on me than I realized. I have seen what life is like in a country that is not all high and mighty.... My experiences overseas showed me something that not most people get. I know how much we do take for granted here, and anytime I start to take things for granted, I just think back to being in Albania."[13]

As Sofia reflected on her migration to America (a "high and mighty" country), I hear the take-nothing-for-granted attitude she expressed as a ten-year-old, only more forcefully. I hear Sofia negotiating her identity in skillful ways—speaking around the edges of American and Albanian identity categories, finding value in both. It strikes me that she is authoring an alternative, "transnational" (Smith, 2006) identity, a sense of self-across-two places. What makes her "different" from American children is her awareness of "what I should be grateful for." At the same time, by referring to her "experience overseas" she is centering America and her sense of belonging, which is expressed by how much "we" (meaning Americans) take for granted. Her affirmation of the value of her early Albanian childhood seems to be an important foil against the taken-for-granted abundance of American society.

Particularly striking in Sofia's characterization of belonging is her need to "work" at many things in her childhood, including learning English while maintaining her native language at home at her parents' insistence. She reflected:

> "That was a lot of pressure to put on a five-year-old child. Yet I broke through it, learned English, and can still speak Albanian fluently. If I wasn't forced to speak Albanian at home for years, chances are I would have forgotten most of it. I have grown up around American culture, so it's like second nature to me, whereas my born culture is something I have to work at knowing."

Again I hear Sofia speaking around the edges of American identification as she refers to growing up "around" rather than "in" American culture that has become "second nature" alongside the inherent nature ("born") of her Albanian identity that takes more work.

I also hear Sofia recognizing the strong association between American identity and English dominance, a connection also reflected in the Pew Research Center's findings that for the United States public, "language matters more to national identity than birthplace" (Stokes, 2017). According to the Pew report, over 90 percent of those surveyed stated that "it is [somewhat or] very important to speak the dominant language to be considered truly a national of" the United States—a number far greater than the 45 percent who believe that sharing national customs and traditions is very important to national identity (Stokes, 2017).

Sofia also had to "work at" friendships (that is, belonging). When she first arrived from Albania, she was the subject of ridicule. It was a short period of duress—two months, as she recalled:

> "Those days of being made fun of are mostly a blur. I couldn't speak with them. I didn't know how. But they were in elementary school, and they didn't exactly grasp the concept that I didn't know how. So, 'okay, then, don't be my friend.' It's funny, because back then, in elementary school, everybody was from America, from Worcester, lived their whole lives there,[14] and I come here to high school where it is more mixed. So here I'm not so much different because people are from all over the place, like Central America, South America. And there are five people here from Albania, so I don't feel so different anymore. Everybody speaks different languages—Spanish, Vietnamese. And then there's English, and then there's Albanian. It feels good to be different because this small group of people can understand what you say."

Sofia's story of belonging recognizes and challenges the construction of boundaries and groupings of people—"immigrants," friendship circles, English language learners who are subject to ridicule—as well as the inextricable links between language, identity, and culture that her parents made sure she grew up to value. Sofia relished her comfort in her "difference" and her belonging, which facilitated her current self-definition as an "all-out American teenager." She took a photograph to convey this sentiment and her sense of wholeness in connection to others (Figure 5.4):

> "I took this picture to show all of us together create one thing—a star. Our hands and feet symbolize all of us in that star. It may be one thing, but inside it there are four of us."

Looking and listening to this picture of belonging highlights another unspoken means of belonging: style. Two of the four girls are wearing identical Ugg-style boots, a major fashion trend at the time, though not something Sofia ever discussed.[15]

Sofia's video *Watch, Learn, Be happy ;)* featured what might be seen as the ordinariness of everyday high school interactions (in sharp contrast to Danny's extraordinary, "interesting" scenes). Her video is shot in documentary style as Sofia walks around the classroom, zooming close

Figure 5.4: A star *Sofia, age 15*

into dyads of students using their calculators (Figure 5.5) who pay her little attention, until one exclaims, "we are doing math and drinking coffee!" and pushes a Dunkin Donuts cup into the camera frame.

Sofia is the only young person to film teachers, including a segment featuring a white, male teacher taking pains while using a bit of dramatic, comedic flare to explain a "hanging indent" in English class. She also films a group of students outside the building holding hands as they surround a young, white, female teacher who is explaining the mathematical dimensions of the slope of the school building's roof. Against these more mundane scenes, Sofia films a multi-cultural and multi-racial group of young women (some wearing hijabs) choreographed in a circle in what appears to be a hallway in the school building. On the count of three, the girls let loose a long, extended scream. Another video segment shows the same group of girls sculpting their bodies into forms as if to represent a sense of unity and harmony. The video articulates both the ordinary and extraordinary texture of everyday high school life as a site of cultural formation and "contact zone" (Pratt, 1991) where various kinds of differences come into play. Georges Perec might designate these as "infraordinary" (quoted in Campt, 2017: 8) practices that go unnoticed or seem insignificant but

Figure 5.5: (Video still) We are doing math and drinking coffee *Sofia, age 15*

require special attention if we are to understand why they are essential to young people's own understanding of development. Whether it is "doing math and drinking coffee," or letting loose a collective, unifying scream in the hallway, or taking in the drama of a teacher's efforts to teach students how to make writing appear more professional, Sofia is revaluing the routine activities of school, asking her audience to "watch, learn, be happy."

Sofia photographed her bedroom wall where she actively curates and memorializes her life, and she featured the photo in her VoiceThread:

> "I took this picture of my wall [Figure 5.6] because I have memories from everything I have done, all kinds of girls (akog) [an after-school organization], track, rising stars, [another extracurricular activity], cross-country, and even pictures of my friends and family. These are things I never want to forget, and show what I have accomplished so far."

Sofia's photograph of the memory/accomplishment wall in her bedroom is akin to Danny's "corner of my room" photograph. Both offer insights into their identities and stakes in their own development, what media studies scholar Sonya Livingstone has called teen bedroom culture (2007). Sofia's wall offers an interesting contrast to stereotypical images of American teenage bedrooms, where walls are covered with pop-music posters and magazine spreads.[16] Sofia's wall is about things she "has done," things she "never wants to forget" (paralleling what she said about her photographs at age ten, reported in Chapter 2). Her wall is a bit like a trophy wall, commemorating not final results

Figure 5.6: My wall *Sofia, age 15*

(medals, awards, or trophies) so much as the doing of the things and the preserving of memories of these activities. I see Sofia's wall as her version of development and identity in time—a commemoration of her cultural ties, social bonds, and everyday activities—the "being" and "doing" that establish her value.

## Valued identities and time

Kim-Ly's video is titled *My life consists of a lot of confusion*, and it opens with her sitting in the passenger seat of a car driven by her "bestie friend," who works with her at a local supermarket chain. Another friend sits in the back seat, and all three are singing along with Katy Perry's hit pop song "Firework," which is playing in the background and continues to play through the entire video. This friendship circle is cross-racial (Black, white and Asian) and the camera zooms in to capture each joyful face as they sing, "baby you're a firework," and laugh. Two minutes later (after what is apparently a long time in the car, "getting lost"), Kim-Ly is alone in her bedroom. "Hiii," she greets her viewers, the camera close-up on her face, "It's 11:02. [p.m.] And … I should be doing my homework, but …" she pauses, rolls her eyes and scrunches her lips as if to say "Oopsy…" then remarks rhetorically, "Guess what I'm on?" The camera spins around to a computer screen with a video still of her looking like a pop-star in her bedroom, wearing the same red striped tank-top. "Facebook. Of course I'm on Facebook, I'm always on Facebook" (Luttrell et al, 2012: 174).

In this meta-moment of her video, viewers see Kim-Ly moving and breathing on the (video) screen, and then frozen in still-image on the smaller computer screen. She is self-consciously documenting herself in this moment and showing us that this mode of self-recording and revelation is part of her everyday practice (Luttrell et al, 2012: 174). It is an exemplary twist on being self-conscious and the game of the gaze, where she is at the same time the subject who takes the picture and the object pictured (Lasén & Gómez-Cruz, 2009: 212).

In a similar spirit to Sofia's bedroom wall, Facebook serves as a forum for young people to curate and memorialize their development and identities in time and to establish their value. What makes Facebook different is its public-facing aspect—and the awareness of multiple audiences in fashioning identities.[17] And as would become a recurring theme throughout the young people's representations, "being on Facebook" is a use of time that is value-laden.

Kim-Ly acknowledges the paradox of both displaying and creating her own digital persona. During the screening session and discussion of her video, Kim-Ly asserts that she draws boundaries to protect her virtual image:

> "Well, my mom isn't on Facebook because she doesn't know about it, which is good, because my family is very strict. So my sisters are the ones who watch over me on Facebook. They look at what I put on my wall and my profile, so I block them from seeing it, not that I put anything so bad on there."

Kim-Ly characterizes her Facebook postings as nothing "bad" but also as restricted, a line she walks—and talks about with keen self-awareness—in her video.

Kim-Ly is the youngest of seven children of immigrant parents from Vietnam. Her father, a landscaper, died in a tragic work accident right before she started fifth grade. Her mother owns and works full time at a nail salon. During our conversation about her childhood photographs, Kim-Ly described the strictness of her family in the following way:

> "I mean, right now my family is still strict on me, because they don't want to see me be a bad girl or anything, but I can still do more stuff than I could have before. Like, I cannot go out longer than like, eight o' clock. No parties at all, which I don't care, cause I'm not a partier. Maybe that's cause I haven't gone out to a party at all, since I've

been alive, but that's fine with me. And, my grades have to be good, all the basic stuff. No boyfriend."

Her reflection on her family expectations provided important context for her video. Immediately after showing herself on Facebook, Kim-Ly turned the camera lens to her bed, piled high with folders and books, and then cut back to her face, as she sighed and spoke haltingly but deliberately:

> "This is how much homework I have … [long pause] I am afraid I am going to fall asleep before it gets done … [another long pause]. But don't get me wrong if I don't finish it, well [pause] … I'll wake up at 3:00 and I'll do it then [another pause and a slight smile, with almost a wink in her eye]. I think I'll go take a shower now, that will wake me up and I'll just finish my homework now."

This conflicted reflection about the use of her time is much like Danny's, and it resonated across the young pe ople's self/media representations. Kim-Ly returned to this tension in her VoiceThread piece. Carefully displaying her makeup on her bed (Figure 5.7), she wrote, "I may not be a good artist, but my face is my canvas & I will gladly waste my time messing around with it."

In the accompanying audio segment about this photograph, she said:

> "I don't really use that much makeup … I'm not a good artist on paper, like writing and stuff, but when it comes down to doing eye stuff, I guess I am good at doing that because it is fun and it's like really cool. But I don't use that much, just eyeliner and mascara."

Kim-Ly seems conscious of the fact that her efforts to shape a particular persona—as artfully and tastefully made up—represents time that she is "glad to waste." Being on Facebook is a bit different, as she suggests that she might use her time better by doing homework ("I should be doing my homework, but …"). Nonetheless, both of these time-consuming "technologies of self" enable her to exercise her authorial agency, even if it is not "productive" or achievement-oriented. As if anticipating judgment or conflict over the daily use of time that saturates popular discourse as well as adult-child relations at home and in school, Kim-Ly seemed ready with her answer. Meanwhile, she makes sure to

Figure 5.7: (VoiceThread) My face is an empty canvass *Kim-Ly, age 18*

tell her imagined audience that she *will* finish her homework, regardless of the time of night.

Kim-Ly's internet use fits into a much larger picture. In the United States, 95 percent of teens use the internet. Youth between the ages of eight and 18 average six and a half hours of screen time a day (Madden et al, 2013), and a quarter of that time, young people are using two or more forms of media at once (Rideout et al, 2010), perhaps watching television while playing a casual game on Facebook. According to a 2015 report, more young people use computers at home than at school.[18] The young people often mentioned adult concerns about or restrictions on screen time, especially time on the internet, frequently describing the strategies they used to get around them. As Kim-Ly told me during her sixth-grade interview, "Most of the time I just lie about going on the computer. 'Cause I'm always like, 'Oh, I'm doing research.' And I talk to people."

Kim-ly's strategy resonates with the axiom that children may have voice (Kim-ly can "just lie," for instance), but adults control the conversation. Considerable media coverage has been given to adult concerns about the risks and consequences of young people's online engagement, from exposure to cyber-bullying and intimidation, to precocious sexuality, to childhood obesity. Worries that young people might put content about themselves online that can compromise their future success (for example, getting into college or getting a job) have led many parents and family members to monitor their teenagers' social media presence. Teenage girls are thought to be at special risk, given their assumed proclivity for "over-sharing" or for posting images that (wittingly or unwittingly) objectify themselves in ways that might lead to unwanted sexual overtures or unnecessary "drama," as it is referred to within youth digital media culture (Marwick & boyd, 2011; Fontaine, 2015). There are two sides of this anxiety coin. On the one hand, young people's online access to digital devices is framed as a matter of safety, a means for parents to keep abreast of their children's movement outside the home or to feel secure that they are safe at home entertaining themselves. On the other hand, young people's self-directed, active use of this technological environment is viewed as inherently risky.

Indeed, a persistent theme in the young people's accounts was their awareness of the double-sided adult discourse about growing up online. And if a single young person could be said to personify this conflict, it would be Mesha. Readers will remember her from Chapter 2 as the girl who chose to photograph the role-playing video game *Final Fantasy X*.

Seeing Mesha approach me in the office of her comprehensive high school took me by surprise. She appeared much older than I anticipated and looked tired. Her hair was pulled into a hair net because she was on her way to her after-school job at the fast-food chain Wendy's. She spoke ever so quickly, as if time might run out before she could fill me in—but she slowed down when I reassured her that I could come back as many times as she might want. The press of time seemed on her mind.

Looking back on her string of photographs of *Final Fantasy X*, Mesha laughed, "WOW, I think I went crazy with the camera. I took a lot of pictures of that one. I was just snapping away. I was obviously young and focused on just one thing … Why did I take so many pictures of this?"

Mesha admitted that her father had been (and continued to be throughout her high school years) critical of her time spent playing video games, but she hoped to prove him wrong when she becomes a video-game designer, which is her life's goal. She believed her father's concern was not only that she was "wasting" her time, but that she might get involved with the "wrong kind of people, like older men. But I tell him I can protect myself." Reflecting on her photographs, Mesha said what is most memorable to her about the role-playing video game was the social bond it forged between her and her best friend:

> "My best friend and I would play it all the time. In sixth grade, when he moved I was heartbroken. People said we were boyfriend and girlfriend but it wasn't like that, we were just best friends."

At the same time that Mesha framed video-gaming as a form of social glue, a means to create and sustain social ties, she also self-consciously used her video-gaming as a means to establish her value—her expertise and advanced skills in the male-dominated world of gaming, a world that she observed is "hard to break into as a girl."[19] As the youngest child and only girl, Mesha used to spend her afternoons at home, while her two older brothers were free to come and go as they pleased. She spoke with a sense of pride about being the main source of technological expertise for her family, the troubleshooter for all things computer-related, whether it was helping her grandmother record her favorite shows, or helping her parents navigate the internet. But she also suggested that it was a burden. She cast her digital engagement not only as a form of entertainment and a means of connection, but as educational and important for her future, and as a duty/obligation to her family—both worth investing her time in.

Much of our conversation sitting with her archive of images revolved around life stresses unrelated to her photographs, including her mother's chronic illness. She mentioned getting "depressed" in freshman year, which caused her grades to drop, but thanks to the help of her "AVID family," she was "hanging in there." (AVID is an academic program dedicated to closing the achievement gap by provided extra support and guidance for students "who are capable of completing a college preparatory curriculum".) She spoke about her desires to attend art school to study video-game design, and about her enrollment in an online commercial art college "that my dad already paid for ($130.00 a month)" to assist her in producing a portfolio. She described her time demands, already anticipating that she might be prevented from attending the NYC event to screen her video. She explained that she was saving her money to move in with her boyfriend, who is "into web-mastering."

The photographs Mesha took in high school featured "*things I do wit my life,*" as she titled her VoiceThread. The presentation opened with the picture of a guitar (Figure 5.8). The guitar represents her investment in making others happy ("I want to play for others to put a smile on their faces") and her commitment to "develop more artistic values within my life"—what I hear as two different kinds of time and value.

In the audio segment of her VoiceThread she stressed her "love and passion" for the sound of the guitar in instrumental music. "It also helps me pass the time when I am not playing video games or drawing." Mesha "passes the time" on artistic pursuits, playing guitar, gaming, or drawing. But "since I don't have free time, my parents let me stay home from church," an important family activity. She said she is grateful for this, especially since she finds church to be "boring." She worries that she has "procrastinated" in her online assignments for her

Figure 5.8: (VoiceThread) Guitar *Mesha, age 18*

commercial art class, and she is trying to "make time" despite an array of demands at school, at work, and at home caring for her mother. What strikes me is Mesha's acknowledgment that her time is not her own—she is caught in a web of time demands with little control. She casts herself in time in multiple ways: aimlessly procrastinating, wasting time, passing time, and "making time" for things that might "develop her artistic values" and life goals.

Her VoiceThread ends with a photograph of her big screen TV (Figure 5.9):

> "Now, you are probably wondering why I took a picture of my TV. Personally? Why not? It is a big TV. I love this TV. I love everything about this TV. I love to have friends over and play movies and play video games and laugh at stupid things on TV and make a lot of noise. And it is very educational, yeah, very educational" [said in a serious yet slightly sarcastic tone of voice].

Mesha is keenly aware of her audience here, addressing the "wonderings" of her viewers about the picture of her television. In her claim that TV is "very educational" set against her "love" for "everything about this TV," I hear again two dueling versions of being in time: the instrumental, purpose-driven kind (including watching television when it is educational); and the relational, "free" kind that is governed by enjoyment, fun, entertainment, sociability. There is a sense of push and pull in these twin experiences of time and its value.

Figure 5.9: (VoiceThread) I love this TV *Mesha, age 18*

One way of being-in-time focuses on self-improvement, accomplishing things, being future-directed; the other focuses on hanging out, the mundane pleasures of "laughing at stupid things and making noise" that cultivate relationships. Compared to how Mesha spoke about her photographs in fifth and sixth grade, there is no doubt that she is overtly and explicitly calling out the dominant and adultist expectation of time ("You are probably wondering") and answering back with playful defiance. The adult perspective is acknowledged, adopted, *and* challenged.

These orientations toward time seem to parallel two forms of time outlined by anthropologist Edward T. Hall in a classic book, *The Dance of Life: The Other Dimension of Time* (1984/1989). His book categorizes cultural systems according to whether cultural members think and talk about time as monochronic (M-time)—time that is linear, oriented toward tasks, schedules, productivity, and concerns about "wasted" time—versus polychronic (P-time) time, which is fluid, flexible, and fundamentally relational, with less concern about completing tasks according to a set schedule. Hall explained that M-time characterizes Anglo-European cultures and is aligned with "official worlds" such as the spheres of government, corporations, and public institutions. Insofar as both experiences of and orientations toward time exist within a single culture, which he claims is true for the United States, the second type of time (P-time) is associated with home and family life; most specifically with mothering. The rhythms of time that it takes to raise children are far from predictable, and require a sense of fluidity and flexibility, a tolerance for chaos, and emotional responsiveness, behaviors that are feminized in a society where M-time predominates.

Since the publication of Hall's book, much has been written to critique but also apply his insights about how these two kinds of time are at odds with and pose difficulties for balancing work and family life. His work has been invoked in examining the frustrations of "stay-at-home" moms who live betwixt and between these unequally valued kinds of time—including descriptions of how stay-at-home moms utilize M-time frameworks (for example, making schedules) to manage the unpredictability of P-time.[20] Here I am interested in how different versions of time are expressed by and resonate with these young people, who are now "workers" in working-class jobs. In their late teens, they are experiencing some of the same tensions and contradictions that they watched their parents confront. Indeed, the dueling versions and values of being-in-time that Mesha points out—much like the discrepancies Hall (1984/1989) identified decades before—were highlighted across the young people's images and accounts, with interesting variations and nuance. Jeffrey, whom readers will remember as my helpful assistant from the outset of the project, provides another of these distinctive yet interwoven temporal perspectives.

## (Re-)valuing practices

I might not have recognized Jeffrey had I passed him on the street, but in his high school setting his welcoming grin was unmistakable. As I reached out my hand to greet him when he entered the office, he moved in with a hug, saying "I don't remember you being so short." I laughed, feeling small in his embrace. He asked if I wanted him to carry my laptop bag—*always the helper*, I thought to myself.

No sooner had we sat down than Jeffrey was exhibiting his technological skills and expertise, helping me bypass the school internet block in order to access the photo website containing the archive of photographs and videos. He laughed at my multi-step way of accessing his gallery of images and took control of the laptop to show me a faster, more efficient way to view the images on slide show. He seemed surprised but pleased by the website. "Wow, I didn't know it would look like this." He laughed at how he used to look, with his buzz haircut and clothes. Not sure of why he might have taken an array of photographs of his room and belongings, Jeffrey sheepishly confessed that he still has his framed baby pictures above his bed and that he has also kept his baby shoes for "memories"—though they are no longer on display on top of his bureau. Of his photograph of the Puerto Rico jersey, he was most certain, "I took it because it is Puerto Rican, because I am Puerto Rican." I take note that he claims an identification as Puerto Rican; no longer the "three halves" ("half Puerto Rican, half Black and half white") he asserted as a child.

Jeffrey's technological skills and expertise were also on display in his VoiceThread, which emphasized his "setup" for playing video games. In his audio segment Jeffrey explained his photographs (Figures 5.10 & 5.11): "This is my setup in my room. This is where I play *Call of Duty, Black Ops*, you already know" (clarifying that his audience is familiar with the game.) "This is my main chair, this is where I spend half of my life sitting with that little cup right next to it, a little beverage [pause] Yep, this is where I spend half my life playing *Call of Duty: Black Ops*."

"Half my life" is undoubtedly an exaggeration of the time he spends. Still, there is no hint of apology about his allocation of time, in contrast to Kim-Ly's acknowledgment that she might better be doing

Figure 5.10: (VoiceThread) This is where I spend half my life *Jeffrey, age 18*

Figure 5.11: (VoiceThread) My gaming chair ... STILL GOOD! *Jeffrey, age 18*

homework than spending time on Facebook or makeup, or Mesha's defense of her time playing video games as preparation for becoming a game designer. Jeffrey added the following comment about his gaming chair (Figure 5.11): "My gaming chair. I got this like 2 Christmas's ago. STILL GOOD!"

I hear this comment as a continuation of the enduring value he places on taking care of his belongings—from the project camera, to the gift of his Yankees jersey, to his baby shoes—a self-positioning reminiscent of his ten-year-old claims, which readers will recall from Chapter 2. Meanwhile, Jeffrey's presentation of himself as an avid gamer drew both humor and teasing from his peer audience as they added comments to his VoiceThread, referring to him as a "gamefreak!" and "nerd."

The graphically violent game *Call of Duty* is a decidedly male-oriented, first-person shooter game.[21] Within the context of contemporary adult discourse, as parents are advised to limit young people's screen time, scrutinize the ratings of video games, and be wary of the "addictive" effects of gaming on kids, *Call of Duty* games in particular might be viewed as cause for alarm.[22] But others see video-gaming as having educational value. At the same time, scholars working in the field of new literacy studies and some school reformers are promoting the connection between (video) gaming, literacy, and learning (Davidson, 2011; Gee, 2003/2007; Gee & Hayes, 2010; Salen, 2011), especially well-designed games that require gamers to navigate complex environments, learn by doing, and produce themselves as flexible learners. The concept of "flow" from positive psychology—defined by Mihaly Csikszentmihaly as "optimal experience … situations in which attention can be freely invested to achieve a person's goals … Thoughts, intentions, feelings, and all the senses are focused on the same goal." (1990: 40–1)—is said to be one possible benefit of gaming. Of the many factors that go into the phenomenon of *flow*, one important one is a sense of timelessness.[23] My point is that the salience of Jeffrey's video-gaming is at the crosshairs of a complex conversation that pivots around multiple issues of time, desire, engagement, technology, and the role of motivation in learning. Again, it is a conversation in which young people may have a degree of agency and voice, but in which adults maintain ultimate control over the terms of the debate.

I find Jeffrey's staging of himself as an avid gamer especially interesting in light of his evolving relationship to schooling. Readers will remember that Jeffrey positioned himself as the quintessential "good" student, as someone who completed his homework and read books on the weekends, not because he *had* to but because he *wanted* to. And he had offered helpful advice for other kids, especially if they were not as fortunate as he was: "Because every kid should like to read at their house if they are bored and have no TV." But in high school, reflecting on his childhood photographs, Jeffrey believes he "set up" certain photographs as a way to make himself "look good for the project," especially the photographs of books—"I would *never* take a picture of a book now," he says, laughing aloud. He is most surprised about the photograph of his homework: "I must have thought I should take a picture like that." In fifth and sixth grade, Jeffrey spoke about a "good" utilization of time, reading rather than watching TV and "doing work" rather "playing around." Even the conclusion of his ten-year-old interview drew on, but also challenged, the adult-sanctioned line between good and bad time use, as he confessed to me with a smile that he usually did his homework in front of the television.

Jeffrey's school-based logic of what would make him "look good" (reading, doing his homework) extends to a photograph he took of one of his learning-group members in fifth grade. Viewing the photograph, he remarks, "Ah, I remember this, I told him to pose like that, like pretend he was working." In the past he had described the photograph as "what is important to me—helping other kids do their work." Then Jeffrey leans in close to examine a blurry and grainy photograph of a classroom—"Cameras back then weren't that good," he says—and then, after studying it for a moment he declares, with excitement in his voice, "I remember this, that is where I used to hang out with the special ed kids! I loved that, just being with them, hanging out." This photograph is not one he thinks he took to make himself "look good," and I detect genuine pleasure laced with nostalgia in his voice. I can't help but wonder what about this activity was so meaningful or significant.

Jeffrey's remembered delight in "spending free time" helping the teacher is worth special consideration because it raises several interconnections between time, identity, and development. As I described in the previous chapter, Jeffrey understood the teacher to be busy (that is, pressed for time, burdened with too much to do); he and his fellow PCS students, in contrast, had time on "free Fridays" to decide what they wanted to do. For Jeffrey, the freedom to "just be" was also the freedom to participate in caring, in helping, in "hanging out," and spending time with others. Spatially the "special ed kids" (as Jeffrey refers to them in retrospect) were marginalized, housed in a classroom in the basement of the school, making Jeffrey's gesture one of inclusion with kids who were not part of his circle of friends. The idea that Jeffrey had the "freedom of time" to spend with kids unlike himself is an idea I will explore more in Chapter 6, but here I want to placemark Jeffrey's past and present allocation of time and its possible meanings for him. First is the value he places on this non-instrumentalist use of time, a relational notion of "just being with." Second is the satisfaction, pride, or pleasure that he gained from this time to care. In juxtaposing the photographs that sixth-grade Jeffrey "set up to make himself look good" with this photograph, which he took to commemorate an activity he loved, two kinds of being-in-time are once more expressed: working-time (time portrayed in a way that would make him "look good" for the project) and relational-time (just "being with" the special ed kids), which involved being present and emotionally attuned to others' needs—as we might remember from his sixth-grade story of consoling the tearful young girl missing her mom.

It strikes me that Jeffrey's association with school and concern about what would make him "look good" are aligned with Hall's (1984/1989) sense of M-time, as is his help keeping learning-group members on task, getting work done. This orientation to time and learning is about efficiency, and its productive focus is absorbed by students and teachers—for example, the "fast" and the "slow" learners discussed in the previous chapter, as well as the distinctions between "free" or "choice" time and recess/"play" time and "work" time. But Jeffrey's memory of joy and pleasure in school was associated with "hanging out" with the special ed kids in ways that were not efficiency-oriented, but care-oriented—affirming the value of P-time within an M-time setting.

Jeffrey's video, entitled *I love Jeffrey Nelson (:* offers an updated version of what matters most to Jeffrey and his efforts to "look good" for the project. It is an interesting variation on the theme of relationships and time. The video consists of a series of interviews with five of his male friends ("my FHS boys") and is artfully shot and edited. Each speaker is framed against a distinctive background at school—a window, a whiteboard, a locker, a white-painted brick wall, and the edge of a green stuffed sofa. The colors are warm and the background school sounds (a bell ringing, shuffling footsteps, muted voices) bring his audience into a space we recognize as school. But what the FHS boys are doing there is at odds with school as a space of adult-directed learning and teaching as depicted in Sofia's video. Instead, "his boys" are cast "hanging out," in control of their time and space. The FHS boys span racial/ethnic groups and skin color (white, Asian, Latino, Black); and viewers get the impression that Jeffrey is at the center even though he is not pictured. The speakers all pay tribute to Jeffrey, praising his generosity, hospitality, loyalty, and spontaneity as a friend. They speak gleefully about the "shenanigans" they have enjoyed together, the boyish pranks they have shared inside and outside of school, and the time they have spent "chillin'" at Jeffrey's home and playing video games. They are not afraid to speak of their affection, to say, "I love you, Jeffrey." The video is a testimony to Jeffrey's enduring self-presentation as "caring" and "cared-for," as special in others' eyes.

Jeffrey's performance not only features himself as a subject of value, it also highlights the importance of sociality (Skeggs, 2011). Jeffrey's self-presentation, his personhood, is not derived solely from school (or his future labor power) but from his *sociality*—the "hanging out" that translates into being connected to, being solidary with, and being loved by his FHS boys. Is Jeffrey positioning himself outside of white, middle-class, college-oriented norms of value that expect him to be investing his time and energy in future employability? Is this also why Jeffrey is so unapologetic about spending "half his life" playing *Call of Duty*? Sociologist Beverly Skeggs might think so. She writes about the moral economy of reality television in a research project she conducted with Helen Wood *Making Class and Self through Televised Ethical Scenarios* (2006–08). They found that:

> [O]ur working-class participants spent most of their time with friends and family in home and local spaces, not involved in improving activities but just 'being', 'with mates', 'chit chatting', and 'hanging out'. In contrast our middle-class participants were anxious to convert all their time into events and activities to generate cultural and social capital. They considered television viewing to be a 'waste of time', suggesting that time was a premium value to be used productively to develop a future. All friendship networks were connected to future enterprise, producing a perfect empirical example of Bourdieu's bourgeois habitus production. (Skeggs, 2011: 505)

I would say that Jeffrey's self-presentation aligns with what Skeggs calls the "valuing practices" of the working-class participants in her study. According to capitalist logic and as further codified in neoliberal policies, the essence of people's value and social worth is economic. To be a "good" person is to be employed, or at least not dependent upon the state for subsistence. "Success" in life is equated with one's wealth; in the hierarchy of economic value, some people's personhood, time, and future are worth more than others'. Skeggs argues that the best chance of value for marginalized and working-poor people, especially those filtered out of the education system, is not financial but moral and affective, and this in part explains the class distinctions she found. I would say that the working-class kids in this project were not overly anxious to convert all their time into events and activities to generate cultural and social capital. They presented themselves as moving between the pull of varied valued activities, from school, to jobs, to family care work, to "self time," "artistry," extra-curriculars, and friend time—all as a means to establish and affirm their value as "proper" and "good" people. Woven into these affirmations were signs of disquiet and self-blame.

## "I don't do much": misrecognizing value

When I reconnect with Kendra, my school tour guide on that first long-ago day at PCS, she can't contain her surprise. We sit in a spare room in her large, comprehensive high school and she keeps repeating, "I can't believe you found me!" She looks much the same as I remembered her, including her signature wide hoop earrings. Her family was forced to move from Terrace Gardens into temporary housing after fifth grade when I last saw her. Despite the principal's efforts to arrange for her to stay at PCS, Kendra attended her last year of elementary school (sixth grade) on the other side of town.[24] Of all the kids participating in the study, Kendra's schooling has been the most disrupted. From kindergarten to grade 12, she has attended seven different schools, including two years in high school in the Midwest while living with her father. Kendra missed her mom "terribly" and so returned sooner than anticipated; as she says, "Worcester is home." Remembering my own experience as a child moving between many schools, cities, and regions of the country, I ask, "Was it hard to adjust to so many moves?"

Kendra nods affirmatively. "Uh huh, I don't know how I did it since I was so shy." She gives a big sigh. "I was so self-conscious because I talked with a lisp. But I guess people liked me. Now I am not that quiet." Indeed, more than the increased volume, I can hear a strong self-assurance in her voice.

Kendra titles her video *The Life of Me*. It opens with a close-up shot of her face against a green-tinted background, her large silver hoop earrings catching the light. An electronic guitar instrumental track plays in the background as she speaks with a flat affect:

> "Hi, my name is Kendra. I am a 17-year-old student at Bridgeport High School, and in a few months I will be attending Worcester State College. I don't really do much because I go to school and work a lot. By watching this

movie you probably won't find out that much about me because my time is…"

Her voice trails off here momentarily, and she rolls her eyes, inviting her audience to fill in the blank.

The sound of an electronic drumbeat and children's voices are heard while the camera cuts to the warmly lit corner of a bedroom. A door is half open and two small boys, perhaps about two and four years old, enter. She introduces them as her nephews and then by name. Her voice is animated and sweetly commanding: "Say hi." The boys move toward the camera and she repeats her request, "Say hi, it's recording." The older boy is playing with a jar of coins and finally obliges her request with a quiet "hi" and a wide grin.

The background music shifts to the pulsing heartbeat rhythm and opening lyrics of Rihanna's ballad "Russian Roulette." The song's bass line ticks like a clock and sets a fitting mood for the next segment of Kendra's video, which is set inside the stainless-steel interior of the industrial kitchen where she works (Figure 5.12).

She moves the camera around the space, zooming in on a refrigerated meal tray (Figure 5.13) and then moves the camera to ask a fellow worker, "What are you doing, Sheryl? Tell them what you are doing."

Sheryl does not look up from her work, nor does she reply to Kendra's question. The camera shakes as it shifts to a large, multi-burner gas stove where a Black woman is texting on her cell phone. She doesn't engage the camera as Kendra introduces her, "This is my sister, the cook." Kendra keeps moving the camera around the kitchen, showing

Figure 5.12: (Video still) Work *Kendra, age 17*

Figure 5.13: (Video still) Tell them what you are doing *Kendra, age 17*

and naming its inventory: "This is the freezer, the coffee.... We don't really do much but make breakfast, lunch and dinner." Her repeated refrain about "not really doing much" puzzles me.

The workplace tour ends abruptly and morphs into a shot of a young Black woman with cornrows, wearing a double-breasted pea coat sitting at a square table in what appears to be a Food Court. She is texting on her cell phone and also does not engage the camera. Kendra says, "this is my best friend eating Chinese food, we are at the mall." The camera zooms into the Styrofoam plates filled with food (Figure 5.14) and then settles on Kendra's face. Shimmering colors refract off the red metal chairs, and the light from store windows casts a dreamy frame around her face where she looks, for a brief moment, alive and energized. But her voice and affect remain flat as Kendra says, "This is what I do with my free time ... when I don't have to work."

Kendra's video foregrounds the theme of work time and its constraints. She warns her viewer from the outset that "you probably won't find out that much about me because my time is ..."; she speaks about "not doing much" at work and ends with "this is what I do with my free time ... when I don't have to work." The steady drumbeat of the background music adds to a sense of Kendra's life as routinized, like clockwork.

I see Kendra's video as an affirmation of her circuits of belonging and being-in-time with family, co-workers, and friends. Contrary to her opening statement, I believe her video *does* in fact tell us much about

Figure 5.14: (Video still) Eating Chinese food at the mall *Kendra, age 17*

her—including her perception that her value might be misrecognized ("I don't do much.") Kendra introduces herself through those closest to her—her nephews, co-workers (including her sister), and best friend. These people correspond to her dwelling spaces: home, work, and "out" at the Food Court; and all are shown engaged in ordinary, everyday activities.

During our interview, Kendra laments her lack of "free time." She has little time for reading (her enduring passion), and there are days she wishes she could get more sleep. She also regrets that she has little time to "be there" for family and friends. Speaking of her efforts to "balance" between high school and work, she sounds as if she is holding herself to some prescriptive model of time management and finding herself falling short. It is as if her "me-time" and "other-time" (her care-oriented time) are being overtaken by "work-time," a situation for which she feels she is to blame. Her way of talking about time seems to me like a very "adult" way of speaking, heavy with the sense of having multiple roles and responsibilities and never having or being enough. It seems to have particular resonance with "mom talk" and the struggle to manage work and family and still have time left for oneself. I take note that Kendra doesn't speak about being "busy" or "overscheduled" with too many activities. She emphasizes that she "doesn't do much" other than work. Her account is also in striking contrast to a discourse that casts typical middle-class teenagehood as "overscheduled" with the stress of extracurricular activities (music lessons, sports, theater, community service activities, private tutoring, SAT prep) and time dedicated to self-improvement (orthodontic appointments, travel, summer camps)—all the activities that constitute achievement culture and a middle-class habitus described by Bourdieu. This deluge of activities, sometimes framed as "resume-building," is most often mandated and managed by middle-class parents as a way to maximize young people's competitive advantage and value in the future (Weis et al, 2014). Kendra, by contrast, "doesn't do much." According to whom? I wonder. Is it because her time is structured around obligation and financial survival, rather than around choice, enrichment, and future marketability?

It is important to keep in mind that Kendra's struggles over time do not belong solely to her; they are shared among many members of her community. For example, Kendra tells me how she is often asked she to "cover for" co-workers who call upon her to work their shifts in the face of family or health crises so they won't get penalized or lose their job. While she appreciates the extra money, it leaves her less time for things she wishes she could do (including the trip to NYC for the project). Similarly, there are occasions when she is asked to stay home with her nephews when they get sick so that her sister can go to work. Kendra's control over time is negotiated collectively with her employer, her family members, and her co-workers. As sociologists Clawson and Gerstel would put it, Kendra is navigating the "micropolitics of the labor process"—the "pushing and pulling, supporting, substituting for, or struggling" required of people as they "try to get the time to do what they want or need to do" (Clawson & Gerstel, 2014: 261). Their extensive research shows that gender and class intersect in shaping the allocation, experience, and control of time. The result is a "time divide" that underwrites social inequality. The authors emphasize that people's time conflicts are not individual or self-imposed, nor is the solution to time conflicts a one-off. Instead, they write, the "allocation and expenditure of time is collective—within and between occupations, within and between organizations, and within and between families" (Clawson & Gerstel, 2014: 14).

Like Kendra, low-wage co-workers (more than managers or employers) are often the ones to create solutions to time-binds in workplaces, especially in workplaces with punitive sick leave policies, by "swapping" or "covering" work schedules. In workplaces with more generous policies, employees need not worry as much about the routine unpredictability of family life—the need to attend a school event or meet with a teacher, take a family member to an appointment, fix a flat tire, or appear in traffic court. The flexibility of time is simply not a resource afforded everyone equally, as the metaphor "time is money" so aptly expresses. Resources available to those in well-paid professional occupations enable more such flexibility, including a sense of more individual control over time. And a greater or lesser ability to "manage" time is likewise not an individual trait, but is embedded in a network of constraints and resources: workplace organization, work schedules, the financial means (or inability) to pay others for an array of family care services, and so on.

This is not to say that husbands and wives in the most advantaged families and working in the highest-paid occupations don't also have time conflicts. They do—and across classes, when conflicts arise, it's more often wives taking up the slack or being in charge of rescheduling, which takes its own time. Gender, class, and race inequalities and time divides are interlaced in complicated ways, especially in care work careers and industries. For example, in the health care industry, nurses, Certified Nurse Assistants (CNAs) and home health care workers—all predominantly women of color —have vastly different resources available for managing the unpredictability of life, as well as different orientations to control over time (from more individual to more collective).

Thus Kendra's orientation toward being-in-time requires her to weigh different strands in the complex and constraining web of time and its relative costs: missing school costs her less than it costs her sister to miss work; taking a co-worker's shift affords her more money but less time for herself, friends, or activities she would like to pursue; and ultimately she blames herself if she doesn't have enough time. She has absorbed the message that time equals social value and that some people's time is worth more than others'—it's an equation reflecting inequality. And this is perhaps the most poignant aspect of her accounting for herself: in her view, her inability to "do much" reflects negatively on *her*, rather than on the unequal social organization of time.

The various framings, experiences, and valuing of time represented by the young people don't fit neatly into M-time versus P-time, although we hear the outlines of these twin temporalities as they spoke about and represented their lives. The first (M-time) is a linear, economic, managerial notion of time as a resource—something to be balanced, saved, spent, accounted for, wasted, invested. The second (P-time) is a relational, non-instrumental notion of time shared: "just being" with others, cultivating social ties, a notion of time that is associated with care, attention, and love. The youth also distinguish between time that can and cannot be controlled. For example, there is the routine of late-night homework time that also mixes with Facebook time or watching movies—activities that the young people have more control over (including swapping sleep time for homework time). That contrasts with time associated with responsibilities that are mandated by family members, supervisors, or co-workers, over which they have little or no control. There is "ordinary" vs. "extraordinary" (that is, interesting) time; school and homework time; work time; family care time; and personal "free-time" that is subdivided into me-time and being-with-others-time.

These variations notwithstanding, across the board, the young people seem compelled to account for what they want to do, what they need to do, and what they think they are supposed to be doing with their time. This is the sense in which I hear and see the young people developing themselves, asserting their social value through their uses of time and defending against the possibility of judgment or devaluation. They seem aware of an expectation that their time should be converted into economic or social value related to future employability. They speak as members of a culture where there is a pervasive "money" metaphor for time (Lakoff & Johnson, 1980). But they also seem to be honoring and valuing a kind of time that, while culturally devalued (that is, "hanging out"), produces a notion of personhood they also wish to affirm. Adhering to more than the capitalist logics of "time is money," the young people seem to be advocating for time to care—elevating the value of time shared for sociability, friendship, camaraderie, and the creation and sustenance of social bonds—without which, after all, society would be unable to sustain itself.

This chapter has developed the theme of temporality and its different types as part of the process of "growing up." Throughout, I have argued that the young people's subjective experience of time is more complex, interpenetrating, and layered than is depicted by adult concerns and anxieties about teenagers' use of time. Nor do available cultural models (M-time and P-time) and metaphors (time is money) fully capture their experiences. In childhood they had characterized themselves on the receiving side of time—time given them by their mothers (she is always there for me), in school by staff members (especially the principal), Free-Friday time, recess time. But as teenagers they were more on the giving and managing side of time—indeed, the language of "balancing" and "managing" time crept into their discourse. Most important, changing demands of time became a key feature in a new and more complex choreography of care. New rhythms created new tensions and pressures within the performances of family, school, work, and community.

As we have seen in this chapter, the young people locate themselves and their teenagehood in multiple spaces (bedrooms, schools, workplaces, cars, malls, social media sites, and so on); varied cultures (racial/ethnic; transnational; social media); time (not enough, lost, managed, in the moment, future-oriented) and affect (love, solidarity, memorializing).

## Digital Interlude #4: Being in Time

⋇ childrenframingchildhoods.com/digital-interludes/being-in-time

Navigating the flow of time and their multiple identities, each person in his/her own way called attention to their development: "times change; that's (not, in some cases) me now."

I conclude this chapter where I started, still lingering over Juan's parting words: "You made us look good, you gave us attention." Reflecting on Juan's/Gabriel's representation of his childhood and multiple identities, I see these are *his* efforts to "look good," not mine. Juan's appreciation for the "attention" I gave—not only to him, but to "us," (his schoolmates, Brown and Black boys like him?)—speaks to more than being given attention: he is acknowledging the significance of being seen as a subject of value. This is a direct challenge to the predominant ways of seeing in schools and in social institutions of social control, where the gaze conveys observation and judgment: "I am looking at you; surveilling you; measuring you; sussing you out as believable, trustworthy, 'good' or not." But it was Juan/Gabriel who used his camera to refuse this gaze, to see and show value and goodness and care as he represented himself, his home, and his mother. His lens was reciprocal and mirror-like: "I see you, I value you; you see me, you value me." This way of seeing also coincides with how the kids of color used their cameras to show certain teachers and the principal, as if to say, "I see you, I value you because you see me, my value and my goodness." His words speak to the subtleties of "looking good" within different systems of value and the yearning to be seen in a positive light.

To consider new, resistive ways of seeing value, care, and goodness requires us to widen our lens and zoom out to consider larger structures and forces of inequality and injustice in schools and society that constrain us. Lois Weis and Michelle Fine might call such lenses— "critical bifocals" (2012) that I take up in the next and final chapter.

# 6

# The freedom to care

As prime sites of social reproduction, schools reflect and reinforce the social processes in which they are embedded. But as critical education scholar Jean Anyon understood, there is liberatory potential here, too. Anyon insisted on looking at schools as sites with "radical possibilities" for resistance, emancipation, and transformation (Anyon, 2005, 2014). She also recognized the power of educational research—particularly as instantiated through ethnography and political economic analysis—to shape, direct, and empower those radical possibilities. Anyon envisioned an agenda for a "new paradigm" of educational research, in which she called on scholars to "document and describe oppression ... study the powerful ... assess efforts of urban communities to create power and opportunity ... study social movements ... study student activists ... and investigate ways to make schools movement-building spaces" (2006: 21–4). Without a perspective that explicitly examines the inequities and injustices in which schooling is implicated, education research is not just limited but can be damaging. As she once noted with characteristic wit, "Attempting to fix inner city schools without fixing the city in which they are embedded is like trying to clean the air on one side of a screen door" (Anyon, 1997: 168).

Jean Anyon was an inspiration to me—as an ethnographer, researcher, colleague, and friend. Her vision and memory are everywhere in this book, but especially in this final chapter. Here I consider what it might mean to "clean the air" that we (and our children) breathe on both sides of the screen door of schooling. I argue that a crucial first step is to acknowledge what the young people in this book went to such lengths to show us: that the promise of public education relies on hidden community and family care work to ensure that children are "school ready." I don't mean this term as it is conventionally understood, as a reference to the literacy and numeracy skills that ensure competitiveness within the school market exchange.[1] I mean a more generous definition of "school ready" as articulated by the children's images and accounts: being loved, housed, fed, clothed, safe from violence, a feeling they belong, and a sense of collective rather than individual engagement in learning. This is the kind of "school readiness" that demands our attention and action.

In this book I have lifted up the counter-narratives and counter-visualities of care that the kids presented about a different version of school readiness. In their depictions and descriptions, the young people challenged deficit perspectives about both working-class upbringings and the under-resourced schools that serve these populations. Equally important, their visual narratives are "counter" because they offer alternative visions of child and youth development in which growth and learning are multidirectional rather than unidirectional, collaborative rather than competitive, social rather than individual. Through their visual narratives, the young people display what I have called their valuing practices—which focus less on individual acquisitions and achievements and more on sociality—and they show how these valuing practices are shaping influences in their own development. Through their pictures and accounts, the kids framed care practices like the air they breathe—as concerted, collective efforts that enable their participation, learning, and belonging at home and in schools. And in these visions of care there are radical possibilities.

In this chapter, I revisit the contours of the kids' perspectives of care as they played out over the course of the project. I examine what these young people have to say about care—its value, its rewards, its invisibilities, and contradictions. Against this backdrop, I consider the current realities of care in a neoliberal capitalist society, limited and structured by gender-, race-, and class-bias; institutional racism and anti-Blackness; and economic strictures that narrow our conceptualizations of time, productivity, and human value. I believe the young people's visions offer much-needed hope—and in their understandings, we can locate possibilities for a new narrative of care. Drawing on the continuing challenges that the PCS students identified and the insights that they offered, I imagine an alternative social orientation in which care and care work take their rightful place at the center of everyday life—highly visible and highly regarded not only in the spheres of family and school, but in the very fabric of democratic society and in our fundamental understanding of freedom and social justice itself.

## Un-covering care: a retrospective view

Remember the school secretary Miss Corey worried that Antonio and Cesar were "covering" for their mother, whose low-wage job required her to be at work before school, leaving them to care for themselves? In that same moment, Miss Corey stretched the rules to accommodate Antonio's lateness to school, and in so doing, "covered" for the unfair demands of low-wage jobs. This metaphor of "covering" struck a chord with me, and its resonance has grown over the course of this project as the kids' images and narratives kept peeling back, *uncovering* both the contours and value of care.

Perhaps the most essential of the young people's insights in this project is their profound basic understanding that care is work: it requires time, effort, resources, and coordination; it demands attention and investment; it is mundane, necessary, and arduous. Its operations (its choreographies) are often complex, intricate, and interdependent—the kids' images and accounts consistently portrayed care as the product of concerted effort nested within social relations (intimate, close, and distant) that are affectively linked with social units and spaces (for example, family, school, friendship circles, workplaces, communities). There is an ecology to this choreography of care, an interdependence between the setting and the way people, time, activities, and objects (the comfort of their things, technology) are arranged. An equally important insight is that care is affective; through caring and being cared for, feelings are mobilized and expressed. These feelings include love, gratitude, reciprocity, obligation, connectedness, and solidarity, as well as pain, anxiety, and fear. And as the young people made clear in their later teen years, the choreographed elements of care shift over time. New constraints of time, resources, and relationships alter the balance and rhythms of care, creating new tensions, pressures, and emotions that are embodied within the performances of family, school, work, and community.

My instruction about the young people's visions of care began on my very first day at PCS in 2003. Though I didn't know it at the time, my fifth-grade tour guides, Kendra and Alanzo, were giving me a first glimpse of the powerful themes that would resonate through all the young people's images and accounts, even a decade later. On that fall day, as they walked me through the halls of their building and pointed out favorite spaces and notable absences, they were proudly drawing my attention to signs of care that would almost certainly have escaped my notice; and at the same time they were also working to address any perceptions I might have of their school as inadequate or lacking. They were priming me to see their school not as a building, but as a dwelling—an assemblage of people, objects, and interactions that could not be reduced to individual elements, but instead worked as a gestalt space of learning, comfort, and relationship. They were directing my vision so I might see where care is hidden: in the nooks and crannies of their dwelling; in efforts to create, sustain, and strengthen the connective tissue between students, parents, teachers, and staff; in the words and gestures, small and large, that made them feel as if they belonged.

The children understood that the connections that enable community don't happen on their own. I devised the term "choreographies of care" to describe the many complex components involved, and to give a name to what the young people seemed to intuit. Different actors are coordinated and set in motion according to the rhythms and demands of family life, workplaces, schools, and a constellation of both private and public resources. The backstage, invisible planning and coordinating of teaching and learning, while not seen, is felt by all those who participate. It was this choreography of care that put the 5 Bs (Be Here; Be Ready; Be Safe; Be Respectful; Be Responsible) in motion, as more than a motto hanging on the wall.

Time-wise, the threads of family, school, and work lives were entangled in a knotty web. Parents' shift work, inflexible work schedules, job loss, the ebb and flow of family activity, family members' comings and goings—all of these created rhythms of time at home that could be out of sync with the rhythms of time required at school. This first became apparent when my guides made the striking assessment that the school's close proximity to their home in Terrace Gardens (a three-minute walk through the concrete school "yard") was better than having playground equipment. This proximity was not trivial. With parents frequently working multiple jobs or double shifts, many children at Terrace Gardens had to feed, clothe, and prepare themselves (and often siblings, cousins, and friends) to be ready to learn. The ability to get to and from school was an essential piece of this preparation for kids who were also in charge of many other tasks: completing homework and collecting parent signatures on school-related materials, organizing their own play, doing domestic chores, caring for younger siblings. While these activities are typically unseen to school personnel, the children made them visible through their photographs and accounts. By the time they were in high school, the distance and movement between home and school had receded from focus. Instead, they depicted an intricate interplay of off- and online time spent navigating school work, family responsibilities, friendships, and, for many, workplace commitments.

In Chapter 2, we saw the children make another gesture of care visible through images of and discussions about their most treasured belongings. The children pointed to beloved objects that often had deep sentimental, if not practical, value: outgrown baby shoes, clothing that they didn't wear, boom boxes that no longer worked, action figures that had never been removed from their packaging, family photographs and drawings—gifts and memorabilia that linked them to their past, to faraway relatives, and to loved ones both present and absent. Photos like these also documented the children's acts of preservation and display, which are themselves crucial forms of care work: honoring relationships, re-telling histories, and maintaining family ties in the face of significant challenges. At the same time, children's peer group discussions about the objects they cherished were opportunities to negotiate—and often agree on—the tokens of value that united them. Big-screen TVs served as evidence of care and belonging, but so did having one's own bed (if not one's own room). Access to cable was universally seen as a cause for celebration; loss of it was likewise jointly mourned. The children's images and accounts reflected a concern for and an engagement with a "politics of belonging" that was deeply social and communal in character. In other words, the young people consistently showed themselves to be far less concerned with "having" than they were with "belonging."

In the photographs of their homeplaces presented in Chapter 3, the PCS youth often chose to focus on the intimate spaces where care work is realized in the form of nourishment. The scenes of small, cozy, dimly lit apartment kitchens had much in common, but the most striking similarity was the predominance of women within them. Mothers and grandmothers stood at counters or over sinks, stirring pots, decorating cupcakes, washing dishes. Many paused mid-motion to glance at the photographer with a half-smile; others posed stiffly and looked straight at the camera. Their expressions suggested their ambivalent feelings as they placed their busy lives on hold for a moment in order to comply with the wishes of children they loved. The kids' eagerness to talk about their mothers (whether pictured in kitchens or not) was striking—in their oral accounts, just as in their images, they gave powerful testimony about the sacrifices, skills, and traits that made their mothers special, and the deep gratitude, appreciation, and reciprocal sense of obligation they felt in return. Even the gestures that accompanied their stories were filled with admiration, tenderness, and love, as they caressed the edges of photographs and held them carefully in their hands. The kids' counter-narratives of family care focused on the intrinsic value of cooking and housework and the skills involved in their production, the pleasure of time spent in one another's company, the difficulties of low-wage employment, and the necessity of "helping each other out." The symbolic capital their mothers embodied and enabled extended to school economies as well, where parental involvement or value might be measured in terms of visibility, or (for many kids) in terms of the quality of homemade goodies for bake sales or school activities, as appraised by teachers and fellow students. One particularly important way for kids to highlight their mothers' value was to assert their educational worth as intelligent and as ardent promoters of literacy, regardless of schooling credentials. Their accounts and images also maintained gendered views about who does what kind of work in what kind of circumstances, offering a window onto discourses in which care work is cast as the "natural," "enjoyable" domain of girls and women, while boys and men demonstrate their masculinity by occasionally "helping out" or "pitching in." Thus even in counter-narratives, hegemonic discourses of gender exert their shaping influence.

In Chapter 4, we saw how these discourses of care as "women's work" also informed the kids' views of school choreographies of care, continuing a long-established cultural conflation of teaching and mothering. Though the school's student population is racially and ethnically diverse and primarily poor and working-class, its teaching staff is overwhelmingly white, middle class, and female. This is consistent with national patterns—the whiteness of faculty in US schools has long been at odds with the diversity of American students.[2] The students did not comment on these differences but instead focused on positively evaluating their teachers—as, for example, "pretty," "nice," "kind," "caring"—and the photos that students took of their teachers showed them smiling, embracing students, adopting silly poses, or otherwise demonstrating good humor and positive attitudes. The children's photographs revealed an effort by their teachers to link *caring* with enjoyment—though the emotional labor that lay behind these displays of enjoyment was unacknowledged and unquestioned. In the racially complex landscape of their school, it was the kids of color who specifically tied teachers' caring to ethical and moral dimensions of belonging: these kids noted how important it was that teachers listened to them, believed them, and believed in their goodness. These same kids were explicit about their sense of vulnerability and worried about fighting and violence, communicating uncertainty and anxiety about their safety as well as a desire to not "be one of them that gets into a fight," to not be perceived as a "bad girl" or a "bad boy." These contours of care are poignant responses to dominant racialized discourses in which Black and Brown children have been systematically denied the "innocent child" status automatically granted to white children.

Many of the children expressed heartfelt appreciation for school staff (nurses, lunch ladies), whose support they saw as an essential part of the community that enabled them to learn. They shared a deep admiration for their principal, whose efforts to secure resources were seen as clear signs that "she really cares about us," and whose disciplinary approach—to "listen to" students, to "calm them down," to "help them resolve problems"—was seen as a particularly powerful form of caring, especially in light of an expectation of more harsh and punitive treatment. And finally, the children repeatedly pointed to the central importance of collaborative and cooperative relationships in their own learning, taking note of how they "help each other learn" in groups. They emphasized that relationality and interdependence are essential elements of a school choreography of care, in which learners are both givers and receivers of help. The ties of mutual regard that we saw so clearly in families apply to schoolmates as well: the children wish to acknowledge the role that others play in their learning and development, rendering visible not only others' acts of caring and helping, but also their own appreciation.

In Chapter 5, as the young people moved from childhood to teenagehood, the choreography of care shifted. In their late teens, their images and accounts featured intra-generational, horizontal care activities, expanding on self-care, obligation, and conflict around the use of time. They photographed things they were explicitly doing to develop themselves and their relationships with others, whether family members, friends, co-workers, or schoolmates. For some of the young people, there was an intensification of their family care responsibilities, including taking jobs to help pay family bills, which compromised their ability to participate in the photography and video part of the project. They described increasing requests from immigrant parents and relatives to translate, connect family members to social institutions (for example, school, health care, social services, local resources), cook and care for ailing grandparents, provide technological assistance, and take part in American popular culture through new media technologies. Those who could participate in the final phase of the project portrayed the hub of their self-care activities taking place in their bedrooms, or in online sites of personal development like Facebook, where they curated and displayed personal affiliations, played with alternative identities, and nurtured social ties. Conflicts over time in relation to care (for self and for others) became more salient, with many young people expressing nostalgia for "free time" and anxiety about the pressures of "productive," task-oriented time. The majority of their time was directed toward school or work, and the easier rhythm of time spent "hanging out" with friends or family was especially missed. As part of their awareness of a constricted web of time, they seemed compelled to account for how they used their time, answering to the negative judgments of an imagined audience (which sometimes included the young people themselves). But despite these conflicts (and perhaps in part because of them), we can see and hear the young people identifying the self-regard, satisfaction, and value that come from both giving and receiving care. The consistency in how they engaged elements of care (of their possessions, friendships, contribution to the family economy), even as the pressures and demands for "productive" school time increased, reveals their sustained ethos of sociality and care.

In the course of the years that I spent with these young people, looking through their camera lenses and listening to their voices, I encountered pictures of care that were at once broader, more complicated, more intimate, more emotionally saturated, and more profoundly discerning than I had anticipated. They shared with me a view of care that was acutely sensitive to individuals, relationships, feelings, timeframes, economic pressures, and scales of value. They recognized where care might be overlooked, and they took steps to address its invisibility, correcting my vision. Again and again, it was as if they said to me and to their audience, "Look here, see? I want to show you that this is important. I don't want you to miss it. This is what really matters."

Of course, that's more or less what I asked for when I devised the initial prompt for that group of fifth-graders in 2003—"Imagine you have a cousin moving to Worcester. Show what's important in your life." But I didn't appreciate at the time how significant the answers would turn out to be, or how far-reaching their implications. In their words and images, the PCS youth offered a vision of care that I believe has revolutionary potential today, in a society where caregivers are chronically unseen and undervalued, where care work has been relegated to the margins and the shadows, and where care itself has often been curtailed, withdrawn, and rescinded where it is most sorely needed.[3]

## Care as public art and engagement

In the PCS students' efforts to render care visible, I see reverberations of work begun decades earlier by the feminist performance artist Mierle Laderman Ukeles. Throughout Ukeles' career, she created installation pieces that forced audiences to confront care practices that would ordinarily take place out of public view (including housework and sanitation work). She characterized her work as describing the tension between two systems of value: on the one hand development, the chief focus of capitalist valuation, representing "pure individual creation; the new; change; progress; advance; excitement; flight or fleeing"; and on the other maintenance, consisting of those efforts that are overlooked or unseen in capitalist logic and in Art: "keep[ing] the dust off the pure individual creation; preserv[ing] the new; sustain[ing] the change; protect[ing] progress; defend[ing] and prolong[ing] the advance; renew[ing] the excitement; repeat[ing] the fight" (Ukeles, www.arnolfini.org.uk/blog/manifesto-for-maintenance-art-1969, n.p.).

Ukeles critiqued the notion that these two could be separated from one another, especially in the art world in which she worked, and she challenged the boundary between "art" and "life." At the time she wrote her influential "Manifesto for Maintenance Art 1969," she had a one-year-old child, and she expressed frustration at the expectation that her identity and work as a mother was expected not to interfere with her identity and "work" as artist. She noted, wryly:

> Maintenance is a drag; it takes all the fucking time (lit.)
> The mind boggles and chafes at the boredom.
> The culture confers lousy status on maintenance jobs = minimum wages, housewives = no pay.
> clean your desk, wash the dishes, clean the floor, wash your clothes, wash your toes, change the baby's diaper, finish the report, correct the typos, mend the fence, keep the customer happy, throw out the stinking garbage, watch out don't put things in your nose, what shall I wear, I have no sox, pay your bills, don't litter, save string, wash your hair, change the sheets, go to the store, I'm out of perfume, say it again—he doesn't understand, seal it again—it leaks, go to work, this art is dusty, clear the table, call him again, flush the toilet, stay young. (1969, n.p.)

Instead of this dichotomy between lauded, innovative, individual public Art and the monotonous, private, invisible, and unappreciated (care) work that enabled, supported, and maintained it, Ukeles proposed an alternative: "MY WORKING WILL BE THE WORK." Ukeles' aim was to elevate maintenance activities in the public consciousness: maintenance, she claimed, *is* art (Figure 6.1).

I see in the PCS kids' visual narratives a parallel aim: to elevate the contours of care in the public consciousness. I do not mean to suggest that the kids were intending to make any particular political, economic, or ideological statement, as Ukeles clearly sought to do. And, as Jillian Steinhauer noted in a recent article on Ukeles' life and career, "Artists—even disempowered female ones—had (and still have) the

Figure 6.1: Mierle Laderman Ukeles, *Washing/Tracks/Maintenance: Outside*, 1973
Part of Maintenance Art performance series, 1973–74. July 22, 1973
Performance at Wadsworth Atheneum, Hartford, CT
Courtesy the artist and Ronald Feldman Gallery, New York

social capital to turn their maintenance work into maintenance art, simply by saying so; [others who do this work, for example, domestic workers, sanitation workers] do not" (2017, n.p.). Unlike Ukeles, a middle-class white artist with a platform from which to advance her views, the young people cannot dictate how their everyday activities will be perceived by others—and they seem to be aware of this, for their remarks about their photographs so often reflect a concern about the perceptions of critical audiences.

The youths' images and accounts also render visible another layer of representation that is distinct from the performance art of Ukeles. The photos capture more than the care work itself; they also demonstrate the young people's regard for creating and maintaining dwellings to accommodate living and learning. They show the figures and markers of honoring care—mothers in tidy kitchens, smiling teachers embracing their students, treasured home furnishings, displays of personal space and belongings in bedrooms—and in the process of viewing each other's photographs they made claims to the dignity of these dwellings. Looking at their photos, we too become witnesses and participants in the children's act of seeing. The process of "picturing care" as I have formulated it here involves subject, photographer, and viewer. Acknowledging the young people's inability to fully dictate the multiple meanings of their images is balanced by the imperative for us, as viewers, to challenge how we see and to value what they are showing us.

What would it mean to take seriously the young people's insights into the centrality of care? What could care look like if care were apparent—if it were publicly acknowledged, appreciated, acclaimed? How might a "carer" identity and ethos be fostered and mobilized in collective, creative activities in schools, workplaces, social policies, and indeed in society at large? And as Ukeles asked in her Manifesto, "what is the relationship between maintenance and freedom; between maintenance and life's dreams"? (1969, n.p.). These are pressing questions that I turn to in the remainder of this chapter. To do so, I stitch together different threads of literature including social theory, social and educational policies, schooling practices, art, and activism with hopes of opening up discussion and debate, and as a consideration of new ways of seeing, valuing, and enacting care.

## Neoliberal capitalism, education, and care injustice

It's essential to note that the young people's counter-narratives and visualities of care, like the narratives and images they challenge, are embedded in larger process of social reproduction. In capitalist societies, these processes take second place to economic production, as if the two were separate and distinct (Davis, 1981; Federici, 2012; Fraser

2013, 2016a, 2016b; Hartmann, 1979; Marcal, 2016). Yet as feminist political theorist Nancy Fraser argues, economic production is only made possible by the processes of social reproduction that lie beneath. She describes social reproduction in terms that echo the themes found in the young people's visions—and counter-narratives—of care:

> Social reproduction is about the creation and maintenance of social bonds. One part of this has to do with the ties between the generations—so, birthing and raising children and caring for the elderly. Another part is about sustaining horizontal ties among friends, family, neighborhoods, and community. This sort of activity is absolutely essential to society. Simultaneously affective and material, it supplies the "social glue" that underpins social cooperation. Without it, there would be no social organization—no economy, no polity, no culture. Historically, social reproduction has been gendered. The lion's share of responsibility for it has been assigned to women, although men have always performed some of it too. (Fraser, 2016b, n.p.)

This view of social reproduction bears on the goals and purposes of public education: how does a democracy produce responsible citizens, support stable relationships, create communities, and sustain social organization? These are precisely the concerns that we saw the PCS principal, staff, and student body embrace through conflict-resolution, non-exclusionary strategies of classroom management, adherence to the "5 Bs," and commitment to group work and peer support, "helping out," "looking out for one another," and "getting to know that person more better." It's clear that the PCS students' investment in social cooperation, relational learning, and interdependence was a core part of their elementary schooling experience—and a fundamental part of their developing identities as learners and "helpers" in their social world. Critical childhood scholars Devine and Cockburn (2018) might refer to these PCS activities as making it possible for children to experience and practice "social citizenship" that among other things relies on a sense of responsibility for others and commitment to the public good.[4]

But while the PCS school community casts these aspects of social reproduction as a central—even *the* central—basis for learning, these are the aspects being squeezed out by the neoliberal policies and discourses shaping American education. For much of the 20th century, the themes of moral citizenship were prominent in the US public education agenda, but in recent decades the focus of policy makers, pundits, and the public has tended instead to be on economic costs and benefits, "winners" and "losers," formulas of monetary investment, the distribution and analysis of national, international, district, school, and individual competitive rankings—all typically reckoned in explicitly quantitative terms.

Among the most influential formulations of neoliberal education ideology was the 1983 report *"A Nation at Risk: The Imperative for Educational Reform,"* released by the Reagan administration's National Commission on Excellence in Education. The report, the result of an 18-month study gathering extensive data,[5] opened with a dire warning and presented education as a critical piece in a zero-sum game of international market advantage:

> Our Nation is at risk. Our once unchallenged preeminence in commerce, industry, science, and technological innovation is being overtaken by competitors throughout the world.... [T]he educational foundations of our society are presently being eroded by a rising tide of mediocrity that threatens our very future as a Nation and a people. What was unimaginable a generation ago has begun to occur—others are matching and surpassing our educational attainments. (National Commission on Excellence in Education, 1983)

The report, at odds with the Reagan administration's own intended policies (for example, tax credits for tuition payments, abolition of the Department of Education), called for changes across five domains: curriculum improvements (stressing math and science as well as foreign language proficiency at early grades); higher standards (addressing grade inflation as well as overall expectations); more *time* in school (a seven-hour day and a 200–220-day school year); improved teaching (and the introduction of performance-based measures); and more federal leadership and fiscal support. At the core of its vision is an image of the ideal schooled child as autonomous and self-sufficient, whose "individual powers of mind and spirit" are developed "to the utmost," whose "own efforts, competently guided" are sufficient to "secure gainful employment." The ability of all children to "manage their own lives" (and serve "their own interests") forms the basis of a calculus in which self-interest rather than social cooperation drives overall social progress. The report rested on the foundations of American individualism—and, it suggested, those foundations were "being eroded by a rising tide of mediocrity."

Part of what is at risk is the promise first made on this continent: All, regardless of race or class or economic status, are entitled to a fair chance and to the tools for developing *their individual powers of mind and spirit to the utmost*. This promise means that all children *by virtue of their own efforts*, competently guided, can hope to attain the mature and informed judgment needed to secure gainful employment, and *to manage their own lives, thereby serving not only their own interests but also the progress of society itself*. (National Commission on Excellence in Education, 1983; emphasis added)

Since the release of this treatise, the focus of US investment in schooling has been on academic achievement, national security, and international competition. Indeed, the "learning/earning" cycle (Feeley, 2014)—that is, the economic returns to education through employment—preoccupies academic study, as well as national and international debate. Global policymakers such as the Organization for Economic Cooperation and Development (OECD)[6] profoundly impact the framing of children's learning in overtly instrumentalist, market-oriented ways. Increasing international competitiveness and an economic "race to the top" have heightened the emphasis on "performance measures" such as standardized test scores.

When education becomes a commodity, narrowly defined arguments of "efficiency," "value for money," and performance objectives take precedence over the idea of education as a transformative experience for an individual that has more than economic value, for example social or cultural value. In neoliberal education, student-consumers are free to choose their paths, free to succeed or fail on their own terms, and individually responsible for their outcomes. The irony of this consumer framework is that it undercuts space for intellectual and social endeavors that don't have obvious metrics or market value. It is important to point out that such neoliberal concepts of education break from earlier paradigms in education at the turn of the 20th century that privileged experiential and critical forms of learning to serve democratic citizenship (broadly defined) and the social good, as in the work of John Dewey, W. E. B Dubois, Jane Addams, and Charlotte Perkins Gillman, to name a few.

The restriction of educational goals and the prioritization of personal (understood as economic) responsibility over social rights and collective engagement has important implications for how learning is being understood and defined, what school curriculum (that is, subject matter and skills) is developed, and whose interests are being served:

> Global business and organizations representing their interests support the idea of the human capital approach to education because ... it emphasizes teaching skills needed in the [corporate] workplace. In this context, human capital goals for education trump other educational goals, such as education for social justice, environmental improvement, political participation, and citizenship training. (Spring, 2015: 5)

Aligned with these human capital goals are narrowing definitions of "child preparation" and "readiness." As Debbie Sonu and Jeremy Benson (2016) observe, these concepts are tools for keeping the next generation of neoliberal subjects firmly in their place within the dominant social order:

> Readiness is not preparedness for participation in the building of a more just and humane society through feminist, anti-racist, and/or anti-capitalist grassroots struggle. Rather, readiness is a mode of socialization that seeks to prepare the child to participate uncritically in the status quo, however detrimental these already existing material and ideological conditions may be to the child's own well-being, let alone the survival of other people. (2016: 238)

Eclipsed from this instrumentalist educational vision are human *care* goals—the meanings, pleasures, responsibilities, and solidarities that fuel social progress. The omission of care goals and the narrow neoliberal conceptualization of "readiness" deny young people and teachers access to powerful instruments of change.

Everyone knows that schools cannot function and children cannot learn without care. Yet the full contours of care have been and continue to be marginalized in, if not absent from, debates about what is "at risk" in the educational foundations of our society.[7] Public discussions and debates about why schools are "failing" do not explicitly address the fundamental care inequities and injustices that undermine children's growth and well-being. These inequities stem from interlocking twin public disinvestments: the failure to invest in low-wage working families and communities of color, and the failure to invest in public education. Steep cutbacks in education spending and the reorganization of public education according to market principles have squeezed out investments in the full contours of care needed in schools. Against the backdrop of unevenly distributed economic growth, those with the fewest care resources (for example, time, money, material goods and services, good health, safe neighborhoods) are held back in an increasingly competitive education system that favors those with the most resources to support children's learning advantage. Those who cannot supplement the system from their own resources suffer the greatest disadvantage. These trends are not limited to the United States; within neoliberal welfare systems around the world, childhood inequality deepens rather than decreases (Cantillon et al, 2017).

Paradoxically, schools are being forced to cut back on the care aspects of children's lives at the very moment when childhood poverty is increasing. According to the Pew Institute, children under the age of 18 are the most impoverished age group of Americans, and African American children are almost four times as likely as white children to be in poverty. A recent UNICEF report found that the US ranked 34th on a list of 35 developed countries surveyed on the well-being of children. Kathryn Edin and H. Luke Shaefer (2015) report that in 2011, about 20 percent of poor American households with children—about 1.46 million households—were surviving on $2 or less per person per day in a given month. They write: "The prevalence of extreme poverty rose sharply between 1996 and 2011. This growth has been concentrated among those groups that were most affected by the 1996 welfare reform." (p. 4) Despite bi-partisan championing of the neoliberal-inspired "welfare reform" (known as Personal Responsibility and Work Opportunity Reconciliation Act, or PRWORA), study after study has shown that it has severely harmed poor families, and driven Black and Latinx children and families into deeper poverty (Schram, 1995; Albelda & Withorn, 2002; Handler & Hasenfeld, 2007; Deprez & Gatta, 2008; Collins & Mayer, 2010; Morgen et al, 2010; Ahn, 2015).

Passed in an era of rising nativism, the PRWORA was a radical piece of legislation that barred immigrants with documentation from receiving major federal benefits (some of which were restored by Congress in subsequent years). The legislation changed public assistance from a federal entitlement program to state block grants, giving states enormous flexibility on how to spend funds. It restricted eligibility for cash welfare (now called TANF, Temporary Aid to Needy Families); introduced a five-year lifetime limit on these benefits; and imposed strict work requirements. Paralleling the *Nation at Risk* ideology that elevated employment goals and economic competitiveness over all else, TANF became singularly focused on work supports rather than family supports. Overseen by federal "Work Participation Rate" regulations, states had to meet targets for getting poor parents into jobs or face losing federal funds. Parents had to meet employment targets or face losing benefits, but four-year college no longer counted as a work-related activity that made a person eligible for benefits.[8] This effectively closed the door to the surest route out of economic hardship for poor women and their children: access to higher education (Adair, 2001; Polokov et al, 2004; Dodson & Deprez, 2017, 2019).[9] And as public investments in education and social welfare declined, demands for family care intensified, falling heavily on the shoulders of already over-stretched, economically excluded and marginalized mothers (Albelda, 2011)—and, by extension, on their children (Dodson & Albelda, 2012).

Care inequalities extend beyond US borders. Hochschild (2002) relates how a "chain of care" propagates care insecurity on a global level as women from the Global South migrate for care-service jobs in the Global North leaving their own children behind in the care of others (Daly & Standing, 2001; Ehrenreich & Hochschild, 2003; Hochschild, 2000, 2002; Yeates, 2004). For these mothers, global capitalism appears to offer a solution to pressing economic need: by providing care work to the privileged global elite, they are able to send remittances home to feed, clothe, and educate their own children. The solution is tainted, however, as migrant mothers who leave their families for work are often subjected to mother-blaming (Lutz, 2011). Rachel Salazar Parreñas (2001) describes how migrant women are caught between a rock and a hard spot, at once subjected to "the ideology of women's domesticity even as the economy promotes the labor market participation of women" (2008: 23). Young people are similarly affected by the chain-of-care cycle. Understanding the complex circulation of care in and through households, Lauren Heidbrink (2018) observes that it is not only mothers but young people themselves who are relied upon to participate in transnational care-giving across borders and generations.

What puts a nation at risk is not mediocrity, but the care crisis—the gendered and racial organization of care work, rooted in the legacies of slavery and colonialism; and the intensification and privatization of care demands.[10] What puts a nation at risk is the way that the human capacity for care and care activities are treated as resources to be stolen, exploited, and treated as limitless, as infinitely available—without need for replenishment or investment. Nancy Fraser draws a parallel to the way nature is treated within capitalist logic: as an "infinite reservoir from which we can take as much as we want and into which we can dump any amount of waste" (2016b: n.p.). The environmental movement has begun to make headway in challenging this logic and to warn of the imminent dangers. However, there has been less focus on the dangers posed by neoliberal capitalism's treatment of the activities of care as individual commodities rather than collective goods, and as a burden to be shouldered by women and children—particularly women of color and their children.

Interrogation of these dangers is, of course, against the interests of those who benefit most directly from the status quo. For those who hold wealth and power, "the commodification of care" has paid accruing dividends. The wealthier you are in the United States, the more you can purchase care services to lessen care obligations and live the myth of "independence." The more economically advantaged a family is, the more they can afford to depend on others to provide basic care needs (food, laundry, housekeeping, child care) and an array of care services (shopping and grocery delivery, shuttling children to and from school and after-school activities, paying bills, doing taxes, home and car maintenance) that facilitate busy family routines and workplace demands. I include myself and my family in this, having relied on house cleaning services and an indispensable childcare worker who smoothed the often frayed edges of a dual career household. But purchasing care establishes more than assistance with maintenance work. When some groups of people are excused from basic caring responsibilities because their work is perceived to be more important, a culture of "privileged irresponsibility" arises (Tronto, 1993: 103–4). The hidden reliance on others' services keeps people from paying attention to the complexity and value of the work that must be done to keep not only family life, but public institutions running smoothly. We become inured to the built-in gendered and racialized inequalities that play out behind the scenes in our families, communities, and institutions.

The artistic practice and interventions of Ramiro Gomez (Figures 6.2–6.5) mentioned in Chapter 3 draw attention to these inequities. His paintings suggest the lack of attention, if not disinterest in those who do the work of care and maintenance. His blurred figures—faceless nannies, housekeepers, gardeners, and handymen—are painted into affluent domestic scenes sometimes taken directly from ads and photo illustrations in magazines like *Architectural Digest*. Though his figures are faceless they are not without identities; Gomez gives them all names in the titles of his pieces (Weschler, 2016: 9).

Gomez's depictions of "homemaking" in affluent America beg the question of whether these people belong or not in the picture—and whether the picture is of home or of nation. For this is one of the ugly secrets of global capitalism: it coerces some people to care in order to allow others to enjoy "privileged irresponsibility." The responsibility to care is "passed on"—whether it is from men to women, from women to poorer and yet poorer women, from white people to people of color, and from wealthier nations to poorer nations.

The core of the problem is that care resources—including such basic resources as clean water, shelter, education, health care—are increasingly framed as private or personal goods to be "freely" purchased through the marketplace, rather than as public goods to be equally distributed as part of social rights.[11] Under a model of social organization that focuses on "personal responsibility" (rather than on "social rights"), significant numbers of parents and children living in poverty and working for poverty wages face untenable choices that cannot be described as "freedom." Readers will recall Antonio and Cesar's mom, for example, whose failure to get her sons to school on time was noted by the school secretary. She cannot "opt out" of work to raise her children, or even shift her hours in order to transport them to school. She is not "free to care" for her children in the same way that those with more "freedom" can "opt out" of work and raise their children or "free" to work and hire help. Those with more "freedom to care" get more of it, while those without it fall deeper into servitude.

Under neoliberal frameworks, "freedom" is construed as the ability to participate in the market, to work as hard as one can, and to accumulate wealth. The ideal employee is available at all times, never late, and never required to leave early or take extended time off to care for others who may depend upon them for various reasons. Ideologically these so-called care-free employees support a particular version of a capitalist work ethic, while serving as justification for blaming and stigmatizing those who can't find or hold a job, or who are shut out of the labor market altogether. This notion of being care-free is so embedded in capitalist requirements of workers that we almost fail to notice it.

A similarly distorted notion of freedom operates in American education, where children and young people are assumed to be "care-free," unencumbered, and able to focus all their time and energy on individual academic achievement. That vision is sustained in middle- and upper-class families, who can afford to arrange chains of care or full-time stay-at-home support to ensure their children's competitive advantage. The success of these care-free children helps to sustain the educational ideology of meritocracy, promoting the idea that those who rise to the top have done so because of their own effort and merit, while those who fail have only themselves to blame. The same ideological implications are extended to schools serving families of means: schools with care-free students support a particular version of school success while serving as justification for blaming and stigmatizing

Figure 6.2: Ramiro Gomez, *Estela and Dylan*, acrylic on magazine, 11x8.5in., 2013

Figure 6.3: Ramiro Gomez, *Esperanza*, acrylic on magazine, 11x8.5in., 2013

Figure 6.4: Ramiro Gomez, *Laura and the laundry*, acrylic on magazine, 11x8.5in., 2014

Figure 6.5: Ramiro Gomez, *Eduardo, the day laborer*, acrylic on magazine, 11x8.5in., 2013

those schools who fail to measure up to imposed standards. According to this logic, then, "failing schools" also have only themselves to blame.

But for countless working-class families and for the schools that serve them, the care-free child is a myth—and neoliberal models of education have refused to acknowledge how this disparity disadvantages children who are not, in fact, care-free. Students who struggle are cast as exhibiting "gaps" in exposure, achievement or motivation, rather than being constrained by the outstanding "debt" owed to them for years of educational neglect and care-less policies (Ladson Billings, 2006). The calculus for what counts as evidence of educational success is individualized and measured by a high-stakes test score, which is de-contextualized and disconnected from the realities and (in)adequacies of care resources. Similar to the main tenet of the capitalist work ethic, the education work ethic is focused on production and productivity, not care and social reproduction. The individualist, competitive performance model requires a self-(rather than other-) oriented stance that justifies leaving the weakest behind.

Most troubling about idealizing the "care-free" student is that it leads to a conception in which freedom means not having to care. Even if it were possible to ensure that all students were "care-free," is this the notion of freedom we want in a democracy? I argue that it is not. Being "free" from care responsibilities—"free" to act on self-interest, "free" to operate, untethered and uninhibited, in the market—corrodes the social fabric of connection, community, and solidarity across differences. Being "free" in this sense depends on care that is commodified, coerced, and invisible. This notion of freedom is impoverished and damaging.

The "passing-on," chain-of-care approach, the resulting culture of "privileged irresponsibility," and the social and educational policies that keep these in place undermine notions of freedom and justice.[12] And perhaps it is because many children of the working poor are linked to this chain that they are so powerfully able to render, in images and in words, the full contours of care and its transformative potential. By making visible the dimensions of care work and signs of care that take place in the privacy of individual lives and homes, the young people invite their viewers to take part in a process of public reflection that puts care and its value squarely at its center.

## Seeing (care) differently: what we learn from Terrance

Figure 6.6: Sometimes we stop at the corner store *Terrance, age 11*

One image made by a fifth-grader named Terrance works especially well to demonstrate both the need for new ways of seeing, and the profound insights that can arise when care becomes visible. Over the years since I began this research, I have presented Terrance's photograph (Figure 6.6) to scores of educators-in-training, teachers in faculty development workshops, graduate students, and conference participants. Following the protocols of collaborative seeing, I ask audiences to reflect on the question, "What is going on here?"

Not once has a viewer's interpretation of this photo come close to the young photographer's account of what is taking place. Most often, viewers read the photograph through the lens of childhood consumption, a snapshot of a "kid in a candy store" on the way to school (or perhaps on the way home from there—the backpack signaling school). Some see the innocence of childhood pleasures. But others have seen the moment as foreboding—a young person (most likely male) in a hooded jacket, arm outstretched to reach for a piece of candy. As if taking on the gaze of a suspicious shopkeeper's surveillance, some viewers have projected an assumption of furtiveness, imagining that the boy is about to steal something.

Terrance, the 11-year-old Haitian American responsible for the picture, offers a different account: he had handed his camera to a local shopkeeper and asked him to photograph a part of Terrance's after-school routine:

"After school I walk my younger cousins home and help them with their homework. Sometimes we stop at the corner store and I get a candy bar so they will get their work done quick, 'cause I have to check it and make sure it is right before my aunt gets home at 6.30 [p.m.]."

Once they are all safely home, Terrance splits the candy bar into pieces, using each bit to bribe his cousins. His effort, much like feeding the family, is *work*. It rests on collective activity and an ethic of care— networks of engagement that include the shopkeeper, who agreed to take the photograph and who, Terrance reports, doesn't charge him for the candy bar. I want to argue that Terrance's care work is of considerable civic significance—yet our eyesight has been pressed into seeing something quite different.

Terrance is among an estimated 1.4 million American children from ages eight to 18 who provide care for a sibling or older adult, including approximately 400,000 children who are between the ages of eight and 11.[13] Aside from routine tasks of cleaning, shopping, laundry, and supervising younger family members, children's care work also extends to caring for ill and disabled family members—dispensing medication, lifting, dressing, bathing, communicating with doctors or nurses, and keeping a care recipient company.

Far too little research has been conducted to help parse out the scope and dynamics of children's care-giving. What roles do gender, race, ethnicity, culture play in young people's care-giving experience? How can we calculate the value of children's care work in filling the gaps of a health care system? How can we calculate the value of children's care work in subsidizing the low-wage work of their parents? And how can we incorporate these calculations into an educational opportunity debt owed (Ladson Billings, 2006) to those children and youth caregivers who are not "free" to learn, and who often fall behind or are forced to leave school?[14]

Overall, the extent of the PCS children's labor to support their own and others' schooling was noteworthy, but it was presented as routine, not occasional or exceptional. We might think of this care work as "education brokering," reminiscent of what Marjorie Falstich Orellana (2010) called "language brokering": the unrecognized work that bilingual immigrant children perform for non-English-speaking family members as part of everyday family life—paying bills, accessing social services, translating at doctor's appointments, and so on. Using a socio-cultural rather than a normative developmental framework to assess children's language brokering, Orellana maintains that the cultural tools that children are afforded as part of this practice—in institutional contexts such as schools, libraries, and hospitals, as well as in other public spaces such as parks or businesses—should be seen as strengths rather than deficits. Even more striking, Orellana casts children's language brokering as a form of valuable civic engagement done for the public good.

What if we were to think of the care work being done by children growing up in poor and working-class families in similar ways? What if we attended to how Terrance and his PCS peers—and millions of working-class youth—work for the public good, brokering educational access, participation, and belonging for themselves and others? How would this shift in seeing children's care work change the way we think about "family involvement," family-school relations and family supports? And what if we put the PCS children's portrayals of their family choreographies of care—including their presentations of self as grateful helpers motivated by love and obligation—into dialogue with cross-cultural and cross-class research about children's work at home?

For more than 40 years, extensive research has been devoted to children's participation in household tasks. Findings in that field suggest that middle-class children in the US contribute far less to family domestic work than children do in other societies around the globe.[15] The class character of children's household responsibilities within the United States has also been documented. Middle-class children's family responsibilities are understood to lie in their accomplishment of academic work rather than housework, reflecting the belief that children are too busy with school and extracurricular activities to help at home (Harkness & Super, 2000; Lareau, 2003; Ochs & Izquierdo, 2009).[16] By contrast, poor and working-class children's lives have been characterized as overburdened by family responsibilities. Sociologist Linda Burton refers to this as a form of "adultification" that is out of sync with the demands of intense and early achievement for future success (Burton, 2007; Burton et al, 1996). And as we saw in the PCS students' discourse in Chapters 3 and 5, their relationship to family care work was complicated—at once a source of pride and self-regard, as well as ambivalence and constraint.

But rather than constructing explanatory or predictive variables about class-based childhoods, I am more concerned that we look and listen carefully to how the PCS children portrayed signs of, anxieties about, orientations toward, and values concerning care as a centerpiece of their lives. The PCS youth have something vital to offer here: like them, we must insist upon the dignity of care work. This means learning to regard care as something beyond routine need. The young people in this study pictured, understood, and appreciated the work of care for its intrinsic value. When asked to take pictures of "what matters most," they trained their lens on what they recognized as good, as valuable, as identity-defining, and as a source of meaning in their lives. Embedded in their pictures and accounts is the understanding that care is more than work, more than duty, and more than obligation—though it is all of these things, too. Care is a social good; it is necessary to civic society in a way that cannot be understated. Care is the basic currency of community—indeed, in a democratic society, it is the precondition of freedom itself.

## Appeals for time and dignity

That mainstay of capitalist theory—the idealized autonomous economic agent who acts exclusively based on rationality and self-interest—underwrites the individualism of the American work ethic and dominates public policy (Folbre, 1994; Folbre and Bittman, 2004). We are more than rational actors and self-sufficient beings; we are interdependent, relational beings who come into human-ness through connection. As Cynthia Willett has written in *The Soul of Justice: Social Bonds and Racial Hubris*, "The deep sources of human meaning, the capacity for alienation and outrage as well as joyful recognition lie in libidinal forces of human connection" (2001: 28). Our freedom rests on the capacity to flourish with others in history, culture, and communities *through care*. We discover who we are by caring, by being cared for, and by creating and maintaining social bonds through relationships of care.

As I noted in the beginning of this book, working-class labor struggles have historically focused on demands for time and the dignity of work. In part this is because capitalism gets in the way of the time caring takes, the dignity caring embodies, and our deep desire to care for loved ones. No one knows this better than poor mothers, who animated the Welfare Mothers' Rights movement in the 1960s and 1970s. Susan Hertz (1977) describes the shared principles that linked together several overlapping welfare rights organizations and activism within states and across the country: 1) self-determination, specifically the right to choose between staying at home as a full-time mother or going to work; 2) human dignity; 3) organizing welfare recipients to achieve their goals; and 4) political influence on the institutions

affecting welfare mothers' lives (1977: 602–3). At the heart of the
National Welfare Rights Organization message was the sense that
"welfare mothers knew more about welfare than [the legislators] did"
(1977: 603) and would provide the best insight into a range of welfare
issues, most especially regarding their children. An important aspect of
this social movement was challenging the stinging, racialized stereotype
of welfare mothers as lazy, nonproductive, and purposefully scheming
ways to secure benefits (a "controlling image" of Black women, to
use Patricia Hill Collins's (1998) term). To make their appeals to the
welfare system and its administrators, welfare mothers mobilized two
discourses: their rights as citizens and their rights as clients.[17] While
the movement's larger goal to change the economic system and create
real opportunities for welfare mothers was not realized, women who
participated in organizing efforts gained a sense of their ability to make
change for themselves and on behalf of others (Hertz, 1977: 610).[18]

In following decades, these principles would be tapped and expanded
by Black women and other women of color who called for reproductive
justice, forming groups such as SisterSong and Asian Communities
for Reproductive Justice. SisterSong identifies three core principles
of reproductive justice, according to which every woman has the
human right to:

> Decide if and when she will have a baby and under what
> conditions she will give birth;

> Decide if she will not have a baby and her options for
> preventing or ending a pregnancy;

> Parent the children she already has with the necessary
> social supports in safe environments and healthy
> communities and without fear of violence from individuals
> or the government. (https://trustblackwomen.org/
> our-work/what-is-reproductive-justice/9-what-is-
> reproductive-justice)

Whether their specific concerns are framed as human rights or as
citizenship claims, social movements like these illustrate that freedom
to care and time to care are inextricably linked to the conditions of
social justice—they are not a question of individual choices and access.
The freedom to care can only be realized if intersecting issues and
oppressions are addressed—from immigrant rights, to economic and
environmental justice, to women's rights to bodily self-determination,

to rights to sovereignty, to criminal (in)justice, to children's rights, which here I define as the rights to safety, protection, self-expression, and the presumption of goodness that is the foundation of self-worth and well-being.

Perhaps it is no accident, then, that appeals for time and dignity were consistent themes in the young people's images and reflections. I believe we must take these appeals seriously. What might it mean to dignify care, to have time to care—for kids, for families, for schools, and for civic society?

Even as our neoliberal policies encourage us to look toward the marketplace for fulfillment and to ignore or devalue tasks and activities that have no practical commercial value, the need for care makes inevitable incursions into everyday life. Socks do not, unfortunately, wash themselves and levitate magically into drawers. Sick children do not schedule illnesses at their parents' convenience. No matter what else we do, we must eat, drink, and sleep. We need clothing, shelter, and some modicum of affection and connection. All of this means that as human beings, we are likely to spend a great deal of time in our lives on earth engaged in one form of care work or another.

Yet somehow this time is neither assessed nor valued in the metrics typically used to characterize societies and economies. Marilyn Waring's (1999) groundbreaking feminist analysis of global economics pointed out that the measures used to calculate Gross Domestic Product (GDP)—and, in turn, to determine qualifying conditions for aid and trade—exclude all work of care for dependents and households, including subsistence farming, on the grounds that none of this work produces "value."[19] By contrast, illegal activities such as prostitution, the arms trade, and the drug trade are counted as activities producing value, because they involve the exchange of money. The result, Waring argues, is a systematically distorted and inaccurate measure of a nation's wealth and welfare—yet this erroneous measure continues to be used to determine international policy. To assess economic value, Waring suggests measuring time use instead.

Time-use studies and census data have shown that housework (including the work of care for dependents, and the care and maintenance of households that sustain them) takes an enormous amount of time and energy. In many cultures, "housework" includes subsistence farming, fetching water, and gathering food; in places where people have been driven off their land, "housework" would also include scavenging. Even in wealthy nations, "housework" dominates, as has been shown by time-use measures and census data in Canada, Australia, New Zealand, and the UK. For example, the first set of household accounts published in the United Kingdom in 1997 showed that people (gender unspecified) spent more time in unpaid work in the household sector than they did in paid employment. While there was considerable dispute about how that unpaid work ought to be valued, "whatever rate was chosen, the value of unpaid work in the household sector was greater than any major industry within the production sector, including the whole of the manufacturing industry." In other words, "*the household was the single largest sector in the economy.*" (Waring, 1999: xxviii, quoted in Weir, 2005: 317). To drive home the point, Allison Weir writes: "If the definition of care work can be broadened to include the work of care for the household that sustains dependents, then care work takes more time and produces more 'value' than any other kind of work on the planet" (p. 317).

We are adept at calculating the output-per-input productivity measures of "clock-time" or capitalist "working hours." But these metrics aren't suitable for measuring care work, and an exclusive focus on time efficiency is utterly incompatible with the valuation of care. The time structures of care work are not rigid and fixed, but flexible and plastic. Imagine how it is to deal with a sick spouse, a child's toothache, a family member who needs a ride, a friend or neighbor or loved one who becomes seriously ill, a friend who needs a favor, a death, a birth, a child's celebration, a holiday, a feast, an impromptu visit or a planned one—care makes different demands of time, and they rarely happen one at a time. Activities can become suspended, juggled, fluidly or abruptly shifted; they can be more or less synchronized, more or less compatible, more or less urgent, more or less enjoyable.

Care work is the biggest investment of time that we make in our lives. Moreover, as feminist economist Nancy Folbre (2008) argues, parenting is one of the most important undervalued contributions people make to the overall economy, ensuring that there will be a next generation of productive citizens to finance the old age of increasing numbers of Americans. Those without children reap the social benefits of parenting, but don't pay its private costs—what Folbre calls "reproductive free riding." Children are not "pets," conceived and reared for private satisfaction. Folbre argues that the "family work" that it takes—in time, energy, and finances—should be rewarded, not penalized as it currently is. In an economy that that does not value care-giving, the high "price" of parenthood (but especially motherhood) is one more factor that pushes women and children in poverty, an unjust penalty.

Second-wave feminists pointed out the degree to which family care work has been leveraged as a form of an oppression—recall Ukeles' bitter observation that maintenance "is a drag." The intersectional feminists of the third wave, however, like the children who walked the halls of PCS and Terrace Gardens and grew up contributing to family survival, pushed the argument in another direction, one that lifts up care as an intrinsic value in its own right and a source of resistance (Moraga & Anzaldúa 1981; Delgado Bernal, 2001; Federici, 2012; hooks, 1984, 1990). How can we avoid participating in economic systems, chains of care, and unjust penalties that erase the invaluable contributions of care—whether by design or by default? The young people's images and insights suggest that the answers lie, first, in learning to see care; and second, in learning to see care differently, in a way that recognizes and values the time, dignity, skill, feelings, and community ethos that care embodies.

## The freedom to care: an urgent need

I noted earlier that the children in this study viewed care as a token of value and a responsibility. This view strikes me as especially poignant as the United States reckons with the current Administration's impact on immigrant families, people of color, women, and trans people. As I write these words, I am aware of the many ways in which care has been not merely overlooked, not merely undermined, but actively impeded through acts of state-sponsored violence and cruelty.

It's important to note that many of the federal policies implemented or suggested since 2016 rely on ways of characterizing public life that separate individuals from communities and divide "us" from "them"—whether it is in terms of the Muslim travel ban, forcible family separation at the border, insisting on dichotomous biological sex assignments as either male or female, criminalizing those who seek refuge/asylum, turning our backs on longtime allies, or the campaign slogan and promise of "America First." These characterizations are neither subtle nor unintentional. During a visit to the US/Mexico border to meet with migrant children, the First Lady famously wore a jacket emblazoned with the words "I really don't care, do U?" This brutal message, the swirl of attention that it garnered in the national and social media spheres, and the surrounding tide of anguished speculation about its intended meaning are all symptoms of an urgent need. We must re-envision care in the United States. We must recognize that care takes diverse forms, carries powerful meanings, and is in itself a distinctive, fundamental collective good, a civic obligation, and a basic human right.

To reclaim and re-envision care would mean shifting reference points from a static focus on individual capacity, production and achievement to a dynamic focus on the power of sociality, connectedness, deep caring, and desire for relationships. These are the kinds of orientations that foster liberation politics in movements like Black Lives Matter.[20] At the same time, re-envisioning care means understanding well-being as more than an individual imperative, as educator Shawn Ginwright suggests:

> Rather than viewing well-being as an individual act of self care, healing justice advocates view healing as political action. Healing is political because those that focus on healing in urban communities recognize how structural oppression threatens the well-being of individuals and communities, and understands well-being as a collective necessity rather than an individual choice. (2016: 8)

It also means shifting understandings of citizenship from "independent worker" to "interdependent caregiver." Both Nancy Fraser and Allison Weir provide models toward this end. Fraser's "universal caregiver" and Weir's "global universal caregiver" conceive of the citizen as enmeshed in local and global webs of interdependence.

In the citizen–as–worker model, we are expected to work for pay, and to have the freedom to do so. In the citizen-as-(global) caregiver model, we are expected to do care work, and to have the freedom to do so. By combining these models, we would both enrich our sense of reciprocal obligations to each other and expand our practical definition of freedom. At the same time, the organization of work would be made compatible with care, and civil society (not only families) would be recognized as a sphere of care. Work would not just be "family-friendly" as we perceive it now, but care-friendly, supported by an equitable distribution of care resources and an infusion of public investment. Meanwhile, if we are to acknowledge that child-rearing and childcare are things that we desire, and not just social burdens, we need to seriously re-think the individualist, childless model of work. And this means re-thinking the nature and purposes of work, and the means of servicing and repairing human needs and desires. A culture of democratic care would endeavor to unlock global care chains and refuse the often-hidden gender, race, class, and anti-immigrant biases that constitute the bedrock upon which social needs are currently met.

One place this work must begin is also the place where this project started, and where the seeds for this book were planted: in the formative, enduring sites of social reproduction that we call schools and childcare facilities.

## Prioritizing time for playful work in school and society

As we have seen throughout the book, time surfaces again and again as an essential precondition for the freedom to care. It's "free time"—like PCS's "Free Fridays"—that enabled kids like Jeffrey to choose to "go help some kids who need help" and to experience the satisfaction and relational fulfillment that caring provides. Time to "just be" or to "hang out"—without instrumental, task-oriented, or measured goals—is something that many of the young people lamented the loss of as they looked back on their childhood photographs. Readers will recall that this kind of time was already fleeting by fifth grade, when on my first day at the school, Alanzo drew my attention to a red tricycle sitting in the middle of the gym. I can still hear the longing in his voice as he reminisced, "I rode this bike all the time during free time when I was little." His poignant request that I photograph the tricycle was prescient of reactions to come.

This kind of "free" time for unstructured play is not only disappearing from schools, but increasingly from childcare facilities, where the nation's youngest children are being prematurely inducted into standardized instruction (Crain, 2003; Ginsburg, 2007; Elkind, 2007; Santer et al, 2007; Pellegrini, 2005; Rogers & Evans, 2008; Brown & Vaughn, 2009; Miller & Almon, 2009; Linn, 2008; Nicolopoulou, 2010; Paley, 2010; Persons, 2017). In the US a recent report from the Alliance for Childhood summed up the situation for kindergarten:

> Too few Americans are aware of the radical changes in kindergarten practice in the last ten to twenty years. Children now spend far more time being instructed and tested in literacy and math than they do learning through play and exploration, exercising their bodies, and using their imaginations. Many kindergartens use highly prescriptive curricula linked to standardized tests. An increasing number of teachers must follow scripts from which they may not deviate. Many children struggle to live up to academic standards that are developmentally inappropriate … At the same time that we have increased academic pressure in children's lives through inappropriate standards, we have managed to undermine their primary tool for dealing with stress—freely chosen, child-directed, intrinsically motivated play. (Miller & Almon, 2009, p. 15, quoted in Nicolopoulou, 2010: 1)

There is a growing, and misguided, consensus that children growing up in poor, working-class, and immigrant families will benefit from more direct instruction in preschool as a means to promote their emergent literacy skills. This view, coupled with the press of accountability measures and the over-reliance on standardized testing, has resulted in a designation of playtime for these children as a lower priority, if not wasted time. Yet it is through play—especially unstructured, all-absorbing, social pretend/fantasy play—that children develop cognitively, creatively, and imaginatively, exercise forms of agency and identity, and develop social competencies, including cooperation, interpersonal understanding, perspective taking, and the like. At the same time, the nature of children's play is shifting as they engage in popular culture and utilize new technologies, creating what some have referred to as "high-tech" childhood (Miller & Almon, 2009)—and these developments are coupled with ever-increasing warnings about the dangers of too much "screen time," whether in the form of computers, televisions, or cell phones.[21]

These trends have been described as the "play gap." In 2002, researchers found that only 79 percent of children had recess time. Looking more closely, racial disparities were revealed: only 61 percent of African American children and 75 percent of other minority students were afforded recess, compared to 85 percent of white students. Class disparities were even starker: only 56 percent of children living below the poverty line enjoyed recess at school, compared to 83 percent of children living above the poverty line (Roth, Brooks-Gunn, Linver, & Hofferth, 2002, quoted in Jarrett, 2003). In 2007, the Robert Wood Johnson Foundation conducted a study looking across a series of factors: school size, location, region, minority enrollment, and eligibility for free and reduced-price lunch. The report shows that playtime is being squeezed out most in large, urban schools located in the Southeast that have high levels of poverty and large minority populations.[22] Added to the play gap is the routine practice of denying recess to children who misbehave, a strategy that has been shown to disproportionately affect Black and Brown children, and especially boys.

Aside from nourishing well-being, play is considered a defining feature of childhood, if not a right for all children, as codified in Article 31 of the UN Convention on Rights of the Child: "Children have the right to relax and play, and to join in a wide range of cultural, artistic and other recreational activities" (UNICEF, 1989). Advocates for the benefits of childhood play understand that there is more at stake in protecting time for play than initially meets the eye. There is liberatory potential arising in and from the site of children's play (Katz, 2011).

Cindi Katz organizes her argument by first reviewing all the ways in which poor, historically marginalized Brown and Black children have been made "disposable" in the United States. Multiple factors are to blame: the disinvestment in their schools and communities and the poor conditions that result; the school-to-prison pipeline that disproportionately affects kids of color; environmental disasters that most directly affect poor and non-white communities; and routine, normalized violence. Around the globe, Katz points to war, famine, and land-grabs that have ravaged local economies and made vast numbers of poor children "disposable" and thus open to recruitment as child soldiers, members of street gangs, and equally dangerous forms of child labor. These influences curtail any semblance of what counts as "childhood," let alone time for play. Against this bleak background, Katz lifts up forms of play she observed in rural Sudan as prefiguring new visions of "playful work" and "workful play":

> For example, they played vivid 'geo-dramatic' games of 'fields,' 'store,' and 'house,' wherein they created miniature landscapes which they animated by enacting the tasks and social relations associated with agriculture, commerce, and domestic life. In these activities the children transformed local debris, domestic waste, agricultural detritus, scraps, and dung into amazing imaginary worlds of farming and economic and social exchange in which they had a place; even a future. They internalized, worked out, and expressed the economic relations they saw around them, but with a little bit of a tweak—a gesture toward utopia—no one went broke, everyone had at least some assets, the exchanges were relatively equal, often riotous and always exuberant. (Katz, 2004, quoted in 2011: 56)

This is what unstructured play and recess afford: time for imaginary worlds of care, for "gestures toward utopia" that are generative and full of possibilities, even in the face of grim realities. If we think about childhood play time as valued—not as time wasted, as it is so often framed—we can begin to reassess educational as well as societal priorities. Perhaps we can imagine childhood time not as a finite era that is "lost" or "stolen." Perhaps instead we can imagine it as a *quality* of time that can be experienced as "playful work and workful play" in educational settings, and that can also be preserved into adulthood.

## Imaginative critical childhood inquiry and pedagogy

As adults who are meant to protect the margins of childhood spaces and facilitate trajectories of learning and socialization, we need to revise our own roles and ways of seeing. This kind of revision won't happen on its own—it must be cultivated over time through research practices and pedagogical methods that are both critical and imaginative.

In this book, I have presented my own attempt at imaginative inquiry, which uses kids' images and accounts as a basis for engaging in a new kind of intersubjective and dialogic reflection that I call collaborative seeing. Through photography, the working-class kids of PCS became agents of visibility, documenting the care they receive, providing and asserting its value, and insisting that their families, homes, friends, teachers, and networks of care receive the attention and recognition they deserve. The project opened dialogue and reflexivity among the kids about their intentions and identities, their audiences, and the "multi-directional interactions between looker, looked-at and selves" (Restler & Luttrell, 2018: 466). Through the acts of discussing, sharing, curating, and exhibiting their images, the children and young people found powerful ways to bridge differences and create solidarities. Through the process of looking back on old images and younger selves, and picturing their current selves in time, they expanded their lens on relations of love, care, and solidarity to reveal new patterns of obligation, constraint, and meaning. Throughout, they took opportunities to resist stigmatizing or deficit-based visions and to assert their valuing practices.

Time and again, adult audiences who interacted with the audio-visual archive found that the experience made them "see differently," forcing them to acknowledge the ways in which their seeing is limited. Collaborative seeing offered them an opportunity to confront the assumptions they held about children and youth, including deficit-oriented ways of seeing, and to challenge and transcend them. The transformative potential of this approach depends on being open to its investigative possibilities: A photograph can suggest answers to questions we might not have thought to ask, nor indeed have otherwise recognized as necessary questions. This is what the kids' ways of framing childhood did so effectively, from my perspective, and it drives the analysis that runs throughout this book—that the kids used their cameras to address and enact an ethical and moral imperative that is not only hidden but actively undermined by contemporary schooling and society: to care and be cared for.

To re-envision contemporary childhoods and practices of care depends, first and foremost, on a leap of imagination. This leap is happening elsewhere, too, and there are other forms and settings in which critical childhood inquiry is inviting and incorporating new ways of seeing care. Marjorie Falstitch Orellana (2016) offers an especially salient example. Her inquiry is based in an innovative after-school program in Los Angeles. The program, called B-club,[23] serves immigrant children from Mexico, Central America, and the Philippines (ages 5–10). All are English learners growing up in low-wage households and living in neighborhoods with limited access to safe play spaces and parks. The adults in the program are UCLA researchers and university students who want to learn *from* and *with* the kids—not to hijack their play in service of what they want the children to learn. One caregiver reports, "We don't try to 'get' kids to learn particular things, but instead seek to move *with* them into a kind of 'flow' experience" (Orellana, 2016: 130, emphasis in original). The adult B-club participants offer some scaffolding for play activities, but not in scripted or standardized ways; and it is love, caring, and curiosity that propel learning, rather than performance goals and measures.[24]

Amazing "playful work and workful play" occurs in B-club. Unlike in school, where time is heavily structured around standardized learning, drilling, and testing, time at B-club is unstructured and kid-directed. Kids are free to move; make noise, art, or other things; take part in or sit out of activities; and make use (or not) of the rich resource materials available (paper, crayons, paint, blocks, cardboard, musical instruments, computers, and so on). "Rules" are covenants created by kids themselves: "Say hi!; be safe; play; listen; be responsible; be over/ understanding; be respectful; be nice; have fun; give advice; say please and thank you; give aliens a chance, too" (Orellana, 2016: 19). As long as they abide by those agreements, they can "do anything they want."

Orellana gives many examples of the kinds of productive, connection-oriented games and activities that the children chose to pursue in their after-school hours at B-club. One particular play activity shows them embracing the freedom to care on the boundaries between home and school, between childhood and adulthood, between private worlds and public display, in ways that resonate deeply with the images and accounts of PCS kids. Taking over tables, chairs, cardboard, tablecloths, and blue plastic tarps, B-club children built, decorated, and "lived in" their own B-club dwellings while their adult caregivers looked on (Orellana, 2018).

From her adult vantage point, Orellana describes the intimacies of the spaces created by the children, the objects they made, and the belongings they put inside the dwellings. She reflects on the dual meanings of home—as fortress, barrier, and protection from the world on the one hand; and as an outward reflection of inner states, experiences, and sentiments on the other. The children's dwellings seemed poised on this boundary of private and public, intimate and open—a complex situation that posed challenges for curious (and, sometimes, concerned) adults.

Members of the research/instructional team had questions about what the homes meant: "What does their play in these homes reveal about [the kids'] understandings of home and their home cultural practices?", "What does their home-making reveal about their understandings of the larger social world?" Answers to these questions would require the kids to invite the adults into their home spaces, and such invitations were not always forthcoming. Despite their curiosity, many of the adult researchers felt voyeuristic, if not invasive or threatening (especially at a time of intensified fear about deportation and the raids on migrant families by US Immigration and Customs Enforcement ICE agents), and they made the conscious decision not to intrude. The university students, by contrast, were concerned about their inability to see inside the dwellings, and raised questions about kids' safety and the need for boundaries and surveillance: "What do the kids do in these homes?", "Why do they want to be in there?", "How can we supervise them?", "What limits should we put on their home-making?" There was a worry, an overtone of anxiety, that fueled the undergraduates' ways of seeing (Orellana, 2018).

Neither group of adults felt comfortable joining into this play to learn how the children were making sense of their home-making. But by exchanging their views, the adults did learn about themselves and the lenses they were using to observe. For all participants—kids and adults alike—Orellana argues that an invaluable transcultural competency is being developed at B-club. She called this "an empathic quality of the heart: a *willingness* to connect across differences, and an *openness* to building such connections." (2016: 81). For B-club staff, this means learning to expand their vision and curiosity. By exchanging their observations and curiosities about the children they move with and alongside in their play, the adults come to see children's learning differently. By asking why their attention is drawn to particular things, people, conversations, and activities and not to others, the adults can discover that they don't all see and hear the same things—and that "we can never see schools, classrooms, or kids with virgin eyes" (Orellana, 2016: 32), nor can we see through children's eyes. This awareness of differences in vision can push adults to examine the assumptions that shape their ways of seeing and to question the conclusions that they might draw about children's learning, dwelling, and being.

## What we owe our children

I see a powerful connection between the home-making play of the kids in B-club, the photographs and videos made by the young people in this study, and the children in Sudan observed by Cindi Katz. Each group of kids freely chose to render visible practices of care, and through their activities, each regarded home-making as a fundamental human capacity to be practiced, celebrated, and valued. Home-making holds "creativity and power" to transform experiences of marginality into an "inclusive space where we recover ourselves" and are fully recognized (bell hooks, 1989: 23). The "radical possibilities" that hooks describes present themselves every day at the borders of home, community, and school. Mundane acts of care—cooking, home-making, helping, teaching—can be the sites and substance of social transformation. They inform our ideas about what it means to live in a social world. More promising still, these acts of care can model, instill, and develop the tools we need in order to negotiate and provide for the needs, interests, equality, and interdependence of *all* children and adults. As the kids in this study understood so clearly, care is at the core of our collective well-being.

I believe that an additional lesson can be learned from the kids of Park Central School and from children like them: they are the architects, inventors, expert witnesses, and creators of their *own* worlds of play, care, and belonging. And although as adults we may not be able to fully apprehend the meanings they are making—the beauty and generosity, the dignity and integrity, the harms, fears, and insecurities of their worlds—it is incumbent upon us to strive to learn from them. This also means unlearning ideas, stereotypes, and deficit perspectives that we have inherited about children and youth, especially young people of color—whether these ideas are about who they are and what we want them to become, or who we believe them already to be.

As adults we can nourish and learn from young people's social and imaginary worlds. We can remain open to the forms of care that young people see and wish us to see; and we can stand ready to honor the goodness, love, and creativity that they identify. We can prepare ourselves to leverage the rights and responsibilities of care in their favor, and to cultivate a freedom to care in our society at large. Our instruction must start from the assumption of goodness, not badness, and we must meet transgressions with care and inclusion, not harm and exclusion. And all of this must be a collective endeavor, not a solitary pursuit. This is the lesson in freedom that educator, activist, and scholar Carla Shalaby writes about: "No single one of us has the creativity, the courage, or the skill enough to teach love and learn freedom alone. This is work that requires an imagination developed together, the courage of a community, and the combined skills of each member of that community" (2017: 179).

We cannot afford the "passing-on" approach to care or the culture of privileged irresponsibility it engenders. We must make time to care a priority, and we must develop a way of seeing that allows us to ask and answer the enduring questions that underpin our social fabric: What is the relationship between care and freedom? What is the relationship between care and life's dreams? What are the responsibilities of one generation to another? And how can we make sure that these relationships are fostered not only in kitchens and classrooms, but also in civil society? We need to fashion more collective settings—childcare centers, schools, after-school programs, youth arts and leadership programs, community centers, religious organizations, civic entities— where children, young people, and adults can address these questions in intergenerational communities of care, fostering solidarity within and across generations.

This is the clean, welcome breeze that should blow through the screen door between schools and society. It is what we owe our working-class youth, our immigrant youth, our minoritized youth, our youth of color. It is what we owe all our children, our families, and ourselves: an orientation to care that acknowledges and celebrates the privileges, responsibilities, and affective dimensions of caring. We owe them, and ourselves, a valuation of time measured not in hours, minutes, or dollars, but in pleasure, fulfillment, and inherent worth. We owe them, and ourselves, an approach to education that focuses more on cultivating growth than on quantifying it, and that makes time to care (and care for relational time) an essential part of everyday learning and citizenship. We owe them, and ourselves, a model of social progress that prizes "workful play and playful work," recognizes the dignity and inherent value of care work, and promotes social policies based on such a model. And finally, we owe them, and ourselves, an unwavering societal commitment to that most basic form of social order and transformation—the universal freedom to care.

# Postlude

# Notes on reflexive methods: past, present, and future

In the Prelude I mentioned that this book is not the one I envisioned when I began this project. This is not the first time in my research career that I had an inkling of a certain kind of project that morphed into something else. Indeed, the same could be said of all of my past work about inequality and education: without fail, the process of reflexive qualitative research has led me to rethink and reshape my questions, my interpretations, and my understanding of my roles and responsibilities as a researcher. In this "Postlude," I offer a personal meditation on these issues, which veers at times into the biographical as well as the methodological, the ethical, and the aesthetic. By doing so, my hope is to more thoroughly account for the choices I've made in the present work, but also to offer a portrayal of reflexivity in action over time—a process that is necessarily particular, but also intersubjective, permeable, and continually evolving.

## Style, not speed: a resonant theme

It is a fair question to ask whether or not the early life of a researcher is of interest to readers of an essay on methods. But the shaping influence of youth exerts itself in uncountable ways, and as the data and characters in this book suggest, the imagery of childhood offers powerful tools for reflexive analysis. My aim in this section is not so much to relay a memory as it is to describe the earliest appearance of a theme that has come to characterize my work in what has come to be known as slow sociology. (Skeptical or impatient readers may find it preferable to skip to the next section.)

In the summer before I started fifth grade, my family made one of our many moves, this time from Texas to New Jersey. To help us meet new kids and make friends, my mother signed my younger brother and me up for the swim team at the town's public pool. I did not know what to expect—in Texas we had learned to swim in a nearby lake, which I found preferable to a swimming pool's closed walls and chlorinated water. But I loved to swim, and I dutifully attended swim practice every morning.

Being painfully shy, I sat at the pool's edge, away from the circle of all-white girls who seemed so comfortable in their blue tank suits and suntanned bodies. Unlike the other girls, I didn't wait for our stocky, middle-aged, white male coach to bellow his orders. I was the first one in the water, eager to begin the regime of our required laps. I loved the meditative rhythm of lap-swimming, the full-body sensation of graceful movement and attention to breath that I never felt on land. I felt buoyed without effort, and my mind was free to wander.

One day, after a few weeks of this pleasant routine, the coach took out his stopwatch. Suddenly, lap-swimming changed. The pressure set in; each day was a race against the time set the day before. I resented this imposition—it made me feel inadequate, unable to measure up. After some weeks, the coach pulled me aside after practice. "I don't think you are trying hard enough; if you don't increase your speed in the next few weeks, you won't be able to compete in the season tournament." His stern voice unnerved me. I was silent for a moment, not sure what to say. Then, lightheartedly, as if to break the tension, I said, "That's okay, I don't swim for speed. I swim for style." I can still hear the mocking tone of the coach's voice. "Ha! You like to swim for *style*, do you?" And then, more gruffly and loud enough for other kids to hear: "Well, don't bother coming to swim team practice anymore."

I felt ashamed and humiliated, but I held his gaze without flinching and then headed for the locker room as my eyes swelled with tears. As I left the pool that morning, I contemplated my situation. I didn't want to compete. I wanted to swim laps, and that certainly didn't require being on a swim team. But I worried that my mother was going to be upset. I considered lying and telling her that I had quit the team, but I couldn't formulate a story that I thought would be acceptable. Maybe I could feign a stomachache and delay the inevitable truth-telling. Later that night, after I had finished washing the dinner dishes, my mother asked me if I had anything I wanted to tell her. "Tell you what?" I said with forced cheer, bracing myself for what was coming next. To my great surprise and relief she smiled and said gently, "That you like to swim for style, not for speed."[1]

My mother was fond of telling her version of this story, especially the part about her conversation with the annoyed coach who had phoned to tell her of her daughter's preposterous remarks. I remember wishing I could fully embrace the positive spin my mother had made of my experience—I was not as confident as the story made me sound.

I share this episode because I think it illuminates two important themes in my work in general, and in this study in particular. First is my confrontation with the tyrannical pressures of the stopwatch, which has echoed through my career. In academia, as in so many other aspects of modern life, the press of time seems constant. The impositions of competition, clocks, schedules, timetables, and calendars are relentless, and scholars' careers, like our investigations, are expected to proceed apace—smoothly, efficiently, without disruption or delay. Like my fifth-grade self, I have at times felt embarrassed and defensive about taking "so long" to complete my research projects, and on those occasions I have asked myself, whose timeline I am judging myself against, and to what end? I firmly believe that our entire educational enterprise from Pre-K through higher education and university life, and indeed our society at large, imposes unrealistic time frames in counterproductive and competitive ways. We over-value the M-time described in Chapter 5—time dedicated to productivity rather than relationality—and we fixate on concerns about "wasted time" or excessive "free" time. Our educational policies emphasize outcomes over process and create assessment practices that obscure the most important and meaningful aspects of learning, teaching, and knowledge creation: the need for "free" and "play" time, for risk-taking, innovation, collaboration, and a sense of the collective good through advocacy and activism. None of this can be captured in measures of efficiency, and none of it will register on a stopwatch. It's about style, not speed.

Second, this story speaks to the challenges of taking up a critical childhood perspective. Recognizing the complexities of children's agency and intentions means also considering how much they rely on, respond to, and sometimes defy adult-controlled activities (like swim teams, schools, and families). The coach, my mother, and I all had different visions and versions of my agency. I remember being more frightened by the coach than I was angry or defiant. I also recall vividly how relieved and supported I felt upon hearing my mother's reaction, even as I recognized that her understanding of me was partial. And wider discourses of gendered expectation as well as class and racial privilege no doubt shaped my agency and form of resistance. I was a white girl among other white girls, coached by a white male coach in a well-resourced suburban town. What might have happened had it been my brother who expressed the same non-competitive inclinations? In New Jersey in the 1960s, how might the same coach have responded to a child of color who professed to swim for style, not speed? A critical childhood perspective means considering possibilities like these, and asking how children's agency reflects, challenges, maintains, and changes the social parameters in which they are cast.

My commitment to "style, not speed" has been foundational to my learning, teaching, and research practice. The word "style" has baggage—it can be understood in class terms, to connote elegance or grandeur, or something "popular" or "in fashion"—but this is not how I mean it. I mean "style" as my particular manner of doing things—my method, in other words. Coming into my style as a researcher has been about being open to taking time, being present in time, persisting over time, aided at times by unearned privilege to do so. This last qualifier is the most problematic. As I've tried to emphasize in this book, time to care—about work, about family, about community—should be free to all for the taking.

## Beyond comparison, toward care: the evolution of a career in slow sociology

I have written elsewhere about the need for qualitative inquiry to be responsive to researcher-researched relationships (Luttrell, 2000, 2010). In my first project, reported in *School-Smart and Mother-Wise: Working-Class Women's Identity and Schooling* (1997), I learned that participants have their own agendas and agency in shaping research. That study focused on white and Black working-class women who completed their schooling later in life.[2] At the outset, I was interested in their reasons for returning to school as adults. What conflicts did they encounter? What supported and what hindered their studies? Why was it important to them? What similarities and differences would be apparent? I spent two years in each of two settings as a teacher and an observer, first working with the all-white participants in a women's education program in Philadelphia that I had co-founded (my dissertation research); and then working with a group of Black women enrolled in a workplace adult education program in North Carolina that I coordinated.

In my efforts to learn about the women's reasons for returning to school as adults, I was met by the familiar refrain: "You want to know about my life? I could write a book about that." I had not expected to elicit life stories or to encounter the narrative urgency with which the women spoke to me about their childhoods and schooling. To receive the women's stories and do them analytic justice, I had to re-tool. I read new literature, crossing from a symbolic interactionist-inspired sociological orientation into an anthropological, life-story orientation that led me into a different form of listening which I identified as psychoanalytic. Despite my awareness of the many criticisms and blinders of psychoanalytic theorizing—including, especially, the flawed notion of a "normal" path against which people's life stories can be evaluated—I found it useful to pay close attention to how the women were making sense of their own stories of development. Their narratives persistently pitted good protagonists against bad antagonists or set good personal attributes against bad in their struggle to achieve a visible, worthy, and credible self. I was struck by unexpected memories and feelings that would sometimes interrupt the flow of their telling in what sounded to me like tangents. Over time, I learned to not only be open to, but to pay close attention to the women's unanticipated tangents and associations—particularly about their mothers—and gradually I came to pay more explicit attention to my own feelings about what the women were expressing and my own tendency to avoid or skim over themes I had not foreseen in my research plans.

With more self-awareness, I returned to all the interview material and uncovered a general pattern of maternal images and mixed feelings about mothers as well as teachers. The women had repeatedly acknowledged and referenced these complex images and feelings, but I had minimized them in my analysis. A new line of questioning emerged from this finding: why had school memories evoked such compelling maternal images and conflicts? What model of schooling was being brought into play as of result of these co-constructed interviews? Considering these questions enabled me to make stronger links between a web of themes and patterns I was hearing about knowledge; race, class, and gender struggles of identity; and desires to "become somebody." Initially I had heard the women's conflicts comparatively; indeed, the study had been designed to highlight similarities and differences. I found several. Both groups claimed not to be school-smart: the white, Philadelphia women spoke of having "common sense," while the Black, North Carolina women spoke of being "mother-wise" or having "real intelligence." Both had mixed feelings about being (or not being) a "teacher's pet": the white women claimed to have rejected or eschewed that label, while the Black women noted that it was denied them because of their darker skin color. Both confronted the sense of being disregarded, but where the white women spoke of feeling silenced, the Black women told about the sting of feeling invisible.

My new way of listening also helped me identify trends that couldn't be exhausted through comparison. I came to understand the women's identificatory struggles as being a personal *and* structural feature of their particular school contexts (all-Black rural community schools compared to all-white urban public and urban Catholic schools), which produced distinctive associations and experiences. Despite these differences, all the women described schooling in terms of a vivid relational world of women (teachers, mothers, daughters) that, among other things, was split between "good" and "bad," "idealized" and "devalued," "us" and "them." My research journey tacked back and forth from group comparisons, to individual lives and feelings (including my own—a topic I had preferred to avoid), to comparing school contexts, back to individual lives, and then to the racially segregated and patriarchal organization of schooling.

As my research evolved along these circuitous paths, I also found myself confronting the joys and anxieties of motherhood. Being pregnant during fieldwork and bringing my two-year-old daughter to play with the Philadelphia women's children as I conducted the interviews at kitchen tables established an important observational and empathic bond between the women and me. My move from Philadelphia to Durham, N.C. disrupted this and shaped the parameters of the second research context. This move was followed by a shifting choreography of care in my life: divorce and shared parenting; job instability and financial stress; re-marriage; and a new baby born with medical issues (my pregnancy and new baby were much fussed over by the North Carolina women, and once again cultivated invaluable, caring connections).

Throughout the research process I felt a strong sense of attachment, reciprocity, and obligation born over time to all the women I had interviewed. Indeed, this sense fueled my commitment to finish a book that had been a very long time in the making. It was not a solitary, but a collective effort driven by reciprocal care (thanks to the women, my family, friends, mentors, institutional resources, and a fellowship award). It left an indelible mark on my career as an academic.

There are interesting parallels between my first project and this one. There is the shared topic—the nexus in which schooling contributes to and reflects powerful constructions of childhood and motherhood, and the complex feelings surrounding these constructions and intersectional identities—but this time my aim has been to center the analysis on children's perspectives. There has been the need to re-tool and revise— just as the women's life stories and the force of maternal images and feelings pushed me in new directions, so did the PCS kids' treasure trove of images and accounts, albeit in different ways. As my relationships with the young people stretched out in time and the world around us changed, I found that my older ways of doing visual analysis were no longer sufficient for the task. My leap into more experimental forms of analysis and representation is due to technological advances and the growth of digital scholarship—and also required creative collaborations, which I describe in more detail later.

And just as major life events shaped my early career, they have also affected this work. Several years into this project, my teenage daughter suffered a traumatic brain injury. Her recovery taught me more about patience, the coordination of care-giving as a collective effort that relies upon a host of resources (including time, money, transportation, flexible work hours, supportive colleagues), and shifts in the choreography of family care to meet new challenges. My daughter had accompanied me at times during the project; she met with the kids and helped them make PowerPoint presentations and videos for the public exhibitions, earning the special affection of girls in the second and third cohort (2004–05; 2005–06) who told me they liked my daughter for her humor, helpfulness, and fashion style. The feelings these connections forged were made evident by the care and concern so many of the kids expressed to me during my daughter's healing. Then came a move and new job that changed the pace of data collection and made it particularly challenging to follow through on my promise to be back in touch with the kids in middle-school. I was fortunate to have the help of the PCS principal (she had taken a new position) and the generosity of the high school principals who helped me get in contact once I had re-settled. The travel from NYC to Worcester also took its toll (time-wise, financially, physically). I don't know what I would have done were it not for Facebook as a means of planning, scheduling, and being in touch once the second stage of data collection was in full swing. Once again, unanticipated life events, reciprocal care, new and enduring relationships, and much-needed resources made the project possible. Extraordinary research team members, invaluable new colleagues, and institutional support converged like planets in a universe bringing new possibilities and collaborations. Finally, a fellowship award[3] secured the time I needed not only to write, but also, as it happened, to recover from a debilitating nine-month illness.

There is a parallel as well as an extension/corrective I wish to draw about my affinity with "slow sociology." It is the concept of being "open to disruption"—a phrase that sociologists Anita Garey, Rosanna Hertz, and Margaret Nelson (2014) offer in their edited volume, *Open to Disruption: Time and Craft in the Practice of Slow Sociology*. I identify with the 17 authors in this volume, who write their own stories about taking (or being forced to take) more time than they had anticipated completing their projects. For several authors, it was *care work* that was disruptive and meeting care and relationship demands with openness that was generative, as it has been in my experience.

I wish to extend this thought further. To make a better world, it is the imperative of and freedom to care in our research—for ourselves, family members, participants, community members, those beyond our proximal relationships, and the world we inhabit—that opens us to disruption. Our method is to meet disruption as necessary, as its own way of knowing and form of repair. Time, craft, and enacting care are the elements of slow, transformative sociology.

## Research as a social art form

In my second research project, upon which the book *Pregnant Bodies, Fertile Minds: Gender, Race and the Schooling of Pregnant Teens* (2003) is based, I turned to visual art-making as a means to elicit participants' perspectives and experiences of being pregnant in school. The teenagers that I worked with were predominately African American (they called themselves Black); all of them had chosen to attend the same self-contained alternative public school for young mothers-to-be. I wanted to know how the "girls," as they called themselves, understood the stigmatizing labels and racialized public debates surrounding teenage pregnancy, and I learned that conducting interviews or collecting life stories was not the best approach. Instead, in addition to the traditional methods of participant observation (which I sustained for a five-year period), I engaged five cohorts of ten girls in a series of creative activities: using teen magazines to make media collages in response to the prompt, "Who Am I?"; creating self-portraits made out of hand-made paste paper and writing personal stories to accompany them; engaging in a theatrical role-playing exercise called the "freeze game" (Boal, 1979), in which the girls enacted a recent life event. These research activities were meant as an opportunity to "play," get "lost in," or "transported by" art-making. All manner of free-floating conversations and associations could occur—there could be no "mistakes," only surprises. I tape-recorded our sessions together so I could trace and analyze the topics, themes, and social interactions that emerged during these activities.

As I began to comprehend the degree to which the data centered on the girls' insights and dilemmas about their self-representations, I also saw my researcher role changing. My agenda began to focus on nurturing creativity and self-expression among the girls, and on providing them "opportunities for appearing" (borrowed from anthropologist Barbara Myerhoff, 1992) as a means to imagine new possibilities. I wanted the research to provide a space for the girls to not only respond to stereotypical images others held about them, but to create images of their own design, imbued with their own meanings.

"Playing" with the girls also transported me. As a participant in one of the role-plays, I was assigned to play the character of a girl at her first clinic visit. In the skit I was harshly treated and demeaned by the "nurse," which took me by surprise and put me on edge. I described the multi-layered insights I had from this dramatic encounter (Luttrell, 2003: 120–3) and the various ways my play-acting and the girls' reception of it could be interpreted: as a test, an invitation to enter the girls' punitive world, an initiation of sorts, a twist on or re-positioning of racial dynamics, an attack on a stigmatized self which I had been unable to defend, and which led to conversations about the importance of my need for a tougher armor, and finally, a keen awareness of my whiteness and white privilege.[4] My embodied participation in the play—as opposed to mere attentive observation—resulted in my refusal to settle on any one interpretation and to hold the possibility of multiple and conflicted emotions.

I came to understand my project as a "social art form," a phrase anthropologist Karen McCarthy Brown (1991) so eloquently employed to describe how the full complexity of human relationships is what drives ethnographic research and must be open to both "aesthetic and moral judgment. This situation is riskier, but it does bring intellectual labor and life into closer relation" (1991: 12). Through my relationships with the girls and through the process and products of the girls' arts-making, I drew inferences and lifted up what I called their "bodysmarts"—a term describing the gap between how they imagined themselves and how they felt they were being objectified and stigmatized by others. (For the girls, this mismatch elicited both insight and pain, so the dual connotations of "smarts" seemed fitting.) I followed formalized methods of the interpretive turn that were forged in the 1980s and 1990s—combining narrative and discourse analysis— but never questioned or experimented with the representational form the research would take. The publication that resulted was a traditional word-driven text with color and black-and-white images of some of the girls' collages that I curated. But the project took other, less traditional forms, including hand-made books of collages and poetry produced by the girls, which we celebrated by holding a book-signing party each of the five years during the project's duration.

My belief in the value of publicly honoring young people's own creative self-representations has carried forward to the present, directly informing the project upon which this book is based.

As I've noted elsewhere (Luttrell, 2016), for this project I was excited by the sociological legacy of using photography and the importance of public exhibitions, most importantly W. E. B. Du Bois' "American Negro" photography exhibit for the Paris Exposition at the turn of the 20th century that challenged racist images that were circulating at the time.[5] I was particularly curious about what I could contribute to the more contemporary context of "giving-kids-cameras research" and how the kids' photographs might complicate conventional ideas and images about working-class childhoods (Luttrell, 2010, 2016). Meanwhile, in each public exhibition of the materials, selected and arranged by the kids themselves, I was learning about the different criteria they used to speak to different audiences, criteria I have described throughout this book including their ideas about ethics, aesthetics, and truthfulness. This, in turn, complicated how I was seeing their photographs. And with each public use of the kids' audio-visual archive—in classes about doing visual research, teachers' professional development workshops, and conference presentations—other people's responses were giving me opportunities to reflect.

This is all to reiterate that the longitudinal aspect of this project is as much about the kids' lives over time as it is about the complex life of their photography and photographs—over time, in different contexts, with different audiences and registers of feeling. This complexity is among the most difficult aspects of my research to communicate—and while I don't claim to have done it full justice, I have made my best effort.

### Seeing and "ensouling": photo analysis and collage-making

Over the years, I experimented with different analytic lenses/strategies to "see" the PCS kids' photographs. I went through three formalized processes. The first was a "cultural inventory" approach aligned with anthropologists John Collier, Jr. and Malcolm Collier (1986). This inventory approach was meant to identify clues to value systems (for example, importance of hospitality, order); race, ethnic, national, or religious identities and affinities; and self-expression through crafts and "do-it-yourself" home furnishings. This examination led to the creation of a "data dictionary" that I enlisted members of a racially and ethnically diverse research team to code (Luttrell, 2010; Tinkler, 2013). Second, I used sociologist Howard Becker's guidelines (1986), briefly described earlier in the book (see also Fontaine & Luttrell, 2015; Luttrell & Clark, 2018). Becker cautions the reader-analyst not to "stare and thus stop looking; look actively … you'll find it useful to take up the time by naming everything in the picture to yourself and writing up notes" (1986: 232). This advice is followed by an invitation to engage in "a period of fantasy, telling yourself a story about the people and things in the picture. The story needn't be true, it's just a device for externalizing and making clear to yourself the emotion and mood the picture has evoked, both part of its statement" (1986: 232).[6]

These forms of analysis grounded what I came to call the children's "counter-narratives" of care. But it wasn't until I made collages from the moms-in-kitchen photographs that I realized what methodological and theoretical advantages could be gained from collage-making and its embodied practice.

In my earlier work I had come to appreciate the value of collage-making as a means of data collection, but now I discovered that it offered a new way of seeing and feeling the data—the tactile sensations and manipulations of cutting, assembling, and reassembling pieces of the photographs that amounted to another layer of visual inquiry. It was my version of putting Tina Campt's notion of "listening to photographs" into practice (2017). Indeed, she uses the language of collage to describe a way of seeing that goes beyond visual scrutiny as "an ensemble of seeing, feeling, being affected, contacted, and moved beyond the distance of sight and observer" (p. 42).

I remember when I first looked at Gina's moms-in-kitchen photograph, and then across the kitchen images, I felt as if I was peering into a familiar space. There is a shared aesthetic about the kitchens—dark wood cabinetry, stainless steel sinks filled with dishes, terry cloth dish towels draped over oven handles, dark patterned linoleum floors—that put me in mind of the kitchens of my youth. As small children, my cousin and I spent evenings sitting under the oblong, wooden kitchen table as our parents played pinochle and drank beer. Maybe it was the darkness set behind curtained widows, the square space warmly lit by overhead lights above the stove and sink that evoked this memory and a sense of intimacy. From the warm, muted colors, to the occasional graininess, and finally to the dark shadows cast across the corner of Gina's "mom-in-kitchen" snapshot, I found myself conjuring up the smells of my grandmother's, aunt's, and mother's cooking, fond memories of baking by her side, as well as some ghosts of my childhood past.

Some years ago, a group of American middle-class families opened their doors to a team of photographers and researchers for a book project (Arnold et al, 2012). The team was interested in documenting the material worlds of 21st-century America, and in creating an archeology of how contemporary "families just like yours (and ours)" "use our homes, … cook for dinner, and … interact with our families each day" (p. vii). The kitchens Arnold et al documented do not look like the ones photographed by the children. The PCS kids' kitchens do not share the same visual vernacular of kitchen islands, marble countertops, porcelain sinks, built-in gas ranges, inset ceiling lighting, or terracotta floor tiles. Juxtaposing the two sets of images, I wondered why I felt more of a sense of voyeurism while viewing the children's photographed kitchens than the middle-class kitchens in the coffee table book—did it have to do with the professional quality of the book's images set against the informal, grainy snapshots the kids made? Or was it to do with the signs of middle-class abundance compared to working-class economic stress portrayed? Still, despite the differences, I also noticed similarities, most especially the kitchen counters lined with evidence of daily family operations (phones, pencil holders, calendars, stacks of paper) and refrigerators full of magnets holding photographs of family activities and grocery lists. In this sense all the kitchens share the look of "command centers" as I mentioned earlier (Arnold et al, 2012: 80).

Collage-making was a means to explore my feelings and responses. I don't remember exactly when I began to "play" with collage-making (or, to put it differently, when I gave myself permission to experiment with another layer of visual inquiry, as I encourage doctoral students to do in the courses I teach on visual and arts-based research). I had marveled at the insightful, creative, imaginative, and respectful impulses of doctoral students as they worked with the audio-visual archive. Students expressed a playfulness and pleasure through the process re-representing and re-purposing images to convey their own attachments and identifications. Oftentimes a doctoral student would declare she/he had "fallen in love" with this or another child and her/his photographs, or they would reflect thoughtfully on what they saw (or didn't see) of themselves in the kids' images and accounts. Witnessing this connection, and love propelled me to a (re)newed awareness about enacting care as part of the research process itself.

I chose the moms-in-kitchen photographs for several reasons, including my own sense of connection as well as discomfort. These images had such rich backstories, including the loving and tender way the children spoke about and touched the photographs. By contrast, these images were often met by viewers as mundane snapshots of traditional gender roles (a view I have to confess I shared at first). And none of the doctoral students had gravitated to this series of images, which surprised me.

Making collages opened the door to another way of paying careful, systematic attention to the details of each photograph. Years ago, I had been inspired by feminist botanist Barbara McClintock's early writings about her coming to "know" her plants intimately and the pleasure she drew from that (as quoted in Fox Keller, 1982: 601). I returned to read Evelyn Fox Keller's classic account (1983) of McClintock's work as the bedrock of a new feminist science:

> The ultimate descriptive task, for both artists and scientists, is to "ensoul" what one sees, to attribute to it the life one shares with it; one learns by identification. (1983: 204)

Collage-making was a means to "ensoul" my connection and feeling about what I had seen, what I had learned with and through my relationships with the kids and my students; it was yet another means to convey the significance of care.

My first step was to make enlarged (6 x 8 inch) color photocopies of all the mom-in-kitchen images. Cutting into these enlarged, color photocopies and not the photographs themselves assuaged my discomfort about destroying the images the children had made. I selected blue, green, and cream-colored matboards to try out as backgrounds and prepared an 8-x-11-inch frame within which to assemble the pieces. Then I took the leap with scissors in hand and began cutting. As I did so, I worried: was I undermining the integrity of the images that the children had made and cherished, and that I had spent so many hours viewing, appreciating, and analyzing? Was it ethical?[7]

I was surprised by the time it took to carefully cut around all the specific elements of the kitchen scenes—the bottles, food items, pots and pans, coffee makers, micro-waves, paper towel holders, dish detergents, cannisters, hanging wire baskets, plastic Tupperware, novelty hooks holding utensils, brooms hung on the wall, sunflower wallpaper edging, and matching window valences. I had to decide where to make the cuts—into or around a cabinet, a window, an edge of a doorway or a refrigerator, a mother's hand or fingers. Sometimes I liked the outlines of the shapes, and sometimes I didn't and tried again. I reveled in the process—its fluidity (opposed to the fixed nature of coding and categorizing), the layering of shapes and colors, the creation of open and closed spaces, the tactile pleasures, the sense of delight when I settled on an arrangement that I liked. The process wasn't belabored, but deliberate and conscious—not entirely unlike lap-swimming, I thought at one point.

Figure E: Mom-in-kitchen collage

The collage-making heightened my appreciation for the temporality and sensory aspects of women's work feeding the family. In reassembling the cut-out kitchen sinks, some filled with dishes to wash and others empty, and doing the same with the plastic dish drainers, some neatly lined with plates and others stacked high with pots and pans, I was reminded of the never-ending cycle of washing, drying, and putting dishes away, and the endless quest for order that battles with the limits of time and energy. The slow work of cutting apart and reassembling forced me to contemplate how creating a sense of family was achieved through so many details. The process also helped me see the work and the unique artistry of mothers' organizational and stylistic choices—choices that make a kitchen space one's own.

The collage-making was my way of attending to the affective registers of the photographs and why these images had moved the kids to speak of their moms as they had. It allowed me to "know" the photographs in a more embodied way. Cutting around the edges of what I could see, touch, and be affected by was a way of slowing down my looking and feeling. My tactile immersion in this way of "knowing" the photographs brought me back to the children's ways of "knowing" their photographs—the tender way Gabriel had caressed the edges of the picture he had taken of his mom in the kitchen, the sigh in his voice as he spoke of his explosive love for her. Collage-making brought to my immediate awareness the intimate, affecting, interlocking sense of my looking at, looking through, and looking with the kids.

## From analysis to representation

Making the collages as a new immersion in the data was the first big step. But I felt if I were to use them as a means of *representation* I would want to put them in motion. I had visions of a depiction of the collages that would show my hands assembling the pieces. I hoped the inclusion of my hands might open a rich space for dialogue about my researcher role and the gap between my social position and those of the mothers and children. I also wanted the collage elements in motion to evoke a version of domestic life that is not fixed, but pulled apart and pieced back together, like the choreography of care born from the routines and rhythms of low-wage, working-class households that had been described by the children as they spoke about their daily lives. I wanted to re-create the emotional valence of the children's expressions of love and admiration for their mothers by using their own words and voices.

This vision was beyond my individual capacity to carry it out, but I found a solution in collaboration. A doctoral student, Emily Clark, had taken my visual research course and produced a stunning 35-second video montage of a series of photographs the kids had taken of the PCS school gym/auditorium, to which she had added a soundscape that included music. When I viewed her montage I thought to myself, "how did she capture the look and feel of this place without ever having been there?" I was reminded of debates within anthropology about the role of images (photography, video, film) versus direct observation and immersion (embodied in the ethnographic imperative to "go and see for oneself") as a means to establish ethnographic authority.[8] Emily's video montage pieced together separate photographs (and different elements of each photograph) into a continuous whole, allowing me to enter the space again as I remembered it. I applied for funds to support time for a joint collaboration (though not nearly enough time, as it turned out),[9] and we carved out time to work together over two summers and a winter break, transforming my dining room and kitchen into a film studio to put the mom-in-kitchen collages into motion and to experiment with other video representations that would become the digital interludes.

Emily and I have written about our collaboration creating a video montage that appears as Digital Interlude #1: Dwelling in School which combines video footage I took of the school with PCS students' photographs (Luttrell & Clark, 2018).

## *Digital Interlude #1: Dwelling in School*

 childrenframingchildhoods.com/digital-interludes/dwelling-in-school

The montage attempts to accomplish a multi-sensory sense of time, space, place, stillness, reflection, light, movement—and to evoke school feelings and memories. This experiment of blurring the border between art-making and research required that we step outside our comfort zones as we considered how much creative/artistic license we would exert in our re-use of the children's photographs. Making the video montage raised all sorts of questions for us about the difference between analysis and evocation, our own selective vision, our ethics and aesthetics, our oscillation between creating different feelings of schooling and its production of memories. Most important for me was the creative disruption to my researcher identity, which opened me up to the creative challenge of playful work and workful play that I have advocated. It also catapulted me into re-thinking my roles as researcher, interpreter, writer, curator, and now also as artistic creator.

Our experiment making Digital Interlude #2: Feeding the Family took even longer. Emily and I played with changing the backgrounds of each collage I had made, utilizing the textures of kitchen materials—a paper towel; a piece of linoleum; a cast-iron surface; a piece of tile flooring; a plastic cutting board. As we tried each background, we discussed its class- and historical-based aesthetic, jettisoning some of the materials in my home (for example, a marble top surface on a wooden bureau in the dining room that could be mistaken for a marble kitchen counter) and using others that referenced the architectural features and visual vernacular of a less-than-modern kitchen. Emily created a soundtrack of a kitchen in motion: the sizzling of food frying, the whirring of washing machines, the alarm bell of a microwave, sounds of rice boiling. She layered in the voices of the children, too, so that audiences can hear the individual inflections of pride and value they bestowed on the love labor that takes place in the space. When my hand shifts a piece of the photo that lays askew, it evokes the kind of care that women and mothers put into making things look a certain way, setting things in their "right" order and place. This performative gesture also echoes the identity work that the children were doing to present themselves and their mothers as "right," "good," and "worthy" of teachers', researchers', and viewers' attention and respect, and to defend against the possibility they might be seen as lacking.

## *Digital Interlude #2: Feeding the Family*

 childrenframingchildhoods.com/digital-interludes/feeding-the-family

One goal of Digital Interlude #2: Feeding the Family is to jolt viewers/audiences into seeing in a new way, including an emphasis on the "making" process rather than on the object/product (that is, the collage) itself. Another goal is to remind viewers that in schools and classrooms, family kitchens are unseen or opaque, yet children move fluidly between those two spaces. The kitchen is a threshold on both sides of which kids have to operate. They have to be an arbiter for themselves between the twin worlds of school and home, carrying the smell of caldo soup and juicy chicken, rice, and beans into the classroom and taking the swish of papers back into the kitchen. Conveying the importance of this homeplace and its care work—its multi-sensory sights and sounds, its overall "aliveness"—was an effort to do justice to the kids' intentions.

To re-represent the kids' images of teachers-in-classrooms photographs that are iconic and yet seemingly mundane, I took a different approach. I was struck by both the similarities and differences in these images from the moms in kitchens. The teachers assumed poses of a certain erectness that seemed to highlight their performative roles. As a group they also seemed more willing to adhere to or were more cognizant of the rules of snapshot photography. This video collage directly asks viewers a question about what they are seeing and what is "nice"—including the troubling questions of what "nice" covers over (including systemic racism, sexism, heteronormativity), just as the individual teacher figures cover over each other. Again, the collage-making process is foregrounded, drawing viewers into a classroom setting that plays with scale, figures, patterns, and negative space. The soundscape, Emily's creation, is a quiet reminder of teachers and students at work with all eyes on teachers.

## *Digital Interlude #3: Nice...?*

 childrenframingchildhoods.com/digital-interludes/nice

Making these videos was an ongoing exercise in interpretation. Emily and I spent two years in a cycle of surprise, revision, and re-assessment;

our ways of seeing, feeling, and understanding were enriched by the process.

My collaboration with Susie Nielsen on Digital Interlude #4: Being in Time was grounded in a different kind of engagement, unrelated to teaching and learning about visual research (which is not to say that we didn't learn and teach each other). As a visual artist, curator, and friend, Susie had listened to me describe my project, and had been drawn to the integrity of the kids' images—not so much for their content (although this fascinated her)—but for their visual elements as photographs. She saw things like illuminance, distortion, and refraction—a journey toward light in the snapshots—that inspired her and gave me a different appreciation. I cherished her vision, trusted her immersion in the online visual archive, and asked whether she would be willing to revisit a video entitled, "Worcester Clips" made by David Chapin.[10] This video was screened with the kids on their trip to New York City and to the Graduate Center. Susie and I sat together in her studio and followed the light, sounds, and movements, sometimes frame-by-frame to get a glimpse of a time, place, ecology of signs, and soundscapes that the kids' had video-taped. I told her stories about the sections of "Worcester Clips" with which the kids' had resonated and sections they felt had been left out from their own video diaries. We toggled back and forth between "Worcester Clips" and an individual kid's video, searching for new lines of light that caught our eyes. Susie made the cuts, transitions, and repurposed a sound track, all under the five- minute limitation we had agreed to.

## Digital Interlude #4: Being in Time

childrenframingchildhoods.com/digital-interludes/being-in-time

I don't see the collage-making or the digital interludes in binary terms, for example, as decentering the kids' images and intentions in order to center my own, but rather as a means to visualize the intimate, dialogic, and reflexive practice of collaborative seeing. My hope in sharing these videos is that they offer an experience of active engagement in looking; that they widen our imagination for ways to "ensoul" research. Through multi-modal research formats perhaps we can be more profoundly affected by, and better respond to, what we learn from research participants.

## Ethics, reciprocity and "response-ability"

I appreciate feminist of science Karen Barad's (2012) formulation of "touching" and "being in touch" as being a form of theorizing as well as a form of ethics. Her work opened new ways of thinking about my own "hand" and "touch" "without any illusion of clean hands" in the discovery process (p. 207).[11] She issues a provocation that resonated strongly with me: "The idea is to do collaborative research, to be in touch, in ways that enable response-ability" (p. 208). It speaks to the way I hope this book and its multiple visual representations will enable audience response-ability—that is, encouraging observers' willingness to look and to respond, not to stare and thus stop asking questions about what else might be possible, imaginable, and desirable.

One of the most frequent questions I get asked about my project has to do with research ethics and securing IRB permission. I explain that my approach necessitates involving participants in discussions about ethics and picture-taking, including, for example, role-plays to practice asking people for permission to photograph them. The kids and I discussed why a person might want to say no and talked about how this also related to their own participation in the project (I reminded them regularly they were free to withdraw at any time, and they didn't need a reason to do so). Later I would learn from some of the kids they had not always asked permission and, as I described in Chapter 1, this became a point of contention in a discussion among the kids about whether a photograph could or should be made public. The question of permissions and release also shaped whether I could use a photograph(s) in publications.

Securing parental permission and informed consent was brokered by various members of the school community (the principal, the teachers, the school secretary) and evolved over time to include permission for release of video and photographic images as parents became more comfortable. Most important, I treated consent, assent, and release as an ongoing process rather than as a one-time event (Luttrell, 2010). As mentioned in Chapter 1, assent and consent for participating and for releasing photographs/videos were built into the project at numerous points: during the active editing of video clips where the kids spoke about their photographs, during the continuation of the project at the beginning of sixth grade, at the conclusion of the initial photo work, when they were asked whether they would be willing to be contacted in the future; and then again when I made contact during high school. The kids were also told they could decide which photographs they did (or did not) wish to discuss with the interviewers, share with their classmates, or select for public viewing.

I believe IRB boards need to be better educated about the relationality and messiness of "consent," "assent," and "release" as processes rather than products (forms to be signed). I suspect that I might not be able to get permission to conduct this study today, as I had been able to do in 2003—even with the explosion of cell phone cameras and the proliferation of posting and commenting on photos in social media, practices that have by now become routine features of young people's lives. I am aware that others have tried to give kids cameras in school, and some (but not all) have met with resistance. In the 15 years since I began the project, I have witnessed a tightening of IRB regulations that I fear has more to do with protecting institutions than actually protecting vulnerable subjects.

Visual research must tackle new and sometimes unanticipated layers of ethical dilemmas and issues. Claudia Mitchell (2011) addresses these quite effectively in her book, *Doing Visual Research*, which I highly recommend.[12] Writing about community-based visual research, she highlights the importance of being conscious of community rights and responsibilities, ensuring protection and advocacy, and being reflexive (essential for both the research team members as well as participants). All of these are issues she believes are inseparable from pedagogy (p. 16). She also writes, "ethical issues can lead to creative thinking about 'alternatives'" (p. 16). Indeed, ethical issues led to several creative alternatives in this project—for instance, blurring the faces of moms so their identities are not so apparent, avoiding the use of certain photographs that would be too identifying of a person or place, and re-purposing some of the kids' images to preserve meanings they intended.

I don't believe in one-size-fits-all principles for visual research; instead I advocate reflexive and flexible frames of ethical engagement. It is important to set parameters for how access to, ownership of, and control of data will be discussed with the communities with whom we work. In this case, the kids' ownership of the camera (both a surprise and "serious responsibility" as I learned from the outset of the project), was a key issue and the children embraced their new possessions with great care and concern (as they later did with the FlipCamcorders). The same was true for the photographs they took (they were given the physical copies and a CD to keep). The materiality of these photographs and the kids' attachments to them figured prominently in the first stages of the research, with kids trading photos with fellow participants in the project, or framing images to give family members as gifts.

Figure F: Banners

In the second stage of the research, their work was housed digitally, and archiving the photographs established a new, enduring form of access. This required a different sort of reciprocal care—on my part, as the organizer of the archive, and on the kids' part to upload, edit, and complete it in their own time. Perhaps this joint involvement contributed to the kids' willingness for me to share in the ownership and control of their images. Or perhaps they weren't thinking so much about what I would do with the visual data as much as they were engaged with the platform and its materials in the moment.

I am eager to learn how the kids from PCS, now grown adults, will receive this book. Just as the kids were attached to their pictures, so was I attached to their images, and, especially, to the young people who made them. I framed a copy of each child's favorite photograph, which I gave as gifts when they graduated elementary school. As a parting gift to the school, the kids designed five large banners that were hung in the auditorium to memorialize the project and their work.

## A provocation

I wish to conclude this essay with a methodological provocation: we can and must use the power of love, care, connection, relationality, regard, and an open-ness to disruption and repair in order to change what is valued and what is achieved in research and in the educational enterprise at large. I write this with hopes for alternative metrics and demands for the time it takes to do care-ful research, teaching, and learning. In such a world, education and research would be public goods—not individual commodities used to leverage competitive advantage or personal gain. In such a world, education and research would challenge narrow ways of seeing, confront artificial divides and actively build solidarities across social differences. To accomplish this, we need to expand our methodological tool kit and theoretical approaches so they are more permeable to alternative ways of perceiving, feeling, knowing, and doing. We need reflexive, embodied, aesthetic practices of research that can bring "intellectual labor and life into closer relation," that can enact care, and "ensoul" knowledge. I believe intersectional, feminist-inspired tools of visual and arts-based research and pedagogy hold promise toward that end, as do many other forms and practices yet to be imagined. If my work to date has shown me anything, it is that research is never complete and there is no "whole" picture to show or tell. But the longer and wider we look, the more viewpoints we seek, and the closer we get a "feel" for our topic of study, the better our chances are for creating new visions and possibilities for change.

# Appendix

Table A1: Cohort 1 (2003–04)

| Name | Race/Ethnicity (School) Self definition | Homeplace |
| --- | --- | --- |
| Allison + | **White** Italian, American, Irish | Duplex |
| Alanzo + | **Hispanic** Puerto Rican | Terrace Gardens |
| Danny * | **Asian American** Vietnamese, American | Three-decker house (living with extended family) |
| Gabriel/Juan + | **Hispanic** Latino | Apartment complex |
| GIna * | **White** Irish and Italian American | Duplex |
| Isaiah * | **Black** African American (age 16) | Terrace Gardens |
| Jack ^ | **White** American | Duplex |
| Jeffrey * | **Hispanic** "Half Puerto Rican, half Black and half white" (age 10) Puerto Rican (age 16) | Apartment complex |
| Kendra * | **Black** African American (age 16) | Terrace Gardens |
| Nadia * | **Other** "I speak Persian" (age 10) | Apartment complex |
| Nia ^ | **Hispanic** Spanish, Dominican | Terrace Gardens |
| Sebastian * | **Hispanic** "My mom is from Colombia" (age 10) Latino (age 17) | Duplex |
| Tina * | **Asian American** Vietnamese | Three-decker house (living with extended family) |

\* Participated in photography and video production in the second phase of the project.

+ Re-viewed childhood photographs but declined to participate in photography and video production.

^ Moved out of Worcester or were unable to be located in 2011.

Table A2: Cohort 2 (2004–05)

| Name | Race/Ethnicity (School) Self definition | Homeplace |
|------|------------------------------------------|-----------|
| Camila + | **Hispanic** "My mom is Dominican and my dad is Puerto Rican" (10) Latina (16) | Terrace Gardens |
| Cheryl ^ | **Hispanic** My dad is Dominican and my mom is Puerto Rican | Duplex Family moved out of state in middle of fifth grade |
| Claire ^ | **White** American, some Irish | Three-decker house (with extended family) |
| Huan * | **Asian American** Asian American | Apartment complex |
| Kim Ly * | **Asian American** Asian American | Apartment complex |
| Ling * | **Asian American** "My parents are from China" (age 10) Chinese American | Duplex |
| Luis ^ | **Hispanic** Dominican | Terrace Gardens |
| Manny ^ | **Hispanic** Puerto Rican | Terrace Gardens |
| Mesha * | **Black** Black (age 17) | Single-family house |
| Natalia * | **Hispanic** "I came here with my mom from Puerto Rico" (age 10) Latina (age 16) | Terrace Gardens |
| Riva ^ | **Other** "I am from Yemen" | Apartment complex (moved back to Yemen) |
| Yanira + | **Hispanic** Latina | Terrace Gardens |

Table A3: Cohort 3 (2005–06)

| Name | Race/Ethnicity (School) Self definition | Homeplace |
|---|---|---|
| Angel + | **Hispanic** Puerto Rican and Black | Terrace Gardens |
| Angeline + | **Black** "Black American but mostly Kenyan though" (age 10) | Apartment complex |
| Christopher * | **Hispanic** Latino | Duplex |
| Crystal + | **Hispanic** Dominican | Terrace Gardens |
| Emily * | **White** White, American (age 10) | Single-family house |
| Junior ^ | **Black** Haitian American (age 10) | Apartment complex Moved after sixth grade |
| Maureen * | **White** "My grandparents are from Ireland, so Irish?" (age 10) American (age 16) | Duplex |
| Nalanie * | **Asian American** "I am from Laos" (age 10) | Duplex |
| Sofia * | **White** "I am from Albania" (age 10) "Immigrant but... "(age 15) "All-out American teenager" (age 16) | Apartment complex |
| Sonya * | **Asian American** Asian American | Duplex |
| Terrance ^ | **Black** Haitian American | Apartment complex Moved in middle-school |
| Vivian * | **Asian American** Asian American | Three-decker house (with extended family) |

# Notes

## Prelude

[1] Throughout this book I will use the terms "kids" and "children" interchangeably; similarly I will use "young people" and "teenagers" interchangeably. "Kids" was the term used most often by the children at ages 10–12 to speak of their age group. Occasionally they referenced themselves and others in reference to school grade, as "my brother is a seventh-grader." Interestingly, often when speaking of adults in relationship to "kids" they most often used the term "children," as in "the teachers care about children at this school." At ages 16–18, when looking back on their childhood images, they shifted between speaking about "being a child" or "when I was a kid" and used a variety of terms to reference their age group as "people," "kids," "teenager" and at times, "high-schoolers."

[2] Throughout this book I use "working class," "wage-poor," and "working-poor" as labels to describe the families and their limited financial resources. I also use a variety of racial/ethnic descriptors throughout, shifting between "Black and Brown," "kids of color," "immigrants of color," and keeping "white" in lower case in an effort to de-center whiteness. But all these labels are loaded; they can be stigmatizing and wholly inadequate to the task of identifying social groups and the intersecting force of class and race. Equally problematic, these are not terms used by the young people. Indeed racial terms will become a focal point of discussion among the kids. My hope is to offer new, more complex angles of vision about intersecting systems of racism, poverty, and immigration through the children's images and accounts.

[3] See Trachtenberg (1980) and Wells (2003) for useful critical reviews of photography and its function, character, and the limits of photographic communication.

[4] The software program VoiceThread allows users to upload photographs and create audio and text-based commentaries or stories within a secure collaborative network. These digital "voice threads" created by the kids are explained more in Chapter 5.

[5] Throughout this book I will refer to neoliberalism and neoliberal policies defined most succinctly as a "political, economical, and ideological system that privileges the market as the most efficient platform for distributing social goods, minimizes the role of government responsibility in assuring collective well-being and highlights instead personal responsibility for assuring individual well-being." (Fabricant & Fine, 2013, p. 4)

## Chapter 1

[1] See R. H. Tawney's (1921) book *The Acquisitive Society*, a critique of capitalism's reliance on selfish individualism, excessive riches, and greed.

[2] This aligned with the "child-saving movement" of middle-class progressive reformers organized around protecting children from the labor market, the streets, poverty, neglect, and physical and/or sexual abuse (Mintz, 2004).

[3] It has been argued that this new approach to thinking about childhood and children is the result of scholars in various countries taking up the challenge of the 1989 United Nations Convention on the Rights of the Child (which has been adopted by all countries except the United States and Somalia). The interlocking Articles of

the Convention offer children an internationally recognized set of rights that they can hold in independence of the interests and activities of the adults that directly surround them (Lee, 2001, p. 92).

4  Understanding the role of the insurance industry in reconceptualizing the meaning and value of children is the subject of Viviana Zelizer's (1994) pathbreaking book, *Pricing the Priceless Child: The Changing Social Value of Children*. Her account of the lucrative but controversial marketing of children's insurance to working-class families who relied on their children for economic stability that began in the 1870s and was criticized by progressive social reformers as a means of condoning child labor, provides insight into how children's value changed from being mostly economic to having sentimental value. Zelizer writes:

> Although monetary compensation for the death of a child was initially justified by the pecuniary loss for the parents, the final success of the industry was based on more than economic rationality. Children's insurance made its appeal primarily as burial insurance for poor children. It offered working-class parents a more dignified alternative than the dreaded pauper burial. (1994: 114–15)

5  https://static1.squarespace.com/static/53f20d90e4b0b80451158d8c/t/54d2d37c e4b024b41443b0ba/1423102844010/BlackGirlsMatterReport.pdf

6  See Noguera, 2003; Morris, 2016; Morris & Perry, 2016; Ayers, Ayers & Dohrn, 2001; and Nolan, 2011 for more discussion of the racialization of school punishment.

7  Sociologist Orlando Patterson (1982/2017) has written about three major tenets of enslavement that constituted the calculation of people as property within a slave society. The first is that enslaved people are natally alienated—that is, their familial ties are not recognized by white society. The second is gratuitous violence and the third is ontological dishonor, an assumption of wrongness. It is interesting to consider how constructions of Black childhood resonate with these tenets.

8  I also say "ordinary" because there was nothing especially "out of the ordinary" in the many daily activities and interactions I witnessed at PCS. Over the course of the 2003–04 school year I was part of an interdisciplinary team of faculty who observed and documented teaching and learning interactions, school improvement initiatives, and collaborations among staff, students, and families. Dr. G., PCS's principal, was interviewed about the school's culture and mission, its improvement process and progress, and its vision and guiding principles. The teaching staff were interviewed and video-taped as they facilitated literacy learning and reflected in small groups about their teaching and assessment practices.

9  Again, these labels are fraught. Throughout the book I will substitute Latinx for Hispanic; Asian American instead of Asian; white instead of White; and will use African American, Haitian American, and Kenyan when referring to students who were collapsed into the category of "Black" within the school records.

10  For an example see *Conditions of America's Public School Facilities: 2012–2013*, Debbie Alexander, Laurie Lewis, and John Ralph (2014).

11  See DeNicolo et al (2017) for their review of the relationship between care and immigrant students' sense of belonging.

12  I noticed that Dr. G. was not explicit about whether these blinders included blinders related to race and colorism, and this would linger in my mind, heightening my interest in how the children would frame their teachers' care. I explore the complexities of the racial landscape of school relationships and care in Chapter 4.

[13] Du Bois wrote in the *The Souls of Black Folk*, "The problem of the twentieth century is the problem of the color-line—the relation between the darker to lighter races of men in Asia and Africa, in America and the islands of the sea" (1903: p. 9).

[14] See Flores and Rosa (2015), who write about linguistic bias that positions the linguistic knowledge of bilinguals as deficient and lacking. They write ". . . from a raciolinguistic perspective, heritage language learners' linguistic practices are devalued not because they fail to meet a particular linguistic standard but because they are spoken by racialized bodies and thus heard as illegitimate by the white listening subject" (2015: 161).

[15] This is an example that bears out Foucault's theory about the internalization of subordination and surveillance. He writes of "An inspecting gaze, a gaze which each individual under its weight will end by interiorising to the point that he is his own overseer, each individual thus exercising this surveillance over, and against, himself" (1980, p. 155). See Luttrell, 2010b for more discussion of what Tina had to say about the photograph and its multiple layers of meaning.

[16] Jack was speaking before the so-called "post-racial" society ushered in by the election of the first African American President. "Post-racial" is a popular discourse that has in part replaced colorblindness and suggests that race is no longer a determining factor in people's life chances and thus there is no need for programs like voting regulation preclearance or affirmative action.

[17] See Luttrell (2010b) for more discussion on my perspective on ventriloquation and the concept of "voice." Briefly, I am wary of essentializing (that is, "this is the essence of what children are like"), universalizing (that is, "all children are like this"), and dichotomizing children's voices in opposition to adults'. I also use the term "voice" in thinking about an individual child's speaking "voice"—its tone, rhythm, and pitch—as a "powerful psychological instrument and channel connecting inner and outer worlds" (Gilligan, 1993: xvi). "Voice" should not be conflated with language, just as silence should not be confused with sound (as in the colloquial phrase, *silence speaks louder than words*). Listening for what might be unspoken or unsayable (Rogers, 2005) in the children's accounts, and considering what might be whispering between the lines of speech, is part of my interpretative and reflective process.

[18] See Wagner (1999) for his introduction to a special issue about how childhood is seen by children through photography that set the stage for doing visual research *with* not just *about* children.

[19] See E. Cavin (1994) for a compelling exception to this rule.

[20] I am grateful to the following people who served in this capacity: J. Poser, E. Mishkin, M. Ticken, and C. Shalaby as interviewers; J. Broussard, S. Deckman, J. Dorsey, J. Hayden, B. Malik, and D. Santill for the first stage of research analysis (including coding the photographs); and V. Restler, R. Silva, C. Fontaine, I. Espinet, and D. Chapin, who took part in the video-making, screening, and data analysis during the second stage of the project.

[21] I wasn't sure what to expect when being introduced as a "Professor from Harvard" and how this would register with the children. I learned that not all the children were aware of Harvard as a university; in one session a child remarked, "Oh, my uncle works at Harvard, it is a big hospital in Boston."

[22] Pugh draws upon Arlie Hoschschild's turn of phrase the "economy of gratitude" to characterize the way spouses recognize each other's gifts of love, care, feelings, work, and time as part of a larger bargain (at times unconscious, unbalanced, ever

changing) about who is responsible for what in maintaining the household and the marriage.

[23] See Pat Thomson (2008: 4–6) for her discussion/critique of "voice" research and its tendency to universalize children and youth experience. She reviews five different kinds of voice to which researchers have paid attention and suggests there may be more: authoritative, critical, therapeutic, consumer, and pedagogic. She also breaks down two different types of approaches to visual research—those in which researchers use visual methods *on* children (where children are framed as the subjects of inquiry) and those that use visual methods *with* children/youth as partners in inquiry.

[24] A discussion about ethics and the dilemmas of consent in school-based projects is well worth mentioning and is the subject of considerable research. The following references are illustrative, but by no means exhaustive: Morrow & Richards, 1996; Thomas & O'Kane, 1998; Valentine, 1999; David et al, 2001; White et al, 2010. I also consider this topic in the Postlude.

[25] These video clips were used during sessions with the Harvard graduate students in the course *Thinking Like an Educator*, in subsequent teacher professional development workshops, and in various doctoral courses as a means for viewers to listen to the children's explanations about their photographs.

[26] Angeline is now attending medical school.

[27] See Penny Tinkler (2008: 259) for a similar reporting.

[28] This is Lutz and Collins' (1993) phrase for talking about the production, circulation, and interpretation of images in *National Geographic* that serve to both reflect and create Western views of cultural difference and hierarchies in the service of imperial power and oppression.

## Chapter 2

[1] See Danny Miller's (2008) book, *The Comfort of Things*, where he describes the importance of organizing objects in the home, not simply for the purpose of tidiness or order, but as an activity of "'a repeated re-acquaintance with each and every object in the home', a way to 'pick up, touch, replace and recollect each item in turn'" (p. 213).

[2] Feeling "at home" isn't necessarily a positive feeling, as Yuval-Davis notes, and can also lead to a sense of anger, resentment, shame, and indignation (Hessel, 2010, quoted in Yuval-Davis, 2011: 10).

[3] See Yuval-Davis (2011) for her discussion of how the concept of belonging has shifted over time. Belonging is no longer tied to civil societies of nations and states, but now takes the form of identity communities.

[4] *The Future of Public Housing in Worcester*, 2001 Report 01–03, www.wrrb.org/wp-content/uploads /2014/07/01-3housing.pdf. Accessed June, 2019.

[5] One or two immigrant parents consciously resist these symbolic displays, and constituted a notable exception.

[6] Pugh identifies these forms of difference as interactional, personal and social (Pugh, 2009, p. 9). Interactional differences arise in peer conversations, like whether one's neighborhood is "safe" or if one has one's own bedroom; personal differences related to individual traits, like having blond hair or being shy; social differences stem from social categories, like class, race, gender, and nationality, to name a few. These three forms of difference can be conflated.

[7] The researchers were also interested in patterns that differentiated some families from others. They found social class differences in the objects mentioned as special, for example, 37 percent of upper-middle-class respondents identified visual art as special compared to only 14 percent of lower-middle-class respondents. At the same time, they found only 8.9 of children compared to 36.7 of parents put special value on visual art, which they speculated might have to do with young people's "inability or disinterest, in finding meanings in forms of two-dimensional representation" (64) (my study did not find this to be true). Their definition of visual art was broadly defined and included any two-dimensional representation other than a photograph—which ranged from "an original Picasso to the cheapest reproduction of the *Last Supper*" (63). Perhaps not surprisingly, visual art was not only valued more frequently by the upper-middle-class respondents, but they owned significantly more art and different types of art (that is, original art objects) than the lower-middle-class respondents who tended to have a higher percentage of mass-produced art. I found these generational and class differences especially intriguing in light of the high percentage of children in my project that took pictures of visual art (primarily mass-produced art, including the *Last Supper*) mentioning that these objects were special to their parents. Upon questioning (*why do you think this painting is important or special to your parent?*) several children mentioned the intrinsic qualities of the piece—its "natural beauty"; "it is bright and cheerful". This breaks from the reasons that adults in the C-R study gave, which instead focused on memories and reminders of relatives, friends, or past events (65). Perhaps the children's photographs of household furnishings, visual art, and plants that signify their parents' special objects are meant to say, "I dwell in my parents' world." Or perhaps these objects, understood to be markers of a kind of middle-class lifestyle, represent their efforts to convince their imagined viewers that their homes are not bereft of visual beauty or things of value.

[8] The children took photographs of family photographs for a range of reasons as will be discussed in Chapter 3.

[9] See others who have addressed similar themes about the complex connections between objects and people, and the various ways in which identity, relationships, and values come to be expressed through personal possessions (for example, Miller, 2008; Croghan et al, 2008; Appadurai, 1986).

[10] The children in the C-R study attach more significance to "activity" objects, that is, objects that engage them in everyday activities (for example, television sets, stereos), than to objects that spark memories. These distinctions were not so clear in my study, as I argue in this chapter.

[11] At age ten, Maureen took 11 out of 27 photographs of family photographs carefully grouped and displayed throughout her home.

[12] The value of individualized watching among children resonates with larger media trends described by David Buckingham (2011).

[13] This realization prompted Claire to conduct further study with four of the female participants about their screen time, online practices and expertise. See her dissertation, *Growing Up Online: Identity, Development and Agency in Networked Girlhoods* (2015).

[14] See Fontaine (2015) for more about Mesha's awareness of and challenge to the male-dominated gaming industry.

[15] Susan Linn's (2004) book, *Consuming Kids: The Hostile Takeover of Childhood* is but one example.

## Chapter 3

[1] See Hochschild (2003) for a discussion of children as eavesdroppers and what they learn from parental negotiations about their care; and see Romero (2001; 2011) about what children learn from being taken by their mothers to their jobs.

[2] See Thorne (2001) for her discussion of reading signs of care across lines of social class, race, and gender, and across cultural divides and child-rearing philosophies.

[3] Mothers and children "do school" in the same manner as people "do gender" (West & Zimmerman, 1987) or "do family" (DeVault, 1991).

[4] I use the term Black here to include African American and immigrant mothers from the African diaspora, and Latina to also include Latin American immigrant mothers.

[5] The kids' descriptions of their families' concerted, collective efforts devoted to dwelling and care work is interesting to consider in light of what Lareau (2003) calls the "concerted cultivation" of children as individuals. In middle-class households, kids' time is highly scheduled in organized enrichment activities that take place outside the home, and children display an "emerging sense of entitlement." In working-class homes, Lareau found that parents tend to rely less on institutionally organized activities and instead foster a "natural growth" environment in which spontaneity flourishes and the focus is more on sociality than on individual development. Children in these settings displayed an "emerging sense of constraint." These diverging perspectives are differently valued in contemporary institutional settings such as school and work, resulting in the continued accumulation of advantage for middle-class families.

[6] Gina's phrasing is interesting. It hints at both pregnancy and labor pain, of course, but also at the long-term burden/pain of intense care-giving and Gina's recognition of that pain and her gratitude for it. It also suggests an understanding that love/care is inherently connected to pain.

[7] See DeVault (1991) for her discussion of research that documents a distinction between meals prepared for socializing in working-class compared to white-collar/professional-class households. Meals prepared for socializing are more likely for family groups in working-class families, while in white-collar/professional households, meals are for "entertaining" guests.

[8] Natalia also linked marriage with exemplary motherhood as she explained the photograph she took of her mother reclining on the sofa with her step-father, "I admire my mom cause it used to be just me and her in Puerto Rico, but when we moved here she got married, so now we are a family."

[9] Two important "outliers" include one child whose parents were both teachers, and another whose (recently widowed) mother was an accountant.

[10] See Fontaine (2015) for her discussion of Fujanese migration patterns and prominence in the Chinese takeout restaurant business, and how they are stigmatized within the Chinese community for a "no-holds-barred" work ethic and culture and a willingness to work longer hours for lower wages, creating intense competition for work within Chinese ethnic enclaves.

[11] As DeVault (1991) contends, women report learning to cook from their mothers, even in households in which men cook. "For most girls, learning about housework begins early. And one of the lessons that most women learn is that housework is "womanly" activity" (DeVault, 1991, p. 106). Also, Angeline's talk is in keeping with research which finds that especially in certain immigrant households, female

children are expected to do the greatest share of domestic work, just as the female parent is expected to do this work for the family (Lopez, 2003).

[12] Angeline's gendered expression of cooking norms is consistent with DeVault's (1991) finding that children in families where the man does most of the cooking consider this to be an aberration from normal family behavior and not a norm. In these homes, the children "referred to these patterns as atypical, discounting the evidence of their own families in favor of assumptions about daily activities in other households" (p. 106). That said, trends regarding the gender division of labor have changed, most notably with fathers spending more time doing child-minding. For a review for these trends and how men and women perceive their labor, see Bianchi et al (2007). Also see Lynch et al (2009), who find that primary care responsibilities continue to fall to women as an assumed natural order of things and to be experienced as a moral imperative.

[13] See Dodson & Dickert (2004) for a review of research about children's family labor—most often girls' labor—as an overlooked survival strategy in wage-poor households.

[14] See Bureau of Labor Statistics (BLS), "American Time Use Survey—2014 Results," 18–19, Tables 8A and 8B.

## Chapter 4

[1] The same could be said about the fields of nursing and social work, where the work of caring for others is tied to cultural assumptions about women's natural aptitudes and desires to bear and raise children.

[2] The phrase "other people's children" references the classic book by Lisa Delpit, *Other People's Children: Cultural Conflict in the Classroom* (2006) to describe forms of miscommunication between predominantly white teachers and children of color. Also, see Kevin Kumashiro (2012) for his discussion of the colonial and racialized positioning of white women as teachers as a means to assimilate and control racially and culturally diverse groups of children.

[3] Women in particular tend to bear the burden of commercialized emotion work associated with low-wage service work and care-related occupations. For example, in face-to-face service work, no matter how poorly one is treated by the customer or client, "the customer is always right." The adage demands that the service worker maintain a smile and courteous behavior at all times—an often-unrecognized form of labor known as commercialized emotion work. This hidden work is not only unacknowledged, but actively devalued in terms of remuneration. Teachers working in poor and working-class communities and in under-resourced schools know better than most about the emotion work required in their jobs, for they must manage their own despair, their sense of impotence about the hardships their students face, their anger about the lack of necessary resources in their schools. This is work that teachers in advantaged communities and schools need not do.

[4] Interestingly, I noticed that Angeline seemed to associate math with the men in her life—her father and his encouragement of math, an uncle who is studying to be a doctor whom she helps with his math homework; her male sixth-grade teacher who "pushes her"; and even in her math classroom photograph, which features only a male student.

[5] See Franziska Vogt (2002) for her research on elementary school teachers' notions of care. She used visual methods to allow teachers to represent their professional identities. In the interpretations of the photos she showed teachers, she observed

that although male and female teachers used different discourses—discipline for males and caring for females—their actions in the classroom were quite similar.

[6] As an example, the implementation of zero-tolerance disciplinary policies in Connecticut led kindergarten suspensions/expulsions to nearly double from 463 in the 2001–02 school year to 901 in 2002–03. This increase included many students who were punished for developmentally appropriate behaviors such as fighting, defiance, and temper tantrums (Schoonover, 2009).

[7] Pitzer's paper was based on a project called "The Smart Kids: Visual Stories," headed by Sari Biklen and Michael Schoonmaker from the Newhouse School of Communication, that took place over three years in "Upstate City" (pseudonym). The qualitative study examined what urban middle school students understand about how urban schools function. The students made films to share their insights. The project began at a school that was struggling, Garber School. Garber was an under-resourced and failing K–8 urban school where most of the students were poor and identified as Black, Latino or immigrants. In the first year, researchers worked with 85 fourth-, fifth-, and sixth-graders, and their three teachers. In the second year, Garber School closed and students were redistributed to other city schools, so in the project's second and third years—the second phase—researchers continued in four of the schools where students transferred. Researchers followed 22 of the students to continue working with them on their visual stories of urban schooling.

[8] The idea of talking, listening, sorting out different perspectives, and seeking connection and reconciliation is part of "restorative justice" alternatives that schools across the country are seeking to employ. The restorative or transformative justice movement in schools is an effort to end "zero-tolerance" school discipline and suspension policies that sustain racism in the educational system.

[9] Steps to Respect is an anti-bullying guidance curriculum designed for students between third and sixth grade to decrease bullying at school while helping students build more supportive relationships with each other. One of the functions of the program is to help provide a school environment that is safe, respectful, and caring. www.blueprintsprograms.com/factsheet/steps-to-respect

[10] Pedro Noguera calls out the damaging stereotypes in his book, *The Trouble with Black Boys: And Other Reflections on Race, Equity and the Future of Public Education*, as "too aggressive, too loud, too violent, too dumb, too hard to control, too streetwise and too focused on sports" (Noguera, 2008, p. xx).

[11] There is research that would suggest that this is unusual, that children are acutely aware of how learning groups are formed according to ability. See Lambert, R (2015 and 2017) for discussion of children's understandings of fast and slow and ability groups.

[12] Also see Sjoberg, 2015; Pinto, 2016; Serder & Jakobsson, 2015.

[13] Wayne Au's (2007) meta-analysis examined 49 qualitative studies to examine how high-stakes testing affects curriculum and found contradictory trends in a minority of cases. He found that certain types of high-stakes tests led to curricular expansion, the integration of knowledge, and more student-centered, cooperative pedagogies. He argues that these special cases suggest the need for a more complicated understanding of the relationships between high-stakes testing and classroom practice.

[14] What the children's pictures of care in school *don't* show is the larger landscape of gender inequality, a continuing historical feature of American public schooling where "women teach and men manage" (Strober & Tyack 1989, quoted in

Restler 2017). For decades women were overrepresented in the teaching force and underrepresented as principals, but this has just begun to change according to 2015–16 figures: https://nces.ed.gov/surveys/ntps/tables/Principal_raceXgender_Percentage&Count_toNCES_091317.asp.

## Chapter 5

[1] I learned that six of these young people had moved out of the city or state. I could not find a trace of the remaining two, only speculations about their whereabouts.

[2] I benefitted from reading Barrie Thorne's (2009) reactions to viewing the *Seven Up!* films, Michael Apted's documentary film series that follows 14 British children from the ages 7–49. Her views about how the series juxtaposes different forms of time expanded my thinking about the longitudinal character of my project.

[3] This group included one Graduate Center faculty member and five doctoral students in Urban Education and Sociology at the City University of New York.

[4] In Foucault's words, technologies of self "permit individuals to effect by their own means or with the help of others a certain number of operations on their own bodies and souls, thoughts, conduct, and way of being, so as to transform themselves in order to attain a certain state of happiness, purity, wisdom, perfection, or immortality" (1988: 16–49).

[5] For a more detailed discussion of Danny's video, as well as the research methods involved in this part of the PCS project, see Luttrell et al (2012). My discussion of Danny's video here both draws on and extends the analysis offered in that article.

[6] "Enhancing" one's life in online media may take various forms and show various emphases. See Pini & Walkerdine (2011), for example, who found that the young women who produced video diaries sought to present their lives as having more "status."

[7] The popularity of the genre has grown in recent years, and there is ongoing debate about whether and to what extent K-pop can be said to be a part of the American mainstream.

[8] In the United States, Vietnamese restaurants in major metropolitan centers mark the presence of Vietnamese culture, but there is very little cultural imagery in the way of music or other media, except for that related to the Vietnam War.

[9] Another way to interpret Danny's performance is through queer theorist Muñoz's concept of "disidentification" (1999). He is writing about "queers of color" and how people who are marginalized by heteronomativity, white supremacy, and/or misogyny create their selves. Neither fully embracing nor rejecting the hegemonic discourses about their minoritized identities, those who disidentify instead "work on and against dominant ideology... to transform cultural logic from within" (1999: 11). There are many ways to theorize how the kids are performing their identities as within and against dominant discourses.

[10] A study of kids' sense of time would undoubtedly need to attend to class differences. Fine et al (2018) asked a group of teenagers in California ("students of color, largely immigrant and all poor" (p. 49)) to draw maps of "how time feels in your body at school." The precarity of time proved to be a major theme. As one boy explained his map, "But it's just a clock with a bunch of question marks, because how I think of time is, it's you can never really know what to expect from, ... I don't know, I think you can never trust, you know. It's always unexpected." (p. 54). The kids in my study did not express the same sense of time as precarious and unpredictable.

[11] Sofia and I co-authored an article together about her "immigration story" (Lico & Luttrell, 2011) upon which I draw in this section.

[12] I assumed Sofia was unfamiliar with this meaning of "foreigner" and wondered from what contexts and communities of speakers she was borrowing the term—friends, family members, school?

[13] See Chapter 2 for Sofia's fifth-grade memories and perspectives on her immigration from Albania.

[14] This perception of PCS as all "American" is at odds with the school's actual demographic profile. It is interesting that Sofia experienced it as so much more homogenous than it was.

[15] Thanks to Victoria Restler for this observation.

[16] For a review of research on teenagers' bedrooms and its historical changes see Jason Reid's (2017) book, *Get Out of My Room!: A History of Teen Bedrooms in America*. Also see Jane Brown et al's (1994) study of teenager's bedrooms as an important site of identity formation and asking teenagers to discuss their rooms as an important means for adult's to gain better insight into their lives.

[17] The conventions of *Facebook* also influenced how the kids presented their lives for the project.

[18] Among those 3–18 who say they use the internet *somewhere*, here are the percentages who say they use at home vs. the percentages who say they use at school (Children's Access to and Use of the Internet, 2015):

| | Use at home | Use at school |
|---|---|---|
| White | 89 percent | 65 percent |
| Black | 80 percent | 66 percent |
| Hispanic | 81 percent | 64 percent |
| Asian | 91 percent | 61 percent |
| Pacific Islander | 69 percent | 59 percent |
| American Indian/Alaskan Native | 74 percent | 75 percent |
| Two or more races | 87 percent | 64 percent |

[19] See Cassell & Jenkins, 1998; Kafai et al, 2007; Taylor, 2006 for discussions of the gendered world of video gaming.

[20] See Gilbert & von Wallmenich 2014 for an excellent discussion of Hall's concept of M-time and P-time and the conflict for working-mothers in the United States as they try to navigate the demands of family and work.

[21] *Call of Duty: Black Ops* is part of a series of combat video games where the player/shooter experiences the action through the eyes of the protagonist undertaking various missions—for example, "Marine One is shot down over Los Angeles, and David Mason must escort President Bosworth to safety as US drones under Menendez' control destroy the city." http://callofduty.wikia.com/wiki/Cordis_Die_(mission). The action of this gameplay includes fast-paced and bloody firefights, as well as quick problem solving to ensure the President's safety. https://en.wikipedia.org/wiki/First-person_shooter

[22] Indeed, nonprofit organizations like Common Sense Media, and grassroots internet vendors like Etsy.com offer advice and guidance, including screen time management charts available for purchase and free download. This is what Common Sense Media writes about *Call of Duty: Black Ops*. It is rated 18+, given 5 stars, and described

as a "superb but violent shooter [which] is definitely for adults only. Parents need to know that *Call of Duty: Black Ops* is a very violent military-themed first-person shooter in which players use a wide variety of weapons and explosives to kill hundreds of enemies in the campaign and countless more human-controlled avatars online. It features violent interrogations, graphic melee combat, and lots of blood. The visceral nature of the action combined with its complex Cold War narrative leave little doubt that it was designed for an adult audience. It is not appropriate for children. Note, too, the online portion of the game supports open voice chat, a feature that Common Sense Media does not recommend for pre-teens. Kids may be talking about this M-rated game because of the ad campaign, which features Kobe Bryant and Jimmy Kimmel holding guns and pretending to play the game." (www.commonsensemedia.org/game-reviews/call-of-duty-black-ops) Interestingly, upon reading the reviews listed on the site regarding the game, one learns that if the blood and gore and language is turned off, then many parent reviewers consider it appropriate for playing in a "family environment."

[23] Both Gee (2003/2007) and Davidson (2011) cite this concept to argue for game-based learning.

[24] Dr. G.'s efforts are an example of the unseen dimensions of the choreography of care in school alongside the school secretary's efforts not to punish Cesar and his brother for being late to school.

# Chapter 6

[1] For an excellent critique of the discourse of "school readiness," see Sonu and Benson (2016). They explain that the notion is quite narrow, focused solely on market demands for 21st-century competitiveness, where children are socialized into accumulating critical thinking and literacy skills in order to improve their market position, their "value" in the global economy.

[2] According to the Schools and Staffing Survey undertaken by the US Department of Education, 56 percent of American students will be non-white by 2024. While this number has grown steadily, the proportion of white teachers has remained almost unchanged for the past 15 years: in 2000, 85 percent of teachers identified as white; in 2012, that number was 82 percent. (US Department of Education, 2016; See also US Department of Education, National Center for Education Statistics. "Public School Teacher Data File," *Schools and Staffing Survey* (SASS)).

[3] I mean "revolutionary" as it is used by feminist Sylvia Federici in her collection of essays, *Revolution at Point Zero* (2012), which points to the alternative and resistive practices of home/dwelling-making as a source of social transformation.

[4] The authors review and provide a critique of the concept of "social citizenship" first offered by Marshall (1992) as a means to re-envision the dynamics of power, equality, and justice between adults and children and among different groups of children (children in poverty, boys and girls, migrant children, and so on). They consider schooling as a prime site where their expanded definition of social citizenship can be practiced. They argue that this is especially crucial in times of economic crisis and austerity where *inter*-generational and *within*-generation social solidarities get strained as different groups compete for limited state resources.

[5] Data included commissioned research; testimonies and discussions of a wide range of stakeholders, including educational and business leaders, schools and families; meta-analysis of existing educational research; and examples from notable programs and promising approaches in education.

6   The OECD is a forum of governments of 34 democracies with market economies that work with each other, as well as with more than 70 non-member economies to promote economic growth, prosperity, and sustainable development.

7   See Beauboeuf-Lafontant (2002), Noddings (1984, 1992), Valenzuela (1999), Thompson (2003), Martin (1992), and Rolón-Dow (2005) for discussions of this absence.

8   Alejandra Marchesvsky and Jeanne Theoharis detailed these effects in their book *Not Working: Latina Immigrants, Low-Wage Jobs, and the Failure of Welfare Reform* (2006) in which they show the especially harmful results of the requirement that TANF recipients accept the first job they are offered—regardless of the pay or working conditions—and that the vast majority of jobs accessible to former recipients were low-paying, "dirty," or contingent jobs that have historically been assigned to women and people of color.

9   The impact of maternal education on children is profound, particularly for children born into the bottom fifth of families. Mothers' education level has been shown to influence children's health, cognitive development, future economic security, and family structure.

10  See Glenn (2010) for her discussion of the history of coercive care and its roots in slavery and settler colonialism. It is vital to note that under the banner of "care" others' goods, property, and labor have been exploited. Uma Narayan (1995) describes how British colonialism in India justified its exploitation through the promise of making natives "better" by their encounter with British, Western, and Christian ideals. Women also were brought into the discursive spread of "good" colonialism in this way. Narayan's example shows how "care" can be deployed discursively to bad as well as to good purpose. It also points to the limits of relying upon a concept, like care, for making judgments about the world.

11  See Arnlaug Leira and Chiara Saraceno (2002) who examine changing sociological, political, and feminist discourses of care that have shifted over time and contexts: as "a public and private responsibility, a relationship of labour, love and power, as personal responsibilities and social rights" (p. 7). Their article reviews what they call "passages in the development of 'care thinking'" (p. 9) and considers public and private caring relationships, the labor of caring, and the "right" to be cared for. Ultimately, the authors explore the notion of care "as a moral and social responsibility and as a basis for entitlements" (p. 27) by examining dilemmas of public and private, labor and economy, and a rights framework. Their review provides an interesting European analysis of care and an important overview of the connections between the personal and the political in care work, in terms of labor and rights. Also see England (2005) and Romero and Pérez (2016) for their review of changing conceptualizations of the care work crisis and globalized care work that emphasizes the intertwining of gender, race, class, and citizenship.

12  See Joan Tronto (2013) for her elaboration of various models of the "passing on" of care—"the protection pass, the production pass, the taking-care-of-my-own pass, the bootstrap pass, and the charity pass"—and how each functions to keep care inequalities in place.

13  These are numbers established by the first large-scale national survey of child caregivers in 2005. See www.apa.org/pi/about/publications/caregivers/practice-settings/intervention/young-caregivers.aspx. The percentage of boy compared to girl caregivers is said to be about equal. There have been no large-scale data collected on child caregivers since 2005, in sharp contrast to several national care-giving surveys of adult caregivers conducted over the same time period (NAC/

AARP 2015). The most recent research, "Unacknowledged Caregivers: A Scoping Review of Research on Caregiving Youth in the United States" (Kavanaugh et al, 2016) reviews 22 articles on the subject, and indicates that little is known about the influence of race and ethnicity on the experience of care-giving for young people or how culture influences family reliance on youth caregivers. There is arguably need for research on this topic.

[14] 2006, The Silent Epidemic: Perspectives of High School Dropouts, a report by Civic Enterprises in association with Peter D. Hart Research Associates for the Bill and Melinda Gates Foundation, by John M. Bridgeland, John J. Dilulio, Jr., and Karen Burke Morison. www.ignitelearning.com/pdf/TheSilentEpidemic3-06FINAL.pdf

[15] Decades ago, Whiting and Whiting's (1975) study found that American children carried out tasks far less often (2 percent of observed time) than children in the Philippines (14 percent), Japan (9 percent), Mexico (8 percent) India (11 percent), and Kenya (41 percent). A recent cross-cultural study had similar findings (Ochs & Izquierdo, 2009).

[16] And historically, compulsory schooling redefined children's responsibilities toward the household economy, diminishing their participation in paid and domestic work.

[17] Examples of the issues that the NWRO newsletter in 1974 featured included forced sterilization and birth control, housing and tenants' rights, medical care, problems of energy conservation, food stamps, child care, and participating in the upcoming Democratic Charter Convention (Welfare Fighter, vol. 4, February 1974) reported in Hertz (1977).

[18] See Nadasen (2005) and Orleck (2006) for accounts of welfare mothers' actions.

[19] Waring drew from a large body of feminist work arguing that housework and childcare produce value. For recent work developing this argument, see Nancy Folbre, The Invisible Heart: Economics and Family Values (New York: New Press, 2002).

[20] Willett borrows Patricia Hill Collins's understanding of Black women's liberation politics as rooted in "mother love"—understood not as an essentialist, biological, natural instinct, but as "the power of intense connectedness" (1998: p. 200).

[21] A new form of digital divide exists where wealthier parents are restricting their children's access to screens in favor of more "free-range" play compared to low-income parents and their children, whose access to safe, outside play spaces are increasingly constricted.

[22] See Robert Wood Johnson Foundation (2007). Recess Rules: Why the undervalued playtime may be America's best investment for healthy kids and healthy schools. Retrieved June 2019 from www.rwjf.org/en/library/research/2007/09/recess-rules.html.

[23] B-club is part of UCLinks (http://uclinks.berkeley.edu/), a larger network of after-school programs, many of which are adaptations of a "Fifth-Dimension" or "Clase-Mágica," Vygotskian approach to informal learning established by Mike Cole and Olga Vásquez in San Diego. The program is a "direct descendent" of one established by Kris Gutiérrez at UCLA in 1994 (Orellana, 2016: x).

[24] Orellana refers to the pedagogy used at B-club as a "pedagogy of heart and mind" that draws on a range of thinkers including Paulo Freire, Lev Vygotsky, bell hooks, Antoine de Saint-Exupéry, and Thích Nhất Hạnh (2016: xi).

## Postlude

[1] I would learn later that my mother knew much about "swimming for style." She had been introduced to synchronized swimming when she was employed as a "mother's helper" for a well-to-do-family who took her on their summer vacation in California. She learned for herself about the strength and endurance as well as the rhythm and grace it takes to do even the simplest moves in synchronized swimming, and she would go on to teach me some of these moves.

[2] In writing about the participants in this study I have used different labels, and explained my reasons for doing so in each case. (See Luttrell 1989, 1993, 2000.)

[3] I am indebted to the American Council of Learned Societies for their enduring support of my work, first in 1994 and then again in 2015.

[4] Arts-based researcher Oikarinen-Jabai might refer to this playing as "performative research." Her description evokes the ethnographic enterprise, too, as she writes, "The "play" becomes interesting when we make ourselves fully present in a space that opens a path for us toward the borders, allowing us to encounter the Other and transgress our boundaries. When we step over the boundary, something is left behind, perhaps to surface again" (2003: 576).

[5] In 1900, W.E.B. Du Bois organized an exhibit on the "American Negro" for the Paris Exposition. The exhibit (which he developed alongside Thomas Calloway and Daniel Murray) consisted of a small library-like installation that included musical compositions and books written by Black authors, charts, models, maps, patents, and plans from several Black universities designed to highlight the advancement of African Americans since slavery. Du Bois' unique contribution to the exhibit was a series of 363 photographs, which he organized into albums, entitled Types of American Negroes, Georgia, U.S.A. and Negro Life in Georgia, U.S.A. Du Bois' albums presented images of middle-class African Americans—at work, reading, and posed for formal portraits. These images directly challenged racist caricatures of the day and the image-discourse of eugenics' "scientific proof" of Black inferiority. Further, the diversity of representations of American Blacks—the different hair textures and styles, skin tones, facial features, and expressions represented in the photos defied racist reductionism and popular claims to a single "Negro type." In Du Bois' public statement about the exhibition he suggested that viewers would encounter "several volumes of photographs of typical Negro faces, which hardly square with conventional American ideas" (1900: 577). Du Bois' albums contested dominant racist logics and frameworks with visual claims about who African Americans were, are, and may become. For all these reasons, Shawn Michelle Smith (2004) refers to these albums as "counterarchives"—images that contest the contents and omissions of official archives.

[6] These two exercises reflect different epistemological approaches to "reading" photographs, one that is grounded in a positivist social science approach of "content analysis" and the other grounded in semiotics and the impact that photographic images have on viewers. See Gillian Rose (2012) for an excellent review of an array of approaches and how these approaches have changed since the 1950s.

[7] We could ask the same question about excerpting or "cutting" a slice of interview text from its larger context. Indeed, researchers can never show the "whole picture" (as there is no whole picture). Collage seems to start from this understanding. I thank Maya Pindyck for this reminder.

# Notes

8   See Grimshaw (2001) and Grimshaw & Ravetz (2005) about the fraught relationship between vision (direct observation vs. photography, video, film) and knowledge in ethnographic inquiry.

9   We are grateful to have received two PSC–CUNY research awards that supported these efforts.

10  See Luttrell et al (2012) for a description of David's video editing.

11  Barad is the next generation of feminist scientists to follow in McClintock and Fox Keller's footsteps along with Haraway (2007, 2016) and de la Bellacasa (2011, 2017). I am not steeped in the feminist post-humanist perspectives of these authors. But I am drawn to the need to challenge the mostly Western hierarchical divisions of bodies and "things" or "matter"; of human and non-human as a means to extend arguments stemming from standpoint theory and the importance placed on thinking from marginalized experiences as key to generating knowledge that challenges oppression (Smith, 1987; Collins, 2000; Hartsock, 1983; Harding, 1991, 2004).

12  Full disclosure: Claudia Mitchell and researchers from her Participatory Cultures Lab https://participatorycultureslab.com/ at McGill University met with me and members of the Collaborative Seeing Studio at the Graduate Center https://collaborativeseeingstudio.commons.gc.cuny.edu/ to discuss our common interests in doing visual research. These meetings (2011, 2012) generated important dialogue around issues of reflexivity, ethics, the meaning and practice of participation, and the legacies and traditions that informed our different practices.

# References

Abrams, L. S. & Gibbs, J. T. (2002) "Disrupting the logic of home-school relations: parent involvement strategies and practices of inclusion and exclusion," *Urban Education*, 37(3): 384–407.

Abu El-Haj, T. R. (2006) *Elusive Justice: Wrestling with Difference and Educational Equity in Everyday Practice*, New York: Routledge.

Abu El-Haj, T. R. (2015) *Unsettled Belonging: Educating Palestinian American Youth after 9/11*, Chicago: Chicago University Press.

Acker, S. (1999) *The Realities of Teachers' Work: Never a Dull Moment*, London: Cassell.

Ada, A. F. & Zubizarreta, R. (2001) "Parent narratives: the cultural bridge between Latino parents and their children," in M. de la Luz Reyes and J. J. Halcon (eds) *The Best For Our Children: Critical Perspectives on Literacy for Latino Students*, New York: Teachers College Press, pp 229–44.

Adair, V. (2001) "Poverty and the (broken) promise of higher education," *Harvard Educational Review*, 71(2): 217–40.

Adler, R. A. & Adler, R. (1986) "Introduction," *Sociological Studies of Child Development*, 1: 3–9.

Ahn, H. (2015) "Economic well-being of low-income single-mother families following welfare reform in the USA," *International Journal of Social Welfare*, 24(1): 14–26.

Alanen, L. (1988) "Rethinking childhood," *Acta Sociologica*, 31(1): 53–67.

Albelda, R. (2011) "Time binds: US antipoverty policies, poverty, and the well-being of single mothers," *Feminist Economics*, 17(4): 189–214.

Albelda, R. & Withorn, A. (eds) (2002) *Lost Ground: Welfare Reform, Poverty and Beyond*, Boston: South End Press.

Alder, N. (2002) "Interpretations of the meaning of care: creating caring relationships in urban middle school classrooms," *Urban Education*, 37(2), 241–66.

Alderson, P. (1995) *Listening to Children: Children, Ethics and Social Research*, London: Barnardo's.

Alexander, D. & Lewis, L. (2014) *Condition of America's Public School Facilities: 2012–13* (NCES 2014-022). U.S. Department of Education. Washington, DC: National Center for Education Statistics. http://nces.ed.gov/pubsearch. Accessed June 2019.

Ambert, A. M. (1986) "Sociology of sociology: the place of children in North American sociology," *Sociological Studies of Child Development*, 1: 11–31.

American Academy of Pediatrics (2013) "Children, adolescents, and the media," *Pediatrics*, 132: 958–961.

American Association of University Women (2000) "*Tech-Savvy: Educating Girls in the New Computer Age*," Washington DC: American Association of University Women Education Foundation.

Antrop-González, R. & De Jesús, A. (2006) "Toward a theory of critical care in urban small school reform: examining structures and pedagogies of caring in two Latino community-based schools," *International Journal of Qualitative Studies in Education* (QSE), 19(4): 409–33.

Anyon, J. (1997) *Ghetto Schooling: A Political Economy of Urban Educational Reform*, New York: Teachers College Press.

Anyon, J. (2006) "What should count as educational research: Notes toward a new paradigm," in G. Ladson-Billings and W. Tate (eds) *Education Research in the Public Interest: Social Justice, Action and Policy*, New York and London: Teachers College Press, pp 17–27.

Anyon, J. (2005/2014) *Radical Possibilities: Public Policy, Urban Education, and A New Social Movement*, 2nd edn, New York: Routledge.

Appadurai, A. (1986) *The Social Life of Things: Commodities in Cultural Perspective: Ethnohistory Workshop & Symposium on the Relationship between Commodities Culture*, New York: Cambridge University Press.

Aries, P. (1962) *Centuries of Childhood: A Social History of Family Life*, New York: Vintage.

Arnold, J. E., Graesch, A. P., Ragazzini, E., & Ochs, E. (2012) *Life at Home in the Twenty-First Century: 32 Families Open Their Doors*, Los Angeles, Calif: UCLA/Cotsen Institute of Archaeology Press.

Arnot, M. & Reay, D. (2007) "A sociology of pedagogic voice: power, inequality and pupil consultation," *Discourse: Studies in the Cultural Politics of Education*, 28(3): 311–25.

Au, W. (2007) "High-stakes testing and curricular control: a qualitative metasynthesis," *Educational Researcher*, 36(5), 258–67.

Auslander, L. (2005) "Beyond words," *The American Historical Review*, 110(4): 1015–45.

Ayers, J., Ayers, R., & Dohrn, B. (2001) *Zero Tolerance: Resisting the Drive for Punishment in Our Schools. A Handbook for Parents, Students, Educators, and Citizens*, New York: The New Press.

Bachelard, G. (1957) *La Poétique de L'espace*, Paris: Les Presses Universitaires de France, 3e édition, 1961, pp 215. Première édition, 1957. Collection: Bibliothèque de philosophie contemporaine.

Baker, B. (1998) "'Childhood' in the emergence and spread of U.S. public schools," in T. Popkewitz and M. Brennan (eds) *Foucault's Challenge: Discourse, Knowledge, and Power in Education*, New York: Teachers College Press, pp 117–43.

Bakhtin, M. M. (1981) *The Dialogic Imagination: Four Essays*, Austin: University of Texas Press Slavic Series.

Ball, S. J. (2003) "The teacher's soul and the terrors of performativity," *Journal of Education Policy*, 18(2): 215–28.

Baltodano, M. (2012) "Neoliberalism and the demise of public education: the corporatization of schools of education," *International Journal of Qualitative Studies in Education*, 25(4): 487–507.

Barad, K. (2007) *Meeting the Universe Halfway*, Durham: Duke University Press.

Barad, K. (2012) "On touching—the inhuman that therefore I am," *Differences*, 23(3): 206–23.

Barthes, R. (1981) *Camera Lucida: Reflections on Photography*, New York: Hill and Wang.

Beauboeuf-Lafontant, T. (2002) "A womanist experience of caring: understanding the pedagogy of exemplary black women teachers," *The Urban Review*, 34(1): 71–86.

Becker, H. (1986) *Doing Things Differently: Selected Papers*, Evanston, IL: Northwestern University Press.

Behrman, S. N. (1954/1982) *The Worcester Account*. Worcester, MA: Tatnuck Bookseller Press.

Berger, J. (1991) *Ways of Seeing*, London: British Broadcasting Corporation.

Berliner, D. & Glass, G. (2014) *Fifty Myths and Lies That Threaten America's Public Schools: The Real Crisis in Education*, New York: Teachers College Press.

Bernstein, R. (2011) *Racial Innocence Performing American Childhood from Slavery to Civil Rights*, New York: New York University Press.

Bianchi, S., Robinson, J. P., & Milkie, M. A. (2007) *Changing Rhythms of American Family Life*, New York: Russell Sage Foundation.

Biklen, S. K. (1995) *School Work: Gender and the Cultural Construction of Teaching*, New York: Teachers College Press.

Bloch, M., Holmlund, K., Moqvist, I., & Popkewitz, T. (2004) *Governing Children, Families and Education: Restructuring the Welfare State*, New York: Palgrave Macmillan.

Boal, A. (1979) *Theatre of the Oppressed*, New York: Erizon Books Theatre Communications Group.

Boix-Mansilla, V. B. (2004) *Thinking Like an Educator: Modeling Integrative Thinking in Educational Analysis-Documentation Plan*, Harvard Graduate School of Education.

Bonilla-Silva, E. (1997) "Rethinking racism: toward a structural interpretation," *American Sociological Review*, 62(3): 465–80.

Bonilla-Silva, E. (2003) *Racism Without Racists: Color-blind Racism and the Persistence of Racial Inequality in America*, Lanham: Rowman & Littlefield Publishers.

Brown, J., Dykers, C., Steele, J., & White, A. (1994) "Teenage room culture: where media and identities intersect," *Communication Research*, 21(6): 813–27.

Brown, K. M. (1991) *Mama Lola: A Vodou Priestess in Brooklyn*, Berkeley: University of California Press.

Brown, S. & Vaughn, C. (2009) *Play: How It Shapes the Brain, Opens the Imagination, and Invigorates the Soul*, New York: Penguin Press.

Buckingham, D. (2011) *The Material Child: Growing Up in Consumer Culture*, Cambridge: Polity.

Bureau of Labor Statistics (2014) "American Time Use Survey—2014 Results," United States Department of Labor: 18–19 Tables 8A and 8B.

Burton, L. (2007) "Childhood adultification in economically disadvantaged families: a conceptual model," *Family Relations*, 56(4): 329–45.

Burton, L., Obeidallah, D., & Allison, K. (1996) "Ethnographic insights on social context and adolescent development among inner-city African-American teens," in R. Jessor, A. Colby and R. Schweder (eds) *Ethnography and Human Development: Context and Meaning in Social Inquiry*, Chicago: University of Chicago Press, pp 395–419.

Campt, T. (2017) *Listening to Images*, Durham: Duke University Press.

Cantillon, B., Chzhen, Y., Sudhanshu, H., & Nolan, B. (2017) *Children of Austerity: Impact of the Great Recession on Child Poverty in Rich Countries*, Oxford: Oxford University Press.

Cassell, J. & Jenkins, H. (1998) *From Barbie to Mortal Kombat: Gender and Computer Games*, Cambridge, Mass: MIT Press.

Cavin, E. (1994) "In search of the viewfinder: a study of a child's perspective," *Visual Sociology*, 9(1): 27–41.

Chalfen, R. (1981) "A sociovidistic approach to children's filmmaking: the Philadelphia project," *Studies in Visual Communication*, 7(1): 3–32.

Chalfen, R. (1987) *Snapshot Versions of Life*, Bowling Green, OH: Bowling Green State University Popular Press.

Charon, R. (2006) *Narrative Medicine: Honoring the Stories of Illness*, Oxford: Oxford University Press.

Clark, C. D. (1999) "The Autodriven interview: a photographic viewfinder into children's experience," *Visual Sociology*, 14(1): 39–50.

Clark-Ibanez, M. (2004) "Framing the social world with photo-elicitation interviews," *American Behavioral Scientist*, 47(12): 1507–27.

Clawson, D. & Gerstel, N. (2014) *Unequal Time: Gender, Class, and Family in Employment Schedules*. New York: Russell Sage Foundation.

Collier, J. & Collier, M. (1986) *Visual Anthropology: Photography as a Research Method* (Revised and expanded edition), Albuquerque: University of New Mexico Press.

Collins, A. (1998) "Mothers as teachers—teachers as mothers," in S. Abbey and A. O'Reilly (eds) *Redefining Motherhood: Changing Identities and Patterns*, Toronto: Second Story Press, pp 92–102.

Collins, J. & Mayer, V. (2010) *Both Hands Tied: Welfare Reform and the Race to the Bottom in the Low-Wage Labor Market*, Chicago: University of Chicago Press.

Collins, P. H. (1998) *Fighting Words: Black Women and the Search for Justice*, Minneapolis: University of Minnesota Press.

Collins, P. H. (2000) *Black Feminist Thought Knowledge, Consciousness, and the Politics of Empowerment*, New York: Routledge.

Conrad, R. (2012) "'My future doesn't know ME': time and subjectivity in poetry by young people," *Childhood*, 19(2): 204–18.

Cook, T. & Hess, E. (2007) "What the camera sees and from whose perspective: fun methodologies for engaging children in enlightening adults," *Childhood*, 14(1): 29–45.

Cooper, C. W. (2003) "The detrimental impact of teacher bias: lessons learned from the standpoint of African American mothers," *Teacher Education Quarterly*, 30(2): 101–16.

Cooper, C. W. (2007) "School choice as 'motherwork': Valuing African-American women's educational advocacy and resistance," *International Journal of Qualitative Studies in Education*, 20(5): 491–512.

Cooper, C. W. (2009) "Parent involvement, African American mothers, and the politics of educational care," *Equity & Excellence in Education*, 42(4): 379–94.

Corsaro, W. A. (1997/2015) *The Sociology of Childhood*, 4th edn, Los Angeles: Sage.

Crain, W. C. (2003) *Reclaiming Childhood: Letting Children Be Children in Our Achievement-Oriented Society*, New York: Times Books.

Crenshaw, K., Ocen, P., & Nanda, J. (2015) *Black Girls Matter: Pushed Out, Overpoliced, and Underprotected*, New York: African American Policy Forum.

Croghan, R., Griffin, C., Hunter, J., & Phoenix, A. (2008) "Young people's constructions of self: notes on the use and analysis of the photo-elicitation methods," *International Journal of Social Research Methodology: Theory & Practice,* 11(4): 345–56.

Csikszentmihalyi, M. (1990) *Flow: The Psychology of Optimal Experience,* New York: Harper and Row.

Csikszentmihalyi, M. & Rochberg-Halton, E. (1981) *The Meaning of Things: Domestic Symbols and the Self,* New York: Cambridge University Press.

Daly, M. & Standing, G. (2001) "Introduction" In M. Daly (ed), *Care Work: The Quest for Security,* Geneva: International Labour Office.

David, M. (1993) *Parents, Gender, and Education Reform, Family life series,* Cambridge: Polity.

David, M., Edwards, R., & Alldred, P. (2001) "Children and school-based research: 'informed consent' or 'educated consent?'", *British Educational Research Journal,* 27(3): 347–65.

Davidson, C. (2011) *Now You See It: How Technology and Brain Science will Transform Schools and Business for the 21st Century,* New York: Penguin.

Davis, A. (1981) *Women, Race, & Class,* New York: Random House.

De Gaetano, Y. (2007) "The role of culture in engaging Latino parents' involvement in school." *Urban Education,* 42(2): 145–62.

de la Bellacasa, M. (2011) "Matters of care in technosience: assembling neglected things," *Social Studies of Science,* 41(1): 85–106.

de la Bellacasa, M. (2017) *Matters of Care: Speculative Ethics in More Than Human Worlds,* Minneapolis: University of Minnesota Press.

De La Vega, E. (2007) "Mexican/Latina mothers and schools: changing the way we view parent involvement," in Montero-Sieburth and Meléndez (eds) *Latinos In a Changing Society,* Westport, CT: Praeger, pp 161–82.

Delgado Bernal, D. (2001) "Learning and living pedagogies of the home: the mestiza consciousness of Chicana students," *International Journal of Qualitative Studies in Education,* 14 (5): 623–39.

Delpit, L. D. (2006) *Other People's Children: Cultural Conflict in the Classroom,* New York: The New Press.

DeNicolo, C. P., Yu, M., Crowley, C. B., & Gabel, S. L. (2017) "Reimagining critical care and problematizing sense of school belonging as a response to inequality for immigrants and children of immigrants," *Review of Research in Education,* 41(1): 500–30.

DeVault, M. (1991) *Feeding the Family: The Social Organization of Caring as Gendered Work,* Chicago: University of Chicago Press.

Deprez, L. & Gatta, L. (eds) (2008) "Beyond the numbers: how the lived experiences of women challenge the 'success' of welfare reform," Special Issue, *The Journal of Sociology & Social Welfare*, 35(3).

Devine, D. (2013) "Valuing children differently? Migrant children in education," *Children & Society*, 27(4): 282–94.

Devine, D. & Luttrell, W. (2013) "Children and value: education in neo-liberal times," Special Issue Introduction, The "valuing" of children in education in neo-liberal times—global perspectives; local practices, *Children & Society*, 27(4): 241–4.

Devine, D. & Cochburn, T. (2018) "Theorizing children's social citizenship: new welfare states and inter-generational justice," *Childhood*, 25(2): 142–57.

Diamond, J. & Gomez, K. (2004) "African American parents' educational orientations: the importance of social class and parents' perceptions of schools," *Education and Urban Society*, 36(4): 383–427.

Dodson, L. (2011) *The Moral Underground: How Ordinary Americans Subvert an Unfair Economy*, New York: The New Press.

Dodson, L. & Dickert, J. (2004) "Girls' family labor in low-income households: a decade of qualitative research," *Journal of Marriage and Family*, 66(2): 318–32.

Dodson, L. & Luttrell, W. (2011) "Families facing untenable choices," *Contexts*, 10(1): 38–42.

Dodson, L. & Albelda, R. (2012) "How youth are put at risk by parents' low-wage jobs," Center for Social Policy, John W. McCormack Graduate School of Policy and Global Studies, University of Massachusetts, Boston.

Dodson, L. & Deprez, L. (2017) "Why higher education is a must for low-income mothers," Scholars Strategy Network, https://scholars. org/brief/why-higher-education-must-low-income-mothers. Accessed January 5, 2019.

Dodson, L. & Deprez, L. (2019) "'Keeping us in our place': low-income moms barred from college success," *Contexts*, 18(1): 36–41.

Du Bois, W. E. B. (1900) "The American Negro at Paris," *The American Monthly Review of Reviews*, 22(5): 575–7.

Du Bois, W. E. B. (1903) *The Souls of Black Folk*, New York: New American Library, Inc.

Du Bois, W. E. B. (1912) "A children's number," W. E. B. Du Bois Papers (MS 312). Special Collections and University Archives, University of Massachusetts Amherst Libraries.

Du Bois, W. E. B. (1923) "A children's number," Editorial, *Crisis*, July: 103.

Dumas, M. J. & Nelson, J. D. (2016) "(Re)imagining black boyhood: toward a critical framework for educational research," *Harvard Educational Review*, 86(1): 27–47.

Edin, K. J. & Shaefer, H. L. (2015) *$2.00 a Day: Living on Almost Nothing in America*, Boston: Houghton Mifflin Harcourt.

Ehrenreich B. & Hochschild A. (eds) (2003) *Global Woman: Nannies, Maids and Sex Workers in the New Economy*, Metropolitan Books: New York.

Elkind, D. (2007) *The Power of Play: How Spontaneous, Imaginative Activities lead to Happier, Healthier Children*, Cambridge: Da Capo Press.

England, P. (2005) "Emerging theories of care work," *Annual Review of Sociology*, 31: 381–99.

Evans, A. E. (2007) "*Changing faces: suburban school response to demographic change*," *Education and Urban Society*, 39(3): 315–48.

Fabricant, M. & Fine, M. (2012) *Charter Schools and the Corporate Makeover of Public Education: What's at Stake?*, New York: Teachers College Press.

Fabricant, M. & Fine, M. (2013) *The Changing Politics of Education: Privatization and the Dispossessed Lives Left Behind*, Boulder: Paradigm Publishers.

Federici, S. (2012) *Revolution at Point Zero: Housework, Reproduction and Feminist Struggles*, Oakland, CA: PM Press.

Feeley, M. (2014) *Learning Care Lessons: Literacy, Love, Care and Solidarity*, London: The Tufnell Press.

Ferguson, A. A. (2000) *Bad Boys: Public Schools in the Making of Black Masculinity, Law, Meaning, and Violence Series*, Ann Arbor, MI: University of Michigan Press.

Fine, M. with C. Greene & S. Sanchez (2018) "'Wicked problems,' 'Flying moneys,' and Prec(ar)ious lives: a matter of time?" in M. Fine, *Just Research in Contentious Times: Widening the Methodological Imagination*, New York: Teachers College Press, pp 49–67.

Fisher, B. M. (2001) *No Angel in the Classroom: Teaching Through Feminist Discourse*, Lanham, Md.: Rowman & Littlefield Publishers.

Flores, N. & Rosa, J. (2015) "Undoing appropriateness: raciolinguistic ideologies and language diversity in education," *Harvard Educational Review*, 85(2): 149–71.

Folbre, N. (1994) *Who Pays for the Kids?: Gender and the Structures of Constraint*, London: Routledge.

Folbre, N. (2002) *The Invisible Heart: Economics and Family Values*, New York: The New Press.

Folbre, N. & Bittman, M. (2004) *Family Time: The Social Organization of Care*, New York: Psychology Press.

Fontaine, C. (2015) *Growing Up Online: Identity, Development and Agency in Networked Girlhoods*, PhD Dissertation, Graduate Center at the City University of New York.

Fontaine, C. & Luttrell, W. (2015) "Re-Centering the role of care in young people's multimodal literacies: a collaborative seeing approach," in M. Hamilton, R. Heydon, K. Hibbert, & R. Stooke (eds) *Negotiating Spaces for Literacy Learning: Multimodality and Governmentality*, New York, Bloomsbury Books, 43–56.

Foucault, M. (1980) *Power/Knowledge: Selected Interviews and Other Writings, 1972–1977*, New York: Vintage.

Foucault, M. (1988) *Technologies of the Self: A Seminar with Michel Foucault*, Amherst: University of Massachusetts Press.

Frankenberg, R. (1993) *White Women, Race Matters: The Social Construction of Whiteness*, Minneapolis: University of Minnesota Press.

Fraser, N. (2013) *Fortunes of Feminism: From State-Managed Capitalist to Neoliberal Crisis*, London & New York: Verso Press.

Fraser, N. (2016a) "Contradictions of capital and care," *New Left Review*, 2(100): 99–117.

Fraser, N. (2016b) "Capitalism's crisis of care," *Dissent*, Fall 2016, www.dissentmagazine.org/article/nancy-fraser-interview-capitalism-crisis-of-care. Accessed March 11, 2018.

Gabriel, T. (2011) "Teachers wonder, why the heapings of scorn?", *New York Times*, March 2, 2011: A1.

García, S. B. & Guerra, P. L. (2004) "Deconstructing deficit thinking: working with educators to create more equitable learning environments," *Education and Urban Society*, 36(2): 150–68.

Garey, A. I. (2011) "Maternally yours: the emotion work of 'Maternal Visibility,'" in A. Garey and K. V. Hansen (eds) *At the Heart of Work and Family: Engaging the Ideas of Arlie Hochschild*, New Brunswick, NJ: Rutgers University Press, pp 171–9.

Garey, A. I., Hertz, R., Nelson, M. (2014) *Open to Disruption: Time and Craft in the Practice of Slow Sociology*, Nashville: Vanderbilt University.

Gartner, A., Kohler, M. C., & Riessman, F. (1971) *Children Teach Children: Learning by Teaching*, New York: Harper & Row.

Gay, G. (2010) *Culturally Responsive Teaching: Theory, Research, and Practice*, New York: Teachers College.

Gee, J. (2003/2007) *What Video Games Have to Teach Us About Learning and Literacy*, New York: Palgrave MacMillan.

Gee, J. & Hayes, E. (2010) *Women and Gaming: The SIMS and 21st Century Learning*, New York: Palgrave Macmillan.

Gilbert, J. & von Wallmenich, L. (2014) "When words fail us: mother time, relational attention, and the rhetorics of focus and balance," *Women's Studies in Communication*, 37(1): 66–89.

Gilligan, C. (1982) *In a Different Voice: Psychological Theory and Women's Development*, Cambridge, MA: Harvard University Press.

Gilligan, C. (1993) "Letter to readers," in *In a Different Voice*, Cambridge: Harvard University Press.

Gilmore, R. W. (2007) *Golden Gulag: Prisons, Surplus, Crisis, and Opposition in Globalizing California*, Berkeley: University of California Press.

Ginsburg, K. R. (2007) "The importance of play in promoting healthy child development and maintaining strong parent-child bonds," *Pediatrics*, 119(1): 182–91.

Ginwright, S. (2016) *Hope and Healing in Urban Education: How Urban Activists and Teachers are Reclaiming Matters of the Heart*, New York: Routledge.

Glenn, E. N. (2010) *Forced to Care: Coercion and Caregiving in America*, Cambridge: Harvard University Press.

Glenn, E. N. (2015) "Settler colonialism as structure: a framework for comparative studies of U.S. race and gender formation," *Sociology of Race and Ethnicity*, 1(1): 52–72.

Goff, P. A., Jackson, M. C., Di Leone, B. A. L., Culotta, C. M., & Ditomasso, N. A. (2014) "The essence of innocence: consequences of dehumanizing black children," *Journal of Personality and Social Psychology*, 106(4): 526–45.

Goffman, E. (1963/1986) *Stigma: Notes on the Management of Spoiled Identity*, New York: Simon and Schuster.

Griffith, A. & Smith, D. (2005) *Mothering for Schooling* (Vol. 2), London: Routledge.

Grimshaw, A. (2001) *The Ethnographer's Eye: Ways of Seeing in Anthropology*, Cambridge: Cambridge University Press.

Grimshaw, A. & Ravetz, A. (2005) *Visualizing Anthropology*, Bristol, UK: Intellect.

Gross, L. P., Katz, J. S., & Ruby, J. (1988) *Image Ethics: The Moral Rights of Subjects in Photographs, Film, and Television*, Oxford: Oxford University Press.

Grumet, M. (1988) *Bitter Milk: Women and Teaching*, Amherst: University of Massachusetts Press.

Hall, E. T. (1984/1989) *The Dance of Life: The Other Dimension of Time*, Garden City, N.Y.: Anchor Press/Doubleday.

Handler, J. L. & Hasenfeld, Y. (2007) *Blame Welfare, Ignore Poverty and Inequality*. New York: Cambridge University Press.

Haraway, D. (2007) *When Species Meet*, Minneapolis: University of Minnesota Press.

Haraway, D. (2016) *Staying With the Trouble: Making Kin in the Chthulucene*, Durham, NC: Duke University Press.

Harding, S. (1991) *Whose Science? Whose Knowledge? Thinking from Women's Lives*, Ithaca, NY: Cornell University Press.

Harding, S. (2004) *The Feminist Standpoint Theory Reader: Intellectual and Political Controversies*, New York: Routledge.

Harkness, S. & Super, C. (eds) (2000) *Parents' Cultural Belief Systems: Their Origins, Expressions and Consequences*, New York: Guilford Press.

Hart, M. (2002) *The Poverty of Life-Affirming Work: Motherwork, Education, and Social Change (Contributions in Women's Studies, No. 194)*, Westport, Conn.: Greenwood Press.

Hartmann, H. (1979) "The unhappy marriage of Marxism and feminism: towards a more progressive union," *Capital & Class*, 3(2): 1–33.

Hartsock, N. (1983) "The feminist standpoint: toward a specifically feminist historical materialism," in N. Hartsock, *Money, Sex and Power: Toward a Feminist Historical Materialism*, New York: Longman, pp 231–51.

Hays, S. (1996) *The Cultural Contradictions of Motherhood*, New Haven: Yale University Press.

Heidbrink, L. (2018) "Circulation of care among unaccompanied migrant youth from Guatemala," *Children and Youth Services Review*, 92: 30.

Hendershot, H. (ed) (2004) *Nickelodeon Nation: The History, Politics, and Economics of America's Only TV Channel for Kids*, New York: New York University Press.

Henry, M. (1996) *Parent-School Collaboration Feminist Organizational Structures and School Leadership (SUNY Series, Social Context of Education)*, Albany, N.Y.: State University of New York Press.

Hertz, S. (1977) "The politics of the welfare mother's rights movement: a case study," *Signs: Journal of Women in Culture and Society*, 2(3): 600–11.

Higonnet, A. (1998) *Pictures of Innocence: The History and Crisis of Ideal Childhood*, London: Thames and Hudson.

Hirsch, M. (1997) *Family Frames: Photography, Narrative, and Postmemory*, Cambridge: Harvard University Press.

Hochschild, A. R. (1983/2012) *The Managed Heart: Commercialization of Human Feeling*, Berkeley, CA: University of California Press.

Hochschild, A. R. (2003) *The Commercialization of Intimate Life: Notes on Family and Work*, Berkeley, CA: University of California Press.

Hochschild, A. R. (2000) "The nanny chain," *The American Prospect*, 11(3): 1–4.

Hochschild, A. R. (2002) "Love and gold," in B. Erenreich & A. R. Hochschild (eds) *Global Woman: Nannies, Maids, and Sex Workers in the New Economy*, New York: Metropolitan Books, pp 15–30.

Hochschild, A. R. (1989/2003) *The Second Shift*. New York: Penguin Books.

Hoffman, N. (1981) *Woman's "True" Profession: Voices from the History of Teaching*, Old Westbury, N.Y.: New York: Feminist Press; McGraw-Hill.

Hollins, W. (2018) "Guilty by association: A critical analysis of how imprisonment affects the children of those behind bars," PhD Dissertation, Graduate Center at the City University of New York.

hooks, b. (1984) *Feminist Theory: From Margins to Center*, Boston: South End Press.

hooks, b. (1989) "Choosing the margin as space of radical openness," *Framework: The Journal of Cinema and Media* (36): 15–23.

hooks, b. (1990) "Homeplace (a site of resistance)," in J. Ritchie and K. Ronald (eds) *Available Means: An Anthology of Women's Rhetoric(s)*, Pittsburgh, PA: University of Pittsburgh Press, pp 383–90.

hooks, b. (1994) *Teaching to Transgress*, New York: Routledge.

Hull, G. A. (2003) "At last: youth culture and digital media: new literacies for new times," *Research in the Teaching of English*, 38(2): 229–33.

Ignatieff, M. (2001) *Human Rights as Politics and Idolatry*, Princeton: Princeton University Press.

Ito, M., Baumer, S., Bittanti, M., boyd, d., Cody, R., Stephenson, B. H., Horst, H. A., Lange, P. G., Mahendran, D., Martínez, K. Z., Pascoe, C. J., Perkel, D., Robinson, L., Sims, C., & Tripp, L. (2009) *Hanging Out, Messing Around, and Geeking Out: Kids Living and Learning With New Media*, Cambridge: MIT Press.

Jackson, I., Sealey-Ruiz, Y., & Watson, W. (2014) "Reciprocal love: mentoring black and latino males through an ethos of care," *Urban Education*, 49(4): 394–417.

James, A. & Prout, A. (1990) *Constructing and Reconstructing Childhood: Contemporary Issues in the Sociological Study of Childhood*, London: Falmer Press.

James, J. H. (2010) "Teachers as mothers in the elementary classroom: negotiating the needs of self and other," *Gender and Education*, 22(5): 521–34.

James, J. H. (2012) "Caring for 'others': examining the interplay of mothering and deficit discourses in teaching," *Teaching and Teacher Education: An International Journal of Research and Studies*, 28(2): 165–73.

Jarrett, K. (2003) "Labour of love: an archaeology of affect as power in e-commerce," *Journal of Sociology*, 39(4): 335–52.

Jenkins, H. (2004) "Interview with Geraldine Laybourne," in H. Hendershot (ed) *Nickelodeon Nation: The History, Politics, and Economics of America's Only TV Channel for Kids*, New York, New York University Press.

Jenks, C. (1992) *The Sociology of Childhood: Essential Readings*, Batsford: London and Gregg Revivals.

Kafai, Y. B., Cook, M. S. & Fields, D. A. (2007) "Blacks deserve bodies too!" Design and discussion about diversity and race in a tween online world in Akira Baba (ed) *Situated Play: Proceedings of the Digital Games Research Association (DIGRA)*, Tokyo: University of Tokyo, pp 269–277.

Kaplan, E. B. (2013) *"We Live in the Shadow": Inner-city Kids Tell Their Stories Through Photographs*, Philadelphia: Temple University Press.

Katz, C. (2011) "Accumulation, excess, childhood: Toward a countertopgraphy of waste and risk," *Documents d'Anàlisi Geogràfica* [en línia], 57(1): 47–60.

Kavanaugh, M., Stamatopoulos, V., Cohen, D., & Zhang, L. (2016) "Unacknowledged caregivers: a scoping review of research on caregiving youth in the United States," *Adolescent Research Review* 1(1): 29–49.

Keeley, B. (2007) *Human Capital: How What You Know Shapes Your Life (OECD Insights)*, Paris, France: OECD.

Kehily, M. J. (2009) *An Introduction to Childhood Studies*, 2nd edn, Maidenhead, UK: Open University Press.

Keller, E. F. (1982) "Feminism and science," *Signs: Journal of Women in Culture and Society*, 7: 589–602.

Keller, E. F. (1983) *A Feeling for the Organism: The Life and Work of Barbara McClintock*, New York: W.H. Freeman.

Koonce, D. & Harper, Jr., W. (2005) "Engaging African American parents in the schools: a community-based consultation model," *Journal of Educational and Psychological Consultation*, 16(1–2): 55–74.

Kumashiro, K. K. (2012) *Bad Teacher!: How Blaming Teachers Distorts the Bigger Picture*, New York: Teachers College Press, Columbia University.

Ladson Billings, G. (2006) "From the achievement gap to the education debt: understanding achievement in U.S. schools," *Educational Researcher*, 35: 7.

Ladson Billings, G. (2011) "Boyz to men? Teaching to restore Black boys' childhood," *Race, Ethnicity and Education*, 14(1): 7–15.

Lakoff, G. & Johnson, M. (1980) *Metaphors We Live By*, Chicago: University of Chicago Press.

Lambert, R. (2015) "Constructing and resisting disability in mathematics classrooms: a case study exploring the impact of different pedagogies," *Educational Studies in Mathematics*, 89(1): 1–18.

Lambert, R. (2017) "'When I am being rushed it slows down my brain': constructing self-understandings as a mathematics learner," *International Journal of Inclusive Education*, 21(5): 521–31.

Lareau, A. (2003) *Unequal Childhoods: Class, Race, and Family Life*, Berkeley: University of California Press.

Lareau, A. & Horvat, E. M. (1999) "Moments of social inclusion and exclusion race, class, and cultural capital in family-like relationships," *Sociology of Education*, 72: 37–53.

Lasch, C. (1995) *Haven in a Heartless World: The Family Besieged*, New York: Norton & Co.

Lasén, A. & Gómez-Cruz, E. (2009) "Digital photography and picture sharing: redefining the public/private divide," *Knowledge, Technology & Policy*, 22:205–15.

Lee, N. (2001) *Childhood and Society: Growing Up in an Age of Uncertainty*, Philadelphia, PA: Open University Press.

Leira, A. & Saraceno, C. (2002) "Care: actors, relationships and contexts," in B. Hobson, J. Lewis & B. Siim (eds) *Contested Concepts in Gender and Social Politics*, Cheltenham/Northampton: Edward Elgar.

Lewis, A. E. & Forman, T. A. (2002) "Contestation or collaboration? A comparative study of home-school relations," *Anthropology & Education Quarterly*, 33(1): 60–89.

Lico, S. & Luttrell, W. (2011) "An important part of me: a dialogue about difference," *Harvard Educational Review*, 81(4): 667– 86.

Link, H., Gallo, S., & Wortham, S. E. F. (2017) "The production of schoolchildren as enlightenment subjects," *American Educational Research Journal*, 54(5): 834–67.

Linn, S. (2004) *Consuming Kids: The Hostile Takeover of Childhood*, New York: New Press.

Linn, S. (2008) *The Case for Make Believe: Saving Play in a Commercialized World*, New York: New Press.

Lipman, P. (2011) *The New Political Economy of Urban Education: Neoliberalism, Race, and the Right to the City* (1st edn), New York: Routledge.

Livingstone, S. (2007) "From family television to bedroom culture: young people's media at home," in E. Devereux (ed), *Media Studies: Key Issues and Debates*, Los Angeles, London, New Delhi, Singapore: Sage, pp 302–19.

Löfgren, R. & Löfgren, H. (2017) "Swedish students' experiences of national testing in science: a narrative approach," *Curriculum Inquiry*, 47(4): 390–410.

Lomawaima, K. T. & McCarty, T. L (2006) *"To Remain an Indian": Lessons in Democracy from a Century of Native American Education*, New York: Teachers College Press.

Lopez, N. (2003) *Hopeful Girls, Troubled Boys: Race and Gender Disparity in Urban Education*, New York: Routledge.

Luttrell, W. (1989) "Working-class women's ways of knowing: effects of gender, race and class," *Sociology of Education*, 62(1): 33–46.

Luttrell, W. (1993). "'The teachers, they all had their pets': concepts of gender, knowledge, and power," *Signs: Journal of Women in Culture and Society*, 18(3): 505–46.

Luttrell, W. (1997) *School-Smart and Mother-Wise: Working-Class Women's Identity and Schooling*, New York: Routledge.

Luttrell, W. (2000) "'Good enough' methods for ethnographic research," *Harvard Educational Review*, 70(4): 499–523.

Luttrell, W. (2003) *Pregnant Bodies, Fertile Minds: Gender, Race, and the Schooling of Pregnant Teens*, New York: Routledge.

Luttrell, W. (2010a) *Qualitative Educational Research: Readings in Reflexive Methodology and Transformative Practice*, New York: Routledge.

Luttrell W. (2010b) "A camera is a big responsibility: a lens for analyzing children's visual voices," *Visual Studies*, 25(3): 224–37.

Luttrell, W. (2012) "Making boys' care worlds visible," *Thymos: Journal of Boyhood Studies*, 6(1–2): 185–201.

Luttrell, W. (2013) "Children's counter-narratives of care: towards educational justice," *Children & Society*, 27(4), 295–308.

Luttrell, W. (2016) "Children framing childhoods and looking back," in J. Moss and B. Pini (eds) *Visual Research Methods in Education Research*, Basingstoke, UK: Palgrave MacMillan, pp 172–88.

Luttrell, W. & Chalfen, R. (2010) "Lifting up voices of participatory visual research," *Visual Studies*, 25(3): 197–200.

Luttrell, W. & Clark, E. (2018) "Replaying our process: video/art making and research," *Qualitative Inquiry*, 24(10): 775–85.

Luttrell, W., Restler, V., & Fontaine, C. (2012) "Youth video-making: selves and identities in dialogue," in E. J. Milne, C. Mitchell, and N. deLange (eds) *Participatory Video Handbook*, AltaMira Press: Lanham, MD, pp 164–78.

Lutz, C. & Collins, J. L. (1993) *Reading National Geographic*, Chicago, University of Chicago Press, pp 87–117.

Lutz, H. (2011) *The New Maids: Transnational Women and the Care Economy*, London, England: Zed Books.

Lynch, K. (2007) "Love labour as a distinct and non-commodifiable form of care labour," *The Sociological Review*, 55(3): 550–70.

Lynch, K. and Lodge, A. (2002) *Equality and Power in Schools: Redistribution, Recognition and Representation*, London: Routledge.

Lynch, K., Baker, J., & Lyons, M. (2009) *Affective Equality: Love, Care and Solidarity Work*, Palgrave Macmillan: New York.

Madden, M., Lenhart, A., Cortesi, S., Gasser, U., Duggan, M., & Smith, A. (2013) *Teens, Social Media and Privacy*, Washington, DC: Pew Internet and American Life Project.

Majors, R. (2001) *Educating Our Black Children: New Directions and Radical Approaches*, London: Routledge/Falmer.

Marcal, K. (2016) *Who Cooked Adam Smith's Dinner? A Story About Women and Economics*, London: Portobello Books.

Marchevsky, A. & Theoharis, J. (2006) *Not Working: Latina Immigrants, Low-Wage Jobs, and the Failure of Welfare Reform*, New York: New York University Press.

Margolis, J. & Fisher, A. (2002) *Unlocking the Computer Clubhouse: Women in Computing*, Cambridge, MA: MIT Press.

Marshall, T. H. (1992) *Citizenship and Social Class*, London: Pluto Press.

Martin, J. R. (1992) *The Schoolhome: Rethinking Schools for Changing Families*, Cambridge, MA: Harvard University Press.

Marwick, A. E. & boyd, d. (2011) "I tweet honestly, I tweet passionately: Twitter users, context collapse, and the imagined audience," *New Media & Society*, 13(1): 114–33.

Matthews, S. H. (2007) "A window on the 'new' sociology of childhood," *Sociology Compass*, 1(1): 322–34.

Mauss, M. (1990) *The Gift*, Translated by W. D. Halls, New York: Routledge.

McBride, N. & Grieshaber, S. (2001) "Professional caring as mothering," in S. Reifel and M. H. Brown (eds) *Early Education and Care, and Reconceptualizing Play*, New York: JAI Press, pp 169–201.

McDermott, R., Goldman, S., & Varenne, H. (2006) "The cultural work of learning disabilities," *Educational Researcher*, 35(6): 12–17.

McFarlane, C. (2011) "The city as assemblage: dwelling and urban space," *Environment and Planning D: Society and Space*, 29(4): 649–71.

McKamey, C. (2011) "Restorying 'caring' in education: students' narratives of caring for and caring about," *Narrative Works* 1(1): 78–94.

Miller, D. (2008) *The Comfort of Things*, Cambridge: Polity.

Miller, E. & Almon, J. (2009) *Crisis in the Kindergarten: Why Children Need to Play in School*, College Park, MD: Alliance for Childhood.

Mink, G. (1996) *The Wages of Motherhood: Inequality in the Welfare State, 1917–1942*. Ithaca, NY: Cornell University Press.

Mintz, N. (2004) *Huck's Raft: A History of American Childhood*, Cambridge: Harvard University Press.

Mirzoeff, N. (2011) *The Right to Look: A Counterhistory of Visuality*, Durham: Duke University Press.

Mitchell, C. (2011) *Doing Visual Research*, London: Sage.

Moll, L. C., Amanti, C., Neff, D., & Gonzalez, N. (1992) "Funds of knowledge for teaching: using a qualitative approach to connect homes and classrooms," *Theory into Practice*, 31(2): 132–41.

Moraga, C. & Anzaldúa, G. (1981/2015) *This Bridge Called My Back: Writings by Radical Women of Color*, Albany: State University of New York Press.

Moreno, R. P. & Lopez, J. A. (1999) "Latina parent involvement: the role of maternal acculturation and education," *School Community Journal*, 9(1): 83–101.

Morgen, S., Acker, J. & Weigt, J. (2010) *Stretched Thin: Poor Families, Work, and Welfare Reform*, Ithaca: Cornell University Press.

Morris, E. & Perry, B. (2016) "The punishment gap: school suspension and racial disparities in achievement," *Social Problems*, 63(1): 68–86.

Morris, M. (2016) *Pushout: The Criminalization of Black Girls*, New York: The New Press.

Morrow, V. & Richards, M. (1996) "The ethics of social research with children: an overview," *Children & Society*, 10(2): 90–105.

Muñoz, J. E. (1999). *Disidentifications: Queens of Color and the Performance of Politics*, Minneapolis and London: University of Minnesota Press.

Myerhoff, B. G. (1992) *Remembered Lives: The Work of Ritual, Storytelling, and Growing Older*, Ann Arbor: University of Michigan Press.

Nadasen, P. (2005) *Welfare Warriors: The Welfare Rights Movement in the United States*, New York: Routledge.

Naples, N. A. (1998) *Grassroots Warriors: Activist Mothering, Community Work, and the War on Poverty*, New York: Routledge.

Narayan, U. (1995) "Colonialism and its others: considerations on rights and care discourses," *Hypatia*, 10(2): 133–40.

National Center for Education Statistics (NCES) Home Page, part of the U.S. Department of Education [WWW Document], n.d. https://nces.ed.gov/. Accessed November 7, 2018.

National Commission on Excellence in Education (1983) "*A Nation at Risk: The Imperative for Educational Reform: A Report to the Nation and the Secretary of Education*," Washington, DC: United States Department of Education.

Nicolopoulou, A. (2010) "The alarming disappearance of play from early childhood education," *Human Development*, 53: 1–4.

Nieto, S. (2008) "Nice is not enough," in M. Pollock (ed) *Everyday Antiracism: Getting Real About Race in School*, New York: The New Press.

Noddings, N. (1984) *Caring: A Feminine Approach to Ethics & Moral Education*, Berkeley: University of California Press.

Noddings, N. (1992) *The Challenge to Care in Schools: An Alternative Approach to Education*, New York: Teachers' College Press.

Noddings, N. (2002) *Educating Moral People: A Caring Alternative to Character Education*, New York: Teachers College Press.

Noddings, N. (2005a) "Caring in education," *The Encyclopedia of Informal Education*, http://infed.org/mobi/caring-in-education/. Accessed July 2019.

Noddings, N. (2005b) *Educating Citizens for Global Awareness*, New York: Teachers' College Press.

Noguera, P. A. (2003) "Schools, prisons, and social implications of punishment: rethinking disciplinary practices," *Theory into Practice*, 42(4), 341–50.

Noguera, P. A. (2008) *The Trouble with Black Boys: Essays on Race, Equity, and the Future of Public Education*, San Francisco: Jossey-Bass.

Nolan, K. (2011) *Police in the Hallways: Discipline in an Urban High School*, Minneapolis, MN: University of Minnesota Press.

O'Brien, M. (2007) "Mothers' emotional care work in education and its moral imperative," *Gender and Education*, 19(2):159–77.

Ochs, E. & Izquierdo, C. (2009) "Responsibility in childhood: three developmental trajectories," *Ethos*, 37(4): 391–413.

Oikarinen-Jabai, H. (2003) "Toward performative research: embodied listening to the self/other," *Qualitative Inquiry*, 9(4): 569–79.

Orellana, M. F. (1999) "Space and place in an urban landscape: learning from children's views of their social worlds," *Visual Sociology*, 14(1): 73–89.

Orellana, M. F. (2010) *Translating Childhoods: Immigrant Youth, Language and Culture*, New Brunswick, NJ: Rutgers University Press.

Orellana, M. F. (2016) *Immigrant Children in Transcultural Spaces: Language, Learning, and Love*, New York: Routledge.

Orellana, M. F. (2018) "Immigrant children making home in an urban after-school program," Paper presented at *Home Matters: Meaning, metaphors and practices, International conference*, Helsinki Collegium for Advanced Studies, University of Helsinki, Finland (May 31–June 1).

Orleck, A. (2006) *Storming Caesars Palace: How Black Mothers Fought Their Own War on Poverty*, Boston: Beacon Press.

Paley, V. (2010) *The Boy on the Beach: Building Community Through Play*, Chicago: University of Chicago Press.

Paris, D. & Alim, H. S. (2014) "What are we seeking to sustain through culturally sustaining pedagogy? A loving critique forward," *Harvard Educational Review*, 84(1): 85–100.

Parreñas, R. S. (2001) *Servants of Globalization: Women, Migration, and Domestic Work*, Palo Alto: Stanford University Press.

Parreñas, R. S. (2008) *The Force of Domesticity: Filipina Migrants and Globalization*, New York: New York University Press.

Patel, L. (2015) *Decolonizing Educational Research: From Ownership to Answerability*, New York: Routledge.

Patterson, O. (1982/2017) *Slavery and Social Death: A Comparative Study*, Cambridge, Mass.: Harvard University Press.

Patterson, O. (2017) "Revisiting slavery, property and social death," in A. Bodel & W. Scheidel (eds) *On Human Bondage: After Slavery and Social Death*, Chichester, UK: Wiley Blackwell, pp 265–296.

Pellegrini, A. D. (2005) *Recess: Its Role in Education and Development*, Mahwah, N.J.: L. Erlbaum Associates.

Persell, C. H. & Cookson, P. W., Jr. (1987) "Microcomputers and elite boarding schools: educational innovation and social reproduction," *Sociology of Education*, 60(2): 123–34.

Persons, M. (2017) "Critical play: Agency, interdependency, and intersectionality in an early childhood classroom," PhD Dissertation, Graduate Center at the City University of New York.

Phillips, M. H. (2013) "The children of double consciousness: from *The Souls of Black Folk* to the *Brownies' Book*," *PMLA*, 128(3): 590–607.

Pini, M. & Walkerdine, V. (2011) "Girls on film: video diaries as 'autoethnographies,'" in P. Reavey (ed) *Visual Methods in Psychology: Using and Interpreting Images in Qualitative Research*, Hove: Psychology Press, pp 139–52.

Pinto, L. E. (2016) "Tensions and fissures: the politics of standardised testing and accountability in Ontario, 1995–2015," *The Curriculum Journal*, 27(1): 95–112.

Piper, H. & Frankham, J. (2007) "Seeing voices and hearing pictures: image as discourse and the framing of image-based research," *Discourse: Studies in the Cultural Politics of Education* 28(3): 373–87.

Pitzer, H. (2015) "Urban teachers engaging in critical talk: navigating deficit discourse and neoliberal logics," *Journal of Educational Controversy,* 9(1): 1–16.

Polakow, V., Butler, S. S., Deprez, L. S. & Kahn, P. eds. (2004) *Shut Out: Low Income Mothers and Higher Education in Post-Welfare America,* Albany: State University of New York.

Pollock, M. (2005) *Colormute: Race Talk Dilemmas in an American School,* Princeton: Princeton University Press.

Pratt, M. L. (1991) "Arts of the contact zone," *Profession,* 33–40.

Prosser, J. & Burke, C. (2008) "Image-based educational research: childlike perspectives," in *Handbook of the Arts in Qualitative Research: Perspectives, Methodologies, Examples, and Issues,* Thousand Oaks: Sage, pp 407–20.

Pugh, A. (2009) *Longing and Belonging: Parents, Children, and Consumer Culture,* Berkeley, CA: University of California Press.

Qvortrup, J., Bardy, M., Sgritta, G., & Wintersberger, H. (1994) *Childhood Matters: Social Theory, Practice, and Politics,* Brookfield, VT: Avebury.

Reay, D. (1998) *Class Work,* (1st edn), London: Routledge.

Reay, D. (2000) "A useful extension of Bourdieu's conceptual framework? Emotional capital as a way of understanding mothers' involvement in their children's education?", *The Sociological Review,* 48(4): 568–85.

Reid, J. (2017) *Get Out of My Room! A History of Teen Bedrooms in America,* Chicago: University of Chicago Press.

Restler, V. G. (2017) "Re-visualizing care: teachers' invisible labor in neoliberal times," PhD Dissertation, Graduate Center at the City University of New York.

Restler, V. G. & Luttrell, W. (2018) "Gaze interrupted: speaking back to stigma with visual research," in P. Alldred, F. Cullen, K. Edwards, & D. Fusco (eds) *The SAGE Handbook of Youth Work Practice,* Thousand Oaks: Sage, pp 454–69.

Rice, J. K. & Croninger, R. G. (2005) "Resource generation, reallocation, or depletion: an analysis of the impact of reconstitution on school capacity," *Leadership and Policy in Schools,* 4(2): 73–103.

Rideout, V., Foehr, U. G. & Roberts, D. F. (2010) "Generation M$^2$: Media in the lives of 8–18-year-olds," A Kaiser Family Foundation Study, the Henry J. Kaiser Family Foundation.

Robert Wood Johnson Foundation (2007) *Recess Rules: Why the Undervalued Playtime May be America's Best Investment for Healthy Kids and Healthy Schools,* http://www.rwjf.org/vulnerablepopulations/product.jsp?id=20591. Accessed February 3, 2011.

Rogers, A. G. (2005) "Interviewing children using an interpretive poetics," in S. Greene & D. Hogan (eds) *Researching Children's Experiences: Approaches and Methods,* Thousand Oaks: Sage, pp 158–74.

Rogers, S. & Evans, J. (2008) *Inside Role-Play in Early Childhood Education: Researching Young Children's Perspectives,* New York: Routledge.

Rolón-Dow, R. (2005) "Critical care: a color(full) analysis of care narratives in the schooling experiences of Puerto Rican girls," *American Educational Research Journal,* 42(1): 77–111.

Romero, M. (2001) "Unraveling privilege: workers' children and the hidden costs of paid childcare." *Chicago-Kent Law Review,* 76: 1651–72.

Romero, M. (2011) *The Maid's Daughter: Living Inside and Outside the American Dream,* New York: New York University Press.

Romero, M. and Pérez, N. (2016) "Conceptualizing the foundation of inequalities in care work," *American Behavioral Scientist,* 60(2):172–188.

Rose, G. (2004) "'Everyone's cuddled up and it just looks really nice': an emotional geography of some mums and their family photos," *Social & Cultural Geography,* 5(4): 549–64.

Rose, G. (2012) *Visual Methodologies: An Introduction to the Interpretation of Visual Materials,* Los Angeles, CA: Sage.

Rosenzweig, R. (1983) *Eight Hours for What We Will: Workers and Leisure in an Industrial City, 1870–1920,* (1st edn), New York: Cambridge University Press.

Salen, K. (2011) *Quest to Learn: Developing the School for Digital Kids,* Cambridge, MA: MIT Press.

Santer, J., Griffiths, C., & Goodall, D. (2007) *Free Play in Early Childhood: A Literature Review,* National Children's Bureau.

Schoonover, B. (2009) *Zero Tolerance Discipline Policies: The History, Implementation, and Controversy in Student Codes of Conduct,* New York, Bloomington: iUniverse Inc.

Schor, J. (2004) *Born to Buy: The Commercialized Child and the New Consumer Cult,* New York: Scribner.

Schram, A. (1995) *Words of Welfare: The Poverty of Social Science and the Social Science of Poverty,* Minneapolis: University of Minnesota.

Serder, M. & Jakobsson, A. (2015) "'Why bother so incredibly much?': student perspectives on PISA science assignments," *Cultural Studies of Science Education,* 10(3): 833–53.

Shalaby, C. (2017) *Troublemakers: Lessons in Freedom from Young Children at School*, New York: The New Press.

Sharpe, C. E. (2016) *In the Wake: On Blackness and Being*, Durham: Duke University Press.

Sharples, M., Davison, L., Thomas, G. V. & Rudman, P. D. (2003) "Children as photographers: An analysis of children's photographic behavior and intentions at three age levels," *Visual Communication*, 2(3): 303–30.

Shwarz, O. (2009) "Good young nostalgia: camera phones and technologies of self among Israeli youths," *Journal of Consumer Culture*, 9(3): 348–76.

Siddle, W. & Tompkins, R. H. (2004) "Caring in the past: the case of a Southern segregated African American school," in V. Siddle Walker & J. R. Snarey (eds) *Racing Moral Formation: African American Perspectives on Care and Justice*, New York: Teachers College Press, pp 77–92.

Sjöberg, G., Silfver, E., & Bagger, A. (2015) "Disciplined by tests," *Nordisk Matematikkdidaktikk, NOMAD*, 20(1): 55–75.

Skeggs, B. (2011) "Imagining personhood differently: person value and autonomist working-class value practices," *The Sociological Review*, 59(3): 496–513.

Smalley, S. Y. & Reyes-Blanes, M. E. (2001) "Reaching out to African American parents in an urban community: a community–university partnership," *Urban Education*, 36(4): 518–33.

Smith, D. (1987) *The Everyday World as Problematic: A Feminist Sociology*, Toronto: University of Toronto Press.

Smith, R. C. (2006) *Mexican New York: Transnational Lives of New Immigrants*, Berkeley: University of California Press.

Smith, S. M. (2004) *Photography on the Color Line: W. E. B. DuBois, Race, and Visual Culture*, Durham: Duke University Press.

Sontag, S. (1977) *On Photography*, (1st Picador USA edn), New York: Farrar, Straus and Giroux.

Sonu, D. & Benson, J. (2016) "The quasi-human child: how normative conceptions of childhood enabled neoliberal school reform in the United States," *Curriculum Inquiry* 46(3): 230–47.

Spring, J. (2015) *American Education*, New York: Routledge.

Stack, C. B. (1974) *All Our Kin: Strategies for Survival in a Black Community*, New York: Harper and Row.

Steedman, C. (1985) "The mother made conscious: the historical development of a primary school pedagogy," *History Workshop*, 20(1): 149–63.

Steinhauer, J. (2017) "How Mierle Laderman Ukeles turned maintenance work into art," *Hyperallergic*, https://hyperallergic.com/355255/how-mierle-laderman-ukeles-turned-maintenance-work-into-art/. Accessed November 20, 2018.

Stephens, S. (1995) *Children and the Politics of Culture, Princeton Studies in Culture/Power/History*, Princeton: Princeton University Press.

Stokes, B. (2017) "What it takes to truly be 'one of us,'" Washington, DC: Pew Research Center.

Stoll, L. C. & Embrick, D. G. (2013) *Race and Gender in the Classroom: Teachers, Privilege, and Enduring Social Inequalities*, Blue Ridge Summit: Lexington Books.

Strack, R. W., Magill, C., & McDonagh, K. (2004) "Engaging youth through photovoice," *Health Promotion Practice*, 5(1): 49–58.

Strauss, V. (2018) "Implicit racial bias causes black boys to be disciplined at school more than whites," *The Washington Post*, April 5.

Strober, M. & Tyack, D. (1980) "Why do women teach and men manage? A report on research on schools," *Signs: Journal of Women in Culture and Society*, 5(3): 494–503.

Tager, M. (2017) *Challenging the School Readiness Agenda in Early Childhood Education*, London: Routledge.

Taubman, P. (2009) *Teaching by Numbers: Deconstructing the Discourse of Standards and Accountability in Education*, New York: Routledge.

Tawney, R. H. (1921) *The Acquisitive Society*, New York: Harcourt Brace and Company.

Taylor, T. L. (2006) *Play Between Worlds: Exploring Online Game Culture*, Cambridge, MA: MIT Press.

*The Future of Public Housing in Worcester*, 2001 Report 01–03, www.wrrb.org/wp-content/uploads /2014/07/01-3housing.pdf. Accessed June 2019.

Thomas, N. & O'Kane, C. (1998) "The ethics of participatory research with children," *Children & Society*, 12(5): 336–48.

Thompson, A. (2004) "Caring and colortalk: childhood innocence in white and black," in V. S. Walker & J. R. Snarey (eds) *Race-ing Moral Formation: African American Perspectives on Care and Justice*, New York: Teachers College Press, pp 23–37.

Thompson, G. L. (2003) *What African American Parents Want Educators to Know*, Westport, CT: Greenwood.

Thomson, P. (2008) *Doing Visual Research with Children and Young People*, New York: Routledge.

Thorne, B. (1987) "Re-visioning women and social change: where are the children?", *Gender and Society*, 1(1): 85–109.

Thorne, B. (1993) *Gender Play: Girls and Boys in School*, New Brunswick, N.J.: Rutgers University Press.

Thorne B. (2001) "Pick up time at Oakdale elementary school: work and family from the vantage points of children," in R. Hertz and N. Marshall (eds) *Working Families: The Transformation of the American Home*, University of California Press: Berkeley, pp 354–76.

Thorne, B. (2007) "Crating the interdisciplinary field of childhood studies," *Childhood*, 14(2); 147–152.

Thorne, B. (2009) "The *Seven Up!* films: connecting the personal and the sociological," *Ethnography*, 10(3): 327–40.

Tinkler, P. (2008) "A fragmented picture: reflections on the photographic practices of young people," *Visual Studies*, 23(3): 255–66.

Tinkler, P. (2013) *Using Photographs in Social and Historical Research*, London: Sage.

Tosolt, B. (2010) "Gender and race differences in middle school students' perceptions of caring teacher behaviors," *Multicultural Perspectives, 12*(3): 145–51.

Trachtenberg, A. (ed) (1980) *Classic Essays on Photography*, New Haven, CT: Leete's Island Books.

Tronto, J. C. (1993) *Moral Boundaries: A Political Argument for an Ethic of Care*, New York: Routledge.

Tronto, J. C. (2013) *Caring Democracy: Markets, Equality, and Justice*, New York: New York University Press.

Tuck, E. (2009) "Suspending damage: a letter to communities," *Harvard Educational Review*, 79(3): 409–28.

Turmel, A. (2008) *A Historical Sociology of Childhood: Developmental Thinking, Categorization and Graphic Visualization*, Cambridge: Cambridge University Press.

Tutwiler, S. W. (2005) *Teachers As Collaborative Partners: Working With Diverse Families and Communities*, Mahwah, NJ: Lawrence Erlbaum Associates.

Ukeles, M. L. (1969) "Manifesto for maintenance art 1969! Proposal for an exhibition 'CARE.'" www.queensmuseum.org/wp-content/uploads/2016/04/Ukeles_MANIFESTO.pdf. Accessed January 5, 2019.

United Nations, Office of the High Commissioner for Human Rights (1989). www.ohchr.or/en/professionalinterest/pages/crc.aspx. Accessed June 2019.

US Census Bureau QuickFacts: Worcester city, Massachusetts [WWW Document], n.d. URL 2018. www.census.gov/quickfacts/worcestercitymassachusetts. Accessed November 7, 2018.

US Department of Education, National Center for Education Statistics (2016) "Public school teacher data file," *Schools and Staffing Survey*.

Valdés, G. (1996) *Con Respeto: Bridging the Distances Between Culturally Diverse Families and Schools: An Ethnographic Portrait*, New York: Teachers College Press.

Valdés, G. (2001) *Learning and Not Learning English: Latino Students in American Schools*, New York: Teachers College Press.

Valencia, R. (2010) *Dismantling Contemporary Deficit Thinking: Educational Thought and Practice*, New York: Taylor and Francis.

Valentine, G. (1999) "Being seen and heard? The ethical complexities of working with children and young people at home and at school," *Philosophy & Geography*, 2(2): 141–55.

Valenzuela, A. (1999) *Subtractive Schooling: U.S.-Mexican Youth and the Politics of Caring*, Albany: State University of New York Press.

Villenas, S. (2001) "Latina mothers and small-town racisms: creating narratives of dignity and moral education in North Carolina," *Anthropology & Education Quarterly*, 32(1): 3–28.

Vinson, K. D. & Ross, E. W. (2003) *Image and Education: Teaching in the Face of the New Disciplinarity*, New York: Peter Lang.

Vogt, F. (2002) "A caring teacher: explorations into primary school teachers' professional identity and ethic of care," *Gender and Education*, 14(3), 251–64.

Wagner, J. (1999) "Introduction: visual sociology and seeing kids' worlds," *Visual Sociology*, 14(1–2): 3–6.

Wakefield, S. & Wildeman, C. (2014) *Children of the Prison Boom: Mass Incarceration and the Future of American Inequality*, Oxford, UK: Oxford University Press.

Waksler, F. (1986) "Studying children: phenomenological insights," *Human Studies*, 9(1): 71–82.

Wald, J. & Losen, D. J. (2003) "Defining and redirecting a school-to-prison pipeline," *New Directions for Youth Development*, (99): 9–15.

Wallace, J. M., Jr., Goodkind, S., Wallace, C., & Bachman, J. (2008) "Racial, ethnic, and gender differences in school discipline among U.S. high school students: 1991–2005," *Negro Educational Review*, 59(1–2): 47–62.

Wang, C. C. (1999) "Photovoice: a participatory action research strategy applied to women's health," *Journal of Women's Health*, 8(2): 185–92.

Wang, C.C. & Burris, M. A. (1997) "Photovoice: concept, methodology, and use for participatory needs assessment," *Health Education Behavior*, 24(3): 369–87.

Waring, M. (1999) *Counting for Nothing: What Men Value and What Women are Worth*, Toronto: University of Toronto Press.

Way, N. (2011) *Deep Secrets: Boys' Friendships and the Crisis of Connection*, Cambridge, MA: Harvard University Press.

Weber, S. & Mitchell, C. (1995) *"That's Funny, You Don't Look Like a Teacher!": Interrogating Images, Identity, and Popular Culture'*, London; Washington, DC: Falmer Press.

Weiner, G. (2002) "Uniquely similar or similarly unique? Education and development of teachers in Europe," *Teaching Education*, 13(3): 273–88.

Weiner, L. (2003) "Why is classroom management so vexing to urban teachers?", *Theory into Practice*, 42(4): 305–12.

Weir, A. (2005) "The global universal caregiver: imagining women's liberation in the new millennium," *Constellations*, 12(3): 308–30.

Weis, L. & Fine, M. (2012) "Critical bifocality and circuits of privilege: expanding critical ethnographic theory and design," *Harvard Educational Review*, 82(2), 173–201.

Weis, L., Cipollone, K., & Jenkins, H. (2014) *Class Warfare: Class, Race and College Admissions in Top-Tier Secondary Schools*, Chicago: University of Chicago Press.

Wells, L. (ed) (2003) *The Photography Reader*, New York: Routledge.

Weschler, L. (2016) *Domestic Scenes: The Art of Ramiro Gomez*, New York: Abrams.

West, C. & Zimmerman, D. H. (1987) "Doing gender," *Gender & Society*, 1(2): 125–51.

Westbrook, R. (2010) "The making of a democratic philosopher: the intellectual development of John Dewey," in M. Cochran (ed) *The Cambridge Companion to Dewey. Cambridge Companions to Philosophy*, New York: Cambridge University Press.

Wexler, L. (2000) *Tender Violence: Domestic Visions in an Age of U.S. Imperialism*, Chapel Hill: University of North Carolina Press.

White, A., Bushin, N., Carpen-Méndez, & Ní Laoire (2010) "Using visual methodologies to explore contemporary Irish childhoods," *Qualitative Research* 10(2): 1–16.

Whiting, B. & Whiting, J. (1975) *Children of Six Cultures: A Psycho-Cultural Analysis*, Cambridge, MA: Harvard University Press.

Willett, C. (2001) *The Soul of Justice*, Ithaca: Cornell University Press.

Willis, P. (2005) "Afterward: Foot soldiers of modernity: the dialectics of cultural consumption in the 21st century school," in C. McCarthy, W. Crichlow, G. Dimitriadis, & N. Dolby, *Race, Identity, and Representation in Education (Critical Social Thought)*, New York: Routledge, pp 461–80.

Yan, W. (2000) "Successful African American students: the role of parent involvement," *Journal of Negro Education*, 68(1): 5–22.

Yates, L. (2010) "The story they want to tell, and the visual story as evidence: young people, research authority and research purposes in the education and health domains," *Visual Studies*, 25(3): 280–91.

Yeates, N. (2004) "Global Care chains," *International Feminist Journal of Politics*, 6(3): 369–91.

Yosso, Tara J. (2005) "Whose culture has capital? A critical race theory discussion of community cultural wealth," *Race, Ethnicity and Education*, 8(1): 69–91.

Yuval-Davis, N. (2011) *The Politics of Belonging: Intersectional Contestations*, Los Angeles, Calif.: Sage.

Zarate, M. E. (2007) *Understanding Latino Parental Involvement in Education. Perceptions, Expectations, and Recommendations*, Los Angeles: Tomas Rivera Policy Institute.

Zelizer, V. (1994) *Pricing the Priceless Child: The Changing Social Value of Children*, Princeton: Princeton University Press.

Zerubavel, E. (2003) *Time Maps: Collective Memory and the Social Shape of the Past*, Chicago, Ill.: University of Chicago Press.

# Index